Dolls of Our Lives

Why We Can't Quit American Girl

Mary Mahoney & Allison Horrocks

Feiwel and Friends
New York

A Feiwel and Friends Book
An imprint of Macmillan Publishing Group, LLC
120 Broadway, New York, NY 10271 • fiercereads.com

Our books may be purchased in bulk for promotional, educational, or business use. Please contact your local bookseller or the Macmillan Corporate and Premium Sales Department at (800) 221-7945 ext. 5442 or by email at MacmillanSpecialMarkets@macmillan.com.

Library of Congress Cataloging-in-Publication Data is available.

First edition, 2023

Book design by Ellen Duda and Mallory Grigg

Feiwel and Friends logo designed by Filomena Tuosto

Printed in the United States of America

ISBN 978-1-250-79283-9 (hardcover)

1   3   5   7   9   10   8   6   4   2

For all fans of American Girl—for anyone who owned a doll, loved the catalogues, or just felt strangely seen by the story of a girl whose history was nothing like your own—this book is for you. While our book may not recreate the lasting bond you had with your childhood doll, we find some comfort in knowing it's priced more competitively.

Table of Contents

Introduction

We don't want to brag, but one day in 2019, we got a table at an exclusive café. While everyone we knew was at work, we sat midday drinking tea and eating finger sandwiches. We barely knew how to act. As we sat among little girls in dresses and tiaras, we were concerned we didn't meet the dress code. Suddenly filled with doubt, we turned to ask our tablemates if we were fitting in, but they weren't talking. Considering that we were surrounded by eighteen-inch dolls in booster seats, that wasn't too much of a surprise.

Where were we? At the American Girl Café, of course.

We were just two adult women historians and podcast hosts casually spending a weekday wandering around the American Girl store with a photographer in tow. We were trying to give "it's not a big deal" energy the entire trip, but the truth was, it *was* a big deal and we had *zero* chill.

We'd started a podcast that year to relive the American Girl series, book by book. What started out as a fun project to do together after finishing grad school hit the airwaves that February as content we truly thought only our friends and family might consume. Maybe our parents, strangers to technology, would respond with praise akin to their commentary on our childhood art projects. "That's nice, girls," they'd tell us. "I don't know what a podcast *is* or what you're doing, but I will put it right up here on the fridge." The pride we'd feel would be overwhelming. Imagine our surprise when we found there were actually a lot of people who wanted to relive the books with us and talk about all things American Girl.

That's how we scored a VIP invite to the American Girl store in New York City. Our college alumni magazine arranged a guided visit where their photographer could take pics of us for a story. Nothing says "take pride in your school" like a story on two historians who abandoned academia to make a doll podcast. We brought our recorder along to, as influencers might say, "create content." Listening back on that day, all we can hear is our total state of wonder. We couldn't believe our good fortune, *and* as people who had not visited the store often (Allison had been to one before) or ever (Mary had not), we were amazed by the sights and sounds of the store that some parents may describe as "sensory overload" and "expensive." We saw a clinic for dolls needing what Goop might call "rejuvenation"; a hair salon for dolls needing an assist after getting some DIY haircuts; the café, where we could dine with dolls of our choice; and more.

As elder millennials, we had aged out of American Girl by the time stores popped up across the country, beginning in 1998 with the flagship Chicago store. Our access to American Girl came solely from its still legendary catalogue. Instead of having high tea in a café with trays and china (including a plate for Allison's Molly doll), we had imaginary meals for our dolls at home or attended birthday parties with friends where we were invited to dress in historical costumes. We also loved the books, which were grouped into six formulaic titles per historic character. The pose of the characters walking across the cover and smiling out at us is iconic and will live in our minds forever.

Sitting in the café, we tried to explain to the photographer what American Girl was all about and what it had meant to us. So much of it is hard to explain to a newbie. How can you tell a stranger that imagining you, too, lived on the prairie in 1854 helped you navigate life as a nine-year-old in the 1990s? Or that some of your first lessons in friendship came from watching how fictional girls forged friendships with one another in the imagined pasts of the books? When we met as adults, just talking about these things instantly brought us closer and was important in our friendship. The relationship between these imaginary girls and our girlhoods felt so vital and obvious to people who'd lived it, but was harder to explain to people who hadn't.

American Girl staff guided us around the store, where we checked out new (to us) characters and their accessories. The staff we met were lovely, but we panicked that they may bristle at some of our reactions to the new displays. On our show, it was not uncommon for us to offer real talk about American Girl, both the brand and the stories it tells. For example: Is the stuff expensive in a limiting way? Yes. Did the brand at one point create its first Black character and focus on an enslaved girl we were then invited to buy? Also yes. Was it "cruel and unusual" to offer dolls with perfect braids that invited restyling without the hope of ever returning them to the perfection of their factory setting? Absolutely.

We were worried the staff would judge us, especially when Mary started shooting hoops in Julie's display and we wondered aloud if her love of basketball and rainbows, and the San Francisco setting of her books, was supposed to *mean* something.

We share all these hot takes and more on our show, and though we have and use PhDs in history, we also use the language of pop culture (perhaps our shared love language) to get at what is going on in the books and with the brand. With that in mind, it's important to say, paraphrasing Julia Roberts in *Notting Hill*, we're just two historians and friends, standing in front of you and asking what it means to be a fan of American Girl.

Yes, loving something can mean learning everything about it and stanning it to friends and family, embracing it over a lifetime in a completely uncritical way. That's not what our fandom looks like. We're not afraid to ask tough questions about it, because we're capable of appreciating its impact on our lives while also acknowledging that it's not perfect.

It's like being a reality-TV fan. You may love *Real Housewives*, *The Bachelor*, *90 Day Fiancé*, or any other premier programming and defend your viewing of it to anyone while also simultaneously screaming at its stars on-screen, "Make better choices!" It's that imaginary space, where we can envision the things the brand might do differently, that leads to such great conversations on our show and with our listeners. For example, we couldn't believe Josefina's approach to grief (mostly, avoiding it), but it did lead us to talk to a therapist who helped us figure out how we should approach it our-selves. Talking about the kinds of stories we wish American Girl would tell (more inclusive and diverse stories in particular) also continues to inspire us to seek out these kinds of stories in other genres of books, shows, and movies. Will we still keep watching reality TV though its stars rarely "make good choices"? Yes. We contain multitudes.

We have had a lot of discussions with listeners over the past few years about what American Girl has meant to them. While the show was centered mainly on our lives and interpretations, we wanted to think about what it means to grow up with American Girl beyond just our own experiences. There are many ways to love American Girl and be a fan.

We wanted to study American Girl fandom in all its facets. Where did it come from? What was it like for other millennials growing up with the brand from its beginnings in 1986? Do other people our age also feel like it shaped them in big ways, and continues to? And where is the work that reinvents the stories of our childhoods in updated and inclusive ways?

We had to find out. We are going to take you on a journey through the wonderful and wild world of American Girl fandom. We'll explore the history of what Pleasant Rowland hoped to create with American Girl and what a generation of people did with it. Some of these expeditions will take us to actual places, like Colonial Williamsburg, where Pleasant Rowland was inspired to invent American Girl; the Smithsonian; a doll museum; and more. Others are more metaphorical journeys through the memories of people who worked for the brand, whether helping to create Felicity, illustrate its books, or edit the *American Girl* magazine.

We wanted to hear from fellow fans about the memories they have of their childhood play and what they make of their fandom now as adults. This goal asked us to confront the true chaos of culture in the '90s: the early internet (we refuse to disclose our AOL screen names at this time), childhood birthday parties, and backyard performances of American Girl plays. We also wanted to include amazing historical and pop culture interpretations happening on social media today. Together, these stories tell us a lot about histories of girlhood, friendship, and American Girl that help us to better understand why these dolls, books, and accessories meant, and continue to mean, so much.

We'll be exploring this over six chapters, following the traditional arc of the historic characters' books—in part because we're in too deep and in part to remind us that this arc can (and should) be reimagined to tell more than just one girl's story. Rather than have one woman's—or, in our case, two women's—stories stand in for all millennials and more, we wanted to emphasize how vast the American Girl universe is. We contain multitudes, and it does, too.

Before we set off to understand what exactly Pleasant Rowland was trying to do, we first want to share a bit of our history. No, we won't be sharing our Venmo history, Gmail archives, or any other terrifying ways to know someone in a digital age. Instead, we're going back to basics and sharing the only true intel you need on us: our American Girl stories.

Meet the Original-Generation American Girls (aka Our OGAGs)

American Girl has released dozens of historical characters since 1986.

The girls listed here are the six that we knew well in our childhoods. When we call them the "original generation" girls, that is a distinction we've totally made up. As Kit fans never hesitate to remind us, there are some really compelling stories that just happened to be released when we stopped reading new American Girl books.

Felicity—Felicity is a wealthy girl living in Virginia during the early years of the American Revolution. In a material world, she is happy to be an imperial girl, but war is coming. Felicity's stories teach us about loyalty, education in the colonies, teatime etiquette, and, of course, the value of a beloved horse. In addition to Penny, the aforementioned horse, Felicity's best friend is a girl named Elizabeth. Felicity is often singled out as the OG horse girl.

Josefina—Josefina's stories begin in 1824. She lives on a rancho in present-day New Mexico. Struggling with the loss of her mother, Josefina tries to adjust to a new life, and the presence of a long-lost aunt (and later stepmother) named Tía Dolores. Josefina's stories teach us about life in a borderland, how to make a good trade, and the support we can get (or not) from family. Mariana is marketed as Josefina's best friend, though her sisters come in a close second. Josefina is best known for her kind heart. Tía D is best known (to us) as perhaps the only serial killer to appear in an American Girl book.

Kirsten—Kirsten is a Swedish immigrant who comes to the United States in the 1840s. While colonizing present-day Minnesota, Kirsten struggles with being the new girl at school, fire, bears, and much more. The Kirsten books are best known for their heartfelt moments, and Kirsten's devotion to her friends, family, and the occasional raccoon. Until her tragic passing, Kirsten's best friend is a fellow immigrant named Marta; later, Marta is replaced by Singing Bird. Lifelong fans are still reeling from Marta's death, and even the most casual reader remembers Kirsten's St. Lucia hair-braids-hot-buns moment.

Addy—Addy is a self-emancipated Black girl who comes north to Pennsylvania during the Civil War. At the start of the series, Addy claims her freedom along with her mother, and they work together to reunite the entire family in Philadelphia. Through Addy's books, readers learn about slavery and racism, along with how to be a good friend and, in some sweeter moments, the importance of ice cream at one's birthday. Addy's best friend is Sarah, who is as loyal as she is smart. Addy is based on a real girl whose story is preserved at Historic Stagville in North Carolina.

Samantha—Samantha is a New Yorker living during the Edwardian era. Though she has everything a girl could dream of and lives in a mansion, Samantha is also an orphan still mourning the deaths of her parents. Through Samantha's stories, we learn about class, poverty, child labor, how trauma lingers, and, in some lighter moments, how to dodge troublesome male neighbors. Her best friend is a girl named Nellie, but Uncle Gard and Aunt Cornelia come in a close second and third place, respectively. Samantha is often perceived to be the spoiled and posh American Girl, but she also has some surprising class-consciousness breakthroughs in her stories.

Molly—Molly is a midwestern girl living during World War II. In addition to a lot of sibling and friend drama, Molly has to navigate war rations, classmate jealousies, and a complex (if colorful and patriotic) dance routine. Her books are meant to inspire appreciation for the children who came of age in the Greatest Generation, or at least the girl bosses who drove local scrap metal drives forward in the 1940s. Molly's best friend, supposedly, is a refugee from England named Emily. We have both long identified most with Molly. This is a lifelong process.

CHAPTER 1

Meet Us

In which we meet Molly, explore our friendship meet-cute,
and create a podcast.

As the immortal Sophia Petrillo, the oldest and best Golden Girl, might say, we want to take you back in time. Picture it: The year is 1995. William "Bill" Clinton is president of the United States. Monica Lewinsky is not yet known for her purse empire. Young girls are often seen carrying backpacks that are far too tiny to be useful but also too adorable not to buy. The 1996 Olympics haven't happened yet. In other international affairs, a second revolution and British invasion is brewing and building to the release of *Spice World*.

We are eight and nine years old, respectively. Both of us are in elementary school, growing our sticker collections and wearing overalls as often as possible. Our bookshelves are full, and we both love historical fiction, especially if it comes in an elaborate binding or contains a ribbon bookmark. We are hearing a cautionary tale about chasing waterfalls on the radio. (Note: TLC dropped "Waterfalls" in 1994 when we were far too young to understand it, though this didn't stop us from wanting to wear an eyepatch like Lisa "Left Eye" Lopes #RIP.) We are also both reeling from the untimely death of Selena Quintanilla-Pérez *#StillDreamingOfYou*. While one of us is thriving in gym class and shooting hoops after school, another is panicking at the mere mention of Presidential Physical Fitness Test challenges (Bill, truly, why?). Tragically, we are not friends yet.

Maybe you're reading this and thinking, "I, too, was dreaming about a spot on the Olympic team while also feeling victimized by the Presidential Fitness exams." And maybe you *also* wished you had the visibility of the Olsen Twins wearing a stylish trench but felt as incognito as Carmen Sandiego (girl, where *are* you?). If you were old enough to understand what was really happening in the TLC music videos, you probably are from Gen X, and a bit older than us. If you didn't get most of your music video knowledge from episodes of *TRL*, and can't explain how we, as Americans, let Carson Daly happen, you're probably younger than we are.

As millennials, we grew up in what some might call the Golden Age of Pleasant Company. Okay, so only *we* call the early 1990s this, but please go with us for a moment. During our childhoods, we both came to love a brand called American Girl, and we weren't alone. These products gave us endless hours of entertainment as young people and, later, a language for connecting with new friends.

We were fortunate enough to be coming of age when the stories they were telling were just right for our age group and interest in history. As adults, we got serious about returning to the brand and its stories after some years away (call it our teenage rebellion), at a moment when podcasting offered an accessible path to revisit sources of childhood nostalgia for an audience of fellow fans. It would be like rereading our childhood diaries but less cringey, and we might learn something about ourselves in rereading books that meant so much to us as kids. As American Girl books taught us, we are all products of our time, but there's also a lot we can learn by stepping into the past.

We didn't become friends until we were adults, but we have learned a lot about each other by talking about our childhood interests. Something we probably all share is the challenge of making, maintaining, and caring for friends at any age. Now, when you meet someone new, and you're trying to get to know them, you probably have your own shortcuts for learning about them. For us, it was a simple question: "Are you a Molly?"

We want to introduce ourselves by telling you about some of the pop culture we loved growing up that led us to American Girl, history, and, eventually, each other.

Meet Mary

It's difficult to begin a story about myself and my relationship with American Girl because I can't recall a time when American Girl wasn't in my life. What I can tell you is that it's never really been about the dolls for me. I've always been in it (and into most things, really) for the stories. If this was a true *Meet Mary* American Girl story and I handed the reins to the likes of Valerie Tripp, iconic American Girl author, or, dare I say it, Pleasant Rowland herself, my story would likely start with an anecdote that placed me in a geographic space and mentioned family and friends with significance in the larger historical moment. "It's 1994, and Mary Mahoney, an acquaintance of Tonya Harding, learns a hard lesson about playing fair."

In reality, I was born in 1986, just like Pleasant Company, and grew up in a suburb of Hartford, Connecticut. Like most people who grew up in the suburbs, I felt like I grew up in a place where nothing happened. While that's not strictly true, the feeling that it was true inspired me to find places where things *were* happening. Books have always been that place for me, particularly when I was small and limited to my local library. I loved the Baby-Sitters Club, the Boxcar Children, and the Matt Christopher books my brothers discarded. These books inspired me to think I, too, could solve crimes *and* start a small business from the sanctity of my childhood bedroom. To this day, the only reason I think this didn't happen is that I wasn't allowed a dedicated phone line in my room (we all know this set Claudia apart, in addition to her killer style).

Even as a nine-year-old, I also spent a lot of time thinking how cool life would be when I hit my teen years. Would it be like *Saved by the Bell* and Sweet Valley High? Elizabeth and Jessica Wakefield drove a Jeep to high school. Could I handle being that cool? (Note: Since I drove a used Saturn LS2 in high school / college / grad school, this would turn out to be an unnecessary fear.)

I also loved *The Witch of Blackbird Pond*, by Elizabeth George Speare. Set in my hometown of Wethersfield, it told the story of a girl accused of being a witch. I was extremely into it. The traits that tipped off the town to the girl's treachery were her unabashed belief in her own mind, her willingness to speak freely, and her gleeful thwarting of the Puritan norm. I had never wanted to be an accused witch so badly. She felt like she didn't fit in, and wouldn't you know, I didn't, either. She also lived in my town, except things happened there! Wow.

In my '90s girlhood, if you drove down the main street of Wethersfield, you would learn quickly that George Washington spent some nights there during the Revolutionary War. I visited the house where he slept on a field trip around the time I read *The Witch of Blackbird Pond* and was disappointed. We didn't hear about one girl my age on the entire tour. Not to let the Leo jump out so early in this book, but how am I supposed to care about this story if it doesn't have someone like me in it? Sure, we learned about the American Revolution, but where was the chaos of a witch hunt? I wanted drama! I wanted history! I wanted stories of a girl who made history while also being dramatic.

I wanted more books that took me back in time to see what other girls' lives were like. If it wasn't too much to ask, I also wanted books that told stories about girls who felt weird and like they were a bit too much.

Enter American Girl.

Christmas Eve 1995 was a big year for me because it's when I met my first American Girl. We spent every Christmas Eve at my paternal grandmother's house in the south end of Hartford. After the 5:00 Christmas Eve mass, we'd head to my grandmother's for dinner, gifts, and general "fun." I put this in air quotes because I found this holiday super stressful. I struggled with dressing up and fitting in at events where appearances and formalities seemed to matter. I had three girl cousins who were a few years older than me, and they seemed much better at being a girl. They rocked '90s fashion (high-waisted everything, a perennial bad idea) and introduced me to New Kids on the Block and Selena cassettes (a true gift to me). They thrived on dressing up for holidays. I hated it. I always saw girls in church wearing velvet dresses, things you'd buy at Caldor, Bradlees, or maybe Lord & Taylor, if you're fancy, and could never fully relate to the joy they seemed to take in those looks. My mom would buy me dresses with care but also knew they were not for me. Seemingly from the womb, my personal brand has been denim (or denim on denim if I'm feeling brave). My grandmother liked to "tease" me for my "tomboy" ways, and I can still full-body flush thinking back to how awkward and embarrassed I felt in those moments.

The one redeeming thing about that night in 1995 was American Girl. I'd never heard of it and have no idea how my grandmother became aware of it. All I know is that she bought each of my girl cousins Molly and her set of books. I realize now how great a financial cost that was for someone who was not wealthy (she was a teacher her entire life), and I'm very grateful to her for it. All the boys got Teenage Mutant Ninja Turtle swords.

I wasted no time in becoming an expert on Molly. In a great act of unconscious self-admiration, I originally prized all of Molly's traits that reminded me of me. A nine-year-old brunette? Check. Who wore glasses? Check. Was sort of nerdy and extra? Check. Molly had pristine twin braids that I was instantly stressed about ruining. I did not know how to braid hair, and if you dared me to French braid hair today, I'd fake my own death and never be found.

I read all her books, slowly. Unlike the Baby-Sitters Club, which I inhaled in an afternoon alone in my room, I read American Girl books with my mom. We'd read one chapter per night, and though my brothers rejected an offer to join because it had "girl" in the title, they would slowly wander in and lie at the end of my bed as my mom read to us about life during World War II. I was so enamored of it all.

The plot of Molly's books had not stayed with me prior to starting the

Dolls of Our Lives podcast. (Note: Our show was initially titled *American Girls* but has shared the title of this book since 2022.) What I do remember is the sensory thrill of this experience: the sound of my mom's voice reading, the looks I'd exchange with my brothers during high-stress moments, the sounds of our protests when my mom said it was time for bed after finishing a chapter. I also loved the way a story like Molly's invited my mom to share some family history. Sometimes she'd tell us about her own father's experience in the war. He'd passed before we were born, and we were hungry for details of his life. It felt magical, the kind of special that allows you to appreciate it while it's happening. These are some of the best memories of my childhood.

Reading all of the American Girl books offered me gateways to history (family and otherwise) and total immersion in the stories. I read all the books for Molly, Kirsten, Felicity, Samantha, and Addy. I still remember how deeply Addy's books affected me. Author Connie Porter described the horrors of slavery in ways I could grasp as someone learning about that history for the first time. I will never forget the moment when the plantation overseer forces Addy to eat worms as a punishment for daydreaming, for example. I have visceral memories of being in school while in the middle of book one and worrying Addy would not remain safe as she and her mother self-emancipated, moving from North Carolina to Philadelphia. I also still think of Addy's books every time I see letter-shaped cookies, recalling how Addy and her mother baked cookies that spelled "LOVE."

This was also one of the first times I asked my mom (a librarian who loves to do research) to help me do a deep dive on a topic I learned about in a book. Like Addy teaching her mother letters and her mother guiding Addy as she grows into her own person, my mom and I had a similar exchange. I taught her the ins and outs of the early internet with Encarta and AOL, and she taught me how to be a good person *and* how to find books on slavery and the Civil War at our local library. This would not be the last time that I asked my mom to be my research partner in trying to figure things out.

Together, we explored rationing, the Revolutionary War, and *Little House on the Prairie*. My *Little House* deep dive (into the books and show) was inspired by the Kirsten books, the plots of which defy any rational attempt at explanation.

Despite my exposure to other characters and their books, Molly remained my favorite. This was in large part because she connected me to my favorite person, my grandmother.

If my maternal grandmother were alive today, she would most want you to know that I'm named after her. We're both Mary-Margaret, though I prefer "Mimi," a family nickname. I never liked being called "Mary" as a kid, let alone "Mary-Margaret," because it felt formal and like I was destined for a convent. Me? Take a vow of obedience? To quote the immortal Cher in *Clueless*, "As if." My grandmother, whom I called "Fluffy," insisted on calling me "Mary" to be reminded of our connection, and it always sounded right coming from her. We were opposites in many ways. I lived for books, and my grandmother didn't keep any in her house. She once asked us to prop up a new TV, and the only books we could find were telephone books from the 1980s in her basement.

The only other book I can think of in her house existed purely in the form of an abstract threat or thought experiment. If you started telling her a story of something you'd done that made her worry or hedged on the boundaries of her Catholic sense of "that's a sin," you'd hear, "Oh, hmm, well, you know, the other day I was reading my book on purgatory . . ." and then a vague instruction to behave yourself or an anecdote about a possibly invented stranger who was murdered, maimed, or had embarrassed her family by doing something in the wheelhouse of what you'd described. I once got this response from her by describing how much I loved my new skateboard.

Needless to say, my grandmother never read an American Girl book. However, talking about American Girl with my grandmother was like being in a book club with someone who refused to read the book but never let that hold her back. I loved Molly so much because she was alive in my grandmother's lifetime and provided a language for us to talk about what life was like when she was a girl. My grandmother grew up during the Depression, and her earliest memory was of sitting up all night with her father's body at age three after he'd dropped dead. This at-home wake is peak #irish family history material, but also spoke to how tough my grandmother was, in part because she'd had to be. She was not the type of person to volunteer these kinds of stories about herself, but I could ask her if she ever grew a liberty garden like Molly or how she dealt with rationing, and she'd share stories I'd never heard before.

Looking back, what strikes me about this time in my life is how much my grandmother made me feel special by sharing so many of her own stories with me and by asking me to share my own with her. This is how she learned about bullies I encountered in school, whom she taught me to combat with wit and some choice gestures (she also offered to meet said bullies in the schoolyard herself). Fluffy also helped me rewrite the stories I'd told about myself, which I can also appreciate helped me to embrace the things that made me who I am. I felt so much shame for being a tomboy and preferring pants to dresses and for loving to play sports more than loving to play with dolls.

My grandmother helped me to figure out how to be my own kind of girl, without apology. She listened to me, took me seriously, and encouraged my instinct for mischief. She taught me to make prank calls. Hers were tame, like "Is your washer running? You better go catch it!" I'd call her and pretend to be the church secretary and ask if she was comfortable flirting in church as much as parishioners reported. I mean, what *would* Jesus do?

While she never read the books, she loved sharing special skills American Girl also encouraged girls to try. She was an epic sewer and made me what I'll call "historic" pieces. I call them "historic" because though I felt super stylish in the corduroy pants / vest / turtleneck combos she made me, I did not realize until later that she sewed them from 1970s patterns she'd used to make my mom's and aunts' clothes when they were girls.

More than anything, she modeled what it looked like to be inherently your-self at all times. She wore a uniform of a sweat suit, a gold chain, and white sneaks 365 days a year like she was the fourth member of Run-D.M.C. That was what she felt comfortable in, so that was what she wore. That inspired me. She always spoke her own mind (even when you wished she'd practice some restraint), loved fiercely, and was the most loyal person I've ever met.

The Molly books helped prompt the conversations that lasted the length of our friendship—that is what my grandmother called it. She liked to say, "We're related, but it's nice because we're friends." That is how I felt, too. Though I still prefer to be called "Mimi" by family and friends, I use "Mary" as my name professionally and on the book you now hold in your hands as a tribute to her. It's one small way I carry my friend with me, especially in the years since her death in 2015.

Friendship has been a vital through line in my life, just as it is in every American Girl book. Friends can teach you things about yourself, inspire you to be a loving and supportive presence in someone else's life, and, if you're Molly McIntire, get you out of scrapes (sometimes of your own making). As anyone who has read the Molly books knows, 90 percent of her drama is self-created (said without judgment of our queen). Knowing my grandmother was like befriending a grown-up Molly who had seen some things. I always wondered what it would be like to befriend another Molly my own age, and then I met Allison.

Meet Allison

What we think matters about any particular date or period in our lives changes over time. I've never really been drawn to nostalgia, though I watched *I Love the '80s* over and over as if I remembered the ~2 years that I spent living in that decade. That exception aside, I *have* always been drawn to finding the hard facts and details about the small things that make up the texture of living in another time. I'm a historian now, but history classes actually used to bore me most of the time. Whether it was the French Revolution or ancient Egypt, I wasn't learning the things I wanted to know about the past. When a major event happened, was the sun shining bright on everyone, or was it one of those days when you'd rather crawl back into bed? What did ordinary people really think about big events, and how did they go to the bathroom?

The line between trivia and history can be blurry, but one of the things I have learned from American Girl is the power of making another time real. All of this is to say that I find something comforting in knowing that Christmas Eve 1995 was cloudy and cold in New England. It is a coincidence of history, and maybe fate, that on the same night that Mary met Molly, my story with American Girl was also just beginning.

Books were always around in my life, and especially during my childhood. Several people in my family are avid readers, and those who aren't so much readers are serious enablers. It's trendy now to talk about the Icelandic tradition of *Jólabókaflóð*, or "book floods," right around Christmas. But the Horrockses were causing their own small book floods on an annual basis long before going to Iceland became a common millennial practice. Overall, holidays were more of a casual thing in my family—our wardrobe often peaked at new pajama sets. We were not the hit-the-road type—for trips or to see family. I remember being horrified at the hijinks of the McCallister family in *Home Alone*. I felt a bit exasperated and thought, "Just stay home and finish those pizza leftovers!" This is probably because my family's holiday memories revolve around being home, waiting for my mom to finish working. She was a nurse, so that meant she spent at least half of the holidays saving lives while we waited impatiently around our kitchen and put olives on our fingertips (don't ask).

I remember a lot of these Christmases in New England being very cold, and snowy, but not in a *White Christmas* kind of way. According to historic weather data (which we can't read too often without weeping), the Christmas of 1995 fell on a gray and winter-weather-filled week. I can't say for sure if that's valid for where I lived, but it tracks with a lot of my memories. I grew up in a semirural area about ninety miles from Mary. I liked to walk in the woods that served as a kind of long ellipsis in the back of my family's property. I loved the way a small brook and a messy stone wall punctuated the open space. Especially when I was with my dolls, I enjoyed the outdoors, but I wouldn't say I was outdoorsy. I was not a punk (too edgy). I did not do ballet (too much coordination required). What more can I say, while continuing to paraphrase Avril Lavigne?

She was a doll. I was a girl. Can I make it any more obvious?

I have tried to distill exactly what I thought when I first saw the eighteen-inch wonder known as Molly McIntire. Most of what I thought has been lost to time, probably because most of us are better off not remembering exactly what it's like to be eight years old. However, I do remember that she was carefully nestled in the distinctive not-quite-red, not-quite-burgundy box that all new American Girls arrived in. Despite not having any of these dolls before, I was somehow aware of who was going to greet me when I ripped off that wrapping paper.

We'd never talked about it out in the open, but I just knew it was an American Girl doll. The products were hard to miss around that time. American Girl was something people talked about at school. I have to imagine I was seeing other, not-so-subtle forms of advertising at bookstores. My mother, who also loves dolls, tells me she chose Molly because she knew she'd like the story, too.

For people who don't love dolls, or are afraid of dolls (fair enough), maybe there's something unnerving about peeling back a layer of tissue paper to see two eyes staring back at you. I've never felt this way. When I received a doll, I felt like I was participating in an exciting ceremonial occasion. Here was a new arrival to the family, ready to take part in any and all adventures I could concoct . . . And trust me, there were many. When I saw *that box*, there was probably a rush knowing that I was getting something I'd hoped for. Dressed to the nines, Molly had arrived at last. Now that she was here, I'm sure I was pleased that this short, bespectacled wonder was dressed exactly like the girl I'd seen in the catalogues. Her eyes were covered by a beautiful pair of glasses I already admired. Once she came out of the box, it was like a new chapter had started in my life. Finally, I had a Molly to call my own.

With gift-receiving, there can be a lot of pressure when opening something from someone you love. I'd like to say that the big reveal of a Molly doll was the highlight of that Christmas, but it wasn't. The gift was just the start of a night I'll always treasure. What I remember most about receiving a Molly doll was what came in the hours after she was opened. By bedtime, she was firmly grounded in my life and there was no turning back.

I should add that I had a habit of bringing dolls with me around the house when I was younger. They also came with me into the car and, whenever possible, into stores to run errands. My parents were incredibly patient with all of this. For whatever reason, they accepted that dolls were not casual accessories for me. Unlike cats, who might run away or bring me a dead animal, dolls were perfectly compliant when playing school or going for a walk. Dolls fit neatly into my bicycle basket and on my swing set. They were genuine companions in a way that non–doll lovers honestly may not understand.

What really made Molly the total package was that she didn't fly solo. Along with a new toy, I had been given six books, kept together in a tight and beautifully packaged set. How *extra* these were! The small ribbon tie and the beautiful font! I felt so mature approaching my bundle with care. When the day was winding down, my mom called me into her bed. I sat attentively in new pajamas and listened as she read *Meet Molly*. She was reading to me about the world inhabited by her parents, when they had been younger. Cracking open that spine, she was also giving me the gift of her time, and herself. Maybe I could have read this chapter book by myself, I'm not really sure. I am so glad I didn't.

Readers know the glow of looking at a beautifully bound friend who sits on the shelf, their whole life made just in the service of opening another world for you. Molly's books came all at once, like a flood, but I remember *Meet Molly* the best. I *loved* this book. I was instantly drawn in by the McIntire family and wanted to know how or if they were going to make it through the war. The story was similar, in some ways, to another favorite of mine from my childhood: *Little Women*. I see now as a women's historian that I was drawn to periods of war, when women had more opportunities presented to them. I had no concept of that in 1995, though. Most of all, I loved the experience of hearing history out loud. Is there a better thrill for a reader than stepping into someone else's world, while still being firmly planted in your own?

Molly was nine and yet, somehow, fully herself. She was interesting, nerdy, and a bit "spunky," to use the American Girl phrasing. Molly sometimes doubted herself, but she wasn't afraid to ask big questions. She also had a kind of cool confidence that I admired. Soon, we'd also share the same hairstyle. By this point, my blond hair had been darkening for a while into a light brown. It was a process that seemed to happen slowly and then all at once. I remember some adults in my life bemoaning the loss of both my curls and my blondness, as if I'd ordered such a change at six. Soon, it would be impossible to imagine myself as anything other than a brunette with chunky bangs.

Molly had something to do with this personal transformation. Upon seeing Molly, I was eager to get a haircut. It's a universally acknowledged truth that bangs change you and choose you, which is something I think I had intuited from just glancing at my older sister's teen magazines. Like Molly, I needed to get fringe that would go straight across. I had also been wishing for glasses to complete the vision of how I saw myself. So much of my life was different from hers, and yet I related to Molly immediately, and wanted to mirror her, too.

Undoubtedly, part of the power of American Girl stories came from the strong writing and the transhistorical connections readers could make between themselves and these people of the past. There are certain things that make us human that don't change even as seemingly everything else does, including our climate (hello, warm Christmases in New England). But I didn't have the language to know any of that back then. I also wasn't aware that this was a turning point in my own life for other reasons. In 1996, my sister graduated high school and went off to college. The following year, my brother did, too. Molly wasn't going through those changes, but her world was changing around her, and she also wasn't sure what to make of it. Years later, I'd learn how to study patterns of upheaval and continuity across American history. But I *could* already see the connections between us and had a growing sense that I could also fashion Molly in my image.

Molly came at just the right time, in more ways than one. My Molly (who now has a bizarrely prominent place in my adult home and life) came along with me into the woods, sat with me during long and tedious sessions of school, and even came to friends' houses. She met other Mollys, and soon was joined by additional American Girl dolls in my bedroom. At night, she slept on a bunk bed that I painted in the family garage. There are still traces of that white paint on the floor, markers of childhood left for another family to find. I saw that bunk bed a few years ago and was surprised by just how bad of a job I'd done painting it. In my memories, it was bright as snow, glossy, and just elegant enough for *my* dolls.

I should note that Molly's other Molly accoutrement has held up better, in part because my mother took charge of the project. By the time I got Molly, I had been receiving dolls for years. Honestly, I had probably also received dolls before I was even born. It was something I shared with my mom, who loved and cherished the dolls she had been given as a child, as well as my toys. In addition to making many of her own clothes for her job as a nurse, my mom would get patterns and figure out how to make American Girl doll clothes. We didn't call this "DIY culture," it was just something we did together. I vaguely knew that American Girl accessories were expensive, but I also had a feeling that it wasn't just about the money. Sometimes at the checkout, I'd marvel at how much we were spending to make a particular thing ourselves (hello, the fancy trim around Molly's bathrobe wasn't cheap). But you couldn't put a price on making something we both could be proud of.

I've kept all those clothes, and they have survived lots of years in stages of storage quite well. My Molly things remain precious to me. Sadly, I do not have most of my original Molly books. These were loaned out to a friend, never to return. But I also didn't actually retain a lot from her books as I got older, despite all she's done for me. I know that part of this forgetting has to do with my own creative revision of her plot points. I would play for hours and make Molly into someone else entirely. Molly becomes Amish? Check! Molly runs a small but successful berry business from the big rock in my backyard? Check! Felicity gets a brand-new strapping colonial outfit because I've decided to repurpose some vest material? Check! After reading the six books, I was just as immersed, years ago, in the stories that I created for her. I didn't need my parents to buy the supplementals, because I had my own workshop right in my room. American Girl had that kind of power for me: It was an invitation to make the past a place I could play in, too.

I can't describe the feeling I had when I first saw Molly. I do feel a sense of wonder now for the way that an eighteen-inch factory-made toy changed my life. Dolls aren't the same as human friends; I know that. I also know with some certainty that dolls have provided a language for me to make some of the most important friendships of my life. Having a Molly to come along for the ride is a bonus.

People often ask us how we met, and presume we were childhood friends (hi, we have a doll podcast). We didn't meet as kids, but we did grow up together. Like the Golden Girls, who were drawn together by shared interests (cheesecake, loungewear, and gossip), we also met and bonded over shared hobbies and dreams (cheesecake, loungewear, gossip, history). When you meet someone who becomes important to you, it's crazy to think about all the things that had to happen to bring you together. Our friendship meet-cute began with the choice to study history.

We attended the same small liberal arts college, but never knew each other. Many grown women meet their best friends in college and/or in their early twenties. These are *prime* years for working on figuring yourself out.

It's also a time when you are learning about coffee (or is that just us?). Our first year of college coincided with the first year Facebook was available on campus. Facebook made it easy for us to know *of* each other. This was in the early days of Facebook, when straight people engaged in fake marriages with friends, everyone was in "it's complicated" relationship with themselves, and no one knew how to self-edit before posting status updates (some things never change). While Facebook may have suggested we should be friends, and we had friends in common, we met only once during senior year.

Given the cool, now grown-ish Mollys that we both became, it's not surprising that we first met after attending the same talk. Huddled in a doorway long after everyone else went home, we talked and learned we enjoyed many of the same history classes, shared a lot of interests, and hit it off immediately. Then, reminiscent of the John Cusack / Kate Beckinsale vehicle *Serendipity*, we did not talk again for years. (In that movie, she puts her phone number in the inside cover of a book and suggests if they're meant to be, it will find its way to him. This seemed insane even upon its release in 2001 and especially now *#RIPLandLines*. This would never work for us, as Allison doesn't do phone calls.)

Now, if you know anything about American Girl, you know that the products are expensive. However, have you tried analyzing the cost of graduating with a liberal arts degree right after the start of a major "once in a lifetime" recession? That is a harder hit. It's a bit of a cliché to say that millennials who aren't sure what to do with their overpriced education and burdensome loans go to graduate school. We took that cliché, spent a few more years analyzing it, mastered it, then added a few more years of hard labor teaching low-level history classes.

Yes, we decided to get PhDs.

Allison started at the University of Connecticut one year before Mary. When Mary started the following year, Allison reached out to offer a tour of campus, intel on the program, and the rundown on grad school life.

We both vividly remember sitting in the student union that day, eating sandwiches and talking about the program. Allison, ever the cool customer, reported, "Don't get attached. I'll probably be out of here in a year." Reader: She wasn't out of there in a year or even five, but that felt very true and real at the time it was said.

There's another aspect of this meeting that's worth repeating. All friendships have elements of an origin story that prove deeply revealing. When Mary called Allison to tell her she was going to be late, Allison didn't answer. In a cinematic version of this meeting, Ja Rule would provide the voiceover. Some people are truly never there when you call, but they are always on time.

Getting a PhD in history often means learning how to be a good researcher, teacher, and graduate student all at the same time. It requires a really intense balancing act. On the one hand, you're learning how to be a historian. Then, once or twice a week, you have to teach undergraduate students as if it's something you've always known how to do. Neither of us looked like teachers, never mind professors. We'd fit in better at a local Baby-Sitters Club meeting than a faculty lounge.

But it wasn't just that.

A big part of grad school is learning how to become a professional without losing your identity (and remaining sanity) in the process. We quickly bonded over the fact that we both watched television (a lot) and enjoyed reading *US Weekly* (as time permitted—hello, we had to read like four books a week). We could swerve between intense historiographical debates (historians explaining how other historians have studied the same topic) and legal dramas such as the divorce between Ryan Phillippe and Reese Witherspoon. We took everything and nothing super seriously, investing huge emotional energy into topics that excited us.

While pushing ourselves to earn PhDs, we were stunned to learn that there were still so many other experts who knew more, such as: random people on Twitter, literally almost any man on Reddit, people who were chatting with us unprompted at the student union, and so on. Sometimes it felt like we could read all day, study all night, and still not be as sharp as That Guy Who Wikipedia-d

This Topic Once. There was also the fact that imposter syndrome was discussed constantly as if it were a plague with no cure. Oh, too bad these gals have it! Whatever can we do? It was a disease that was planted through systemic imbalances for which no higher ed Typhoid Mary was ever held responsible.

We didn't carry a kind of built-in authority. We weren't tall, male, or from academic families. We did have family support, white privilege, and friends we made in our cohorts. Over time, though, we learned just how much we got through it because of each other and the intrepid services of Mary's red Saturn, Stephanie (Stephy). Looking back, it would be convenient to say that we didn't fit into academia, or we were too much for it. But is anyone really a good fit with a dumpster fire?

While we have figuratively set many of our graduate school projects ablaze, we look back on one particular project much more fondly. As with many great American Girl stories, it started with a party invite. Early in our friendship, we got invited to a mutual friend's birthday party. We know that kindness and politeness matter when invitations to high-profile events such as this one come in. The question of the hour was suddenly quite urgent: What would we bring? Instead of going to Target to buy a candle (no shade to candles, they make great gifts), we decided that our contribution would be homemade.

By a twist of fate, and likely because we often shared food, this party happened the same week as we both caught a stomach bug. While we were recovering at home, inspiration struck during one of our many conversations over GChat. We decided we could write a book . . . as if we had time for that. It felt natural to write a kind of American Girl story that would be perfectly suited to our mutual friend. At the time, she studied the Reformation (not the clothing brand but the religious and political upheaval of the 1500s). Cut to the first draft of what we called *Reformation Girl*.

The story that we said would center our friend in a fictional Reformation setting devolved into something our AP History teachers would have called "interesting" or "spirited," two ways of saying "wrong." We knew enough (sort of) about what she studied to know that Martin Luther was involved. Allison had taken a theology class in college, so she knew a bit more about the Ninety-Five Theses. Mary was raised Catholic and at one point wanted to be a medievalist, so she brought saint-relic intel to the table. Pooling our knowledge, we spun a tale around one essential punch line: Martin Luther simply had to walk up to a door and cry, "I have ninety-nine theses, but this ain't one!" Tragically, this is likely not the saddest appropriation of Jay-Z lyrics by white girls.

Surprisingly, we didn't win a Caldecott Medal. We did make our friend happy and, more importantly, laughed harder than we had in months. Like all great authors, we quickly made this story about us. Imagining ourselves as sixteenth-century booksellers, we made Allison and Mary characters who sell saint relics while running a bookstore as a front. One of our mentors once said of a prolific local historian, "He writes without fear or research." We let this be our guide when writing *Reformation Girl*. In the words of another mentor, perhaps we'd become "unhinged," but we had a lot of fun doing it.

As we both got deeper into our areas of expertise, it was becoming harder to come up for air, to get away from argument and accuracy and actually just enjoy what we were learning about. Learning how to take our real work but not ourselves seriously was something that we shared. As we presented *Reformation Girl* to our friend with great solemnity at a run-down bowling alley, we were surprisingly proud of this thing we'd made together. It didn't hurt that we'd gone all out with ribbon and stickers. (Hi, '90s girls, we know how to say "Lisa Frank, take the wheel!")

From that moment on, we weren't afraid to let our proverbial freak flag fly when the time was right. Did we sign a birthday card as if we were Martin Van Buren? Yes. Did we usurp a relatively normal recipe exchange at a bridal shower and pretend to be colonial cookbook writers? Yes. Did Mary transform a literally and figuratively dark (wood-paneled) basement into a Gilded Age retreat for Allison's surprise bridal shower? Yes. Were all of these acts of friendship and perhaps shared insanity appreciated? Not always.

Toward the end of grad school, we each had defining moments that forced us to think about ourselves and what we might want for our futures. For Mary, it was a dismissive comment that came when she cited American Girl as one of the reasons she became a historian. For Allison, it was being told she sounded like a cheerleader when talking about history. What women care about is often denigrated or devalued by society, as if their loves, their interests, are somehow less worthy. There's nothing wrong with loving American Girl, or being inspired by it, just as there's nothing wrong with sounding cheerful about a topic that excites you. But it wasn't just that. There was also the academic culture that we found ourselves in. Was it really better to write something that only a few people would read or find interesting? Is that what we'd spend twenty-four years in school to do?

By the time we were finishing graduate school, we'd developed areas of expertise and had various side hustles. While studying the history of home economics, Allison also worked at a series of house museums and historic sites. Mary was studying the history of the book and how books were used as medicine. On the side, she was also learning how to podcast and work with audio. We found ourselves approaching the end of our degree programs not wanting the supposed brass ring of tenure-track jobs (as if those exist anymore, LOL, but we digress). Rather, we wanted to share what we knew with a broader audience, and to start by talking about a shared inspiration, American Girl.

We knew it was time to put academia's expectations back on the shelf, pull down our dusty American Girl books, and, in the words of Kelly Clarkson, "Breakaway." We thought about sending out a mass survey to people who worked in history jobs to measure the impact of American Girl. But as Carrie Bradshaw might say, we couldn't help but wonder: Was there not something BIGger we could do?

We knew we wanted to make something that spoke to a broader audience that sounded like us. A lot of what academics produce comes from an idea that you can separate yourself from the work that you do, that who you are doesn't seep into what you write. (Many scholars do this anyway with no self-awareness, producing a me-sis more than a thesis.) We actually wanted to share something of ourselves with other people, and in an accessible format.

It has quickly become something of a cliché for two friends with a lot to talk about to start a podcast. For us, podcasting just made a lot of sense. Mary had already made a podcast, and Allison had recorded people with her Fisher-Price microphone when she was younger, which is kind of the same thing. We hoped other people who didn't think about American history all the time might enjoy hearing historians riff on Molly's beret and Felicity's horse girl aesthetic. We could talk in depth about girlhood, gender, and book culture, and reach a wider audience interested in revisiting American Girl. The real Martin Luther once allegedly advised: "If you want to change the world, pick up your pen and write." We figured this might work for a podcast microphone, too.

Part of the joy of doing this podcast would be making it together and empowering each other. We felt just like Pleasant Rowland and Valerie Tripp, another great duo. Pleasant Rowland and Valerie Tripp each brought something important to their friendship. Rowland had made (really) good investments throughout her career and was ready to bankroll a huge enterprise that would be named in her honor. Tripp had an impressive résumé as an educator and author. Together, they would do big things, although they would come in eighteen-inch packages.

Channeling our heroes, we recorded a few test episodes of the podcast in the winter of 2019. We were trying to find a format that felt like us. The history shows we saw in the top-ten lists were mostly men offering monologues about wars, and that was decidedly not our vibe. We played around with different formats, recording from the comfort of our living rooms, and ended up with a format that reflected our friendship. Listeners would get to listen in on what our actual conversations sounded like: catching up on new developments in our lives, sharing recent pop culture things we loved, and diving into an American Girl book and the history behind it.

It is difficult to explain the degree to which we did not anticipate the reaction we would receive when we released our first episode in February 2019. We genuinely believed our real-life friends and family would listen, and maybe a few strangers who stumbled on our show. Imagine our surprise when we were hanging out with friends watching *The Bachelor*, and one of our fellow members of #BachelorNation told us we had collected thousands of followers on our show's Instagram account. Within a few episodes, listeners found the show and told their friends, and our listenership increased exponentially.

Our inbox was inundated with stories from listeners about what their dolls meant to them. People shared photos of themselves dressed as Samantha and stories of pursuing a career in public history because they wanted to interpret the worlds Felicity and Addy lived in. We loved hearing from new moms who listened as they sat up with their babies at night. One listener started listening when she found out she was expecting, and wrote to us when her daughter—our youngest listener to date—was born.

Lots of listeners who didn't grow up to pursue history as a career wanted to be part of this burgeoning community. What bound us together was the fact that these stories still seemed to have a lot to teach us. It seemed like every day, we got treated to new lessons, and new interpretations, coming from listeners. We spent time connecting with women who grew up to identify as queer rereading queerness into the books. We also read long messages from people who could still find Kirsten "sure, let's let a raccoon in the house" Larson's confidence aspirational. Best of all, we watched as strangers became friends.

We would be foolish to think a write-up of our show in the *New York Times* and other outlets was merely a testament to the show we produced. Revisiting American Girl clearly touched a nerve with the people for whom the dolls and stories mattered. While we knew our own Molly stories, and how American Girl shaped (and continues to shape) us, we wanted to know more about this American Girl generation of which we were a part. We also wanted to know more about what inspired American Girl in the first place. But where to begin?

It made sense to start with the original American Girl, Pleasant Rowland.

We didn't actually want to meet Pleasant, because that would be too real for us, and we're not sure she'd understand our desire to compare Felicity's gender politics to Britney Spears's "Toxic." However, we *did* want to understand what went into making the American Girl world she created.

Origin stories, including our own, can be filled with mythmaking. We knew that Pleasant Rowland had the idea for American Girl while on vacation at Colonial Williamsburg. We wondered what influence Colonial Williamsburg had on Pleasant, and the stories her brand told about American history. We also wanted to walk around Williamsburg and imagine how Pleasant saw a museum and imagined something so innovative for kids. Would we sound like Disney Adults walking around the park and talking about Walt "It all started with a mouse" Disney? It's really too late for us to say.

Going there might help us separate myth from reality *and* let us go on vacation at the same time. With that in mind, pack your bags and prepare yourself. We're going back in time to find a hot tub, a good time, and the truth—in that order.

Important Social Media Profiles

The original American Girls did not know about social media. They would have written letters and connected with friends in other ways. But that won't stop us from imagining who among them would have been most invested in Tumblr and why.

Felicity is bizarrely into LinkedIn for reasons unclear to anyone except Elizabeth, who's joined her in the mercantile business. She is staying off other platforms to avoid talking about Ben on social media. Their breakup was publicized on a small local gossip page.

Josefina is still using Facebook to stay in touch with family and friends even though almost everyone else her age has given up on it. She is doing her best to stay out of the Santa Fe community groups and inexplicably loves making deals on Facebook Marketplace.

Kirsten is totally devoted to her complex and beautiful Pinterest board. She spends hours making sure she's crafted the right cottagecore aesthetic. Although she has a lot of followers, Kirsten is really only happy when her friends are copying her best ideas.

Addy is using Instagram to push for social justice and avoiding the meme-ification of civil rights movements. She tries her absolute hardest to keep up with her best friend Sarah's posts while also creating her own content. Addy can definitely be counted on to share petitions with her whole network.

Samantha is trying to get more people to follow her Grandmary-financed Flickr account that exposes social issues. She is also dabbling in some Mercari exchanges (hello, there was a lot of stuff in that family attic) as a way to supplement her trust fund. Though she has tried to sell some of her Piney Point paintings, they have not done well on Etsy.

Molly is fully addicted to making TikTok videos about her life after having one niche post go viral. She is always looking for new ways to connect with friends from college. Emily, who spent one summer with Molly, refuses to friend her back on any platforms.

CHAPTER 2

We Learn a Lesson
Making Memories at Colonial Williamsburg

In which we meet Pleasant, take a trip,
and learn what makes American Girl so special.

For many, the year 1984 conjures images of a dystopian future from the eponymous novel. For Pleasant Rowland, it was the year that changed everything.

In that year, she took one trip to a mall and another to Colonial Williamsburg, the largest living history museum in the country, located in Williamsburg, Virginia. As a result of visits to these decidedly different spaces—one, a place where people like to flex money and buy things that make them seem cultured, and the other, a mall—Pleasant invented a brand that has clearly kept our attention well beyond our childhood years.

Before we get into what our generation (and others) did with the world she made, we wanted to take a sentimental (and literal) journey to the place that inspired her. By retracing her steps, we wanted to capture what so captivated her about the kind of storytelling offered at Colonial Williamsburg. Thinking about American Girl in that place also helped us to understand the true measure of her innovation.

Colonial Williamsburg is a living museum that interprets the history of the revolutionary era. It offers visitors the chance to explore artifacts, spaces, and stories either from the era or inspired by it. Pleasant built on the potent combination of storytelling and artifacts used there and made a scalable living history museum of her own, combining dolls and books to tell an often triumphant (and white) version of American history. Kids could re-create the past (and invent any number of fictional scenarios) in the comfort of their own homes through play. She was so inspired by this place she returned there in 1991 to launch a character set in Williamsburg: Felicity Merriman, a revolutionary-era shero.

Exploring her story, her relationship with this place, and what it inspired her to create helped us to appreciate just how much she truly is the face of her brand (literally, as we will learn). Her memories of her own girlhood and her belief in the importance of making memories were foundational to American Girl. Yes, she wanted kids to learn about history, but from the beginning Pleasant emphasized the importance of memory making as a central element of what American Girl could offer the children she hoped to reach.

Now, we know what you might be thinking: Couldn't we just go to the mall if that also inspired Pleasant? First of all, we love a historical vacation. We've toured Shaker communities, Revolutionary War–era sites in Philadelphia and Boston, and countless house museums with the excitement of bachelorette parties hitting Vegas. Walking around historic spaces is one of our favorite pastimes and is also where we work out some of our best ideas. Second, revisiting the malls of our '90s and early 2000s youths is increasingly difficult. As blogs and Insta accounts document, the number of abandoned malls is growing, and that is not the kind of ghost tour we had in mind.

We want to take you on what *The Bachelor* might call a "real journey" and find examples of what Pleasant adopted from Williamsburg and what she invented herself. But first, we want to introduce you to the OG American girl boss herself and the early years of American Girl, which was called Pleasant Company at its founding. Her story will help you understand how a person could go on a vacation and emerge with a business plan (a thing that has literally never happened to us).

Meet Pleasant

Everything we've read and know about Pleasant suggests her personality entirely suits her name, although a better name may have been "Professional." Born in 1941, and raised in Chicago, Pleasant grew up the daughter of an advertising executive. This lineage, she'd later claim, made her a visual learner and creator. "I grew up kind of osmosing a visual approach to the world," she once explained to a reporter. Graduating from Wells College in 1962, Pleasant worked as an elementary school teacher in five different states before 1968. At that point, she pivoted to become a television news anchor and reporter at San Francisco's KGO-TV, working her way up from field reporter.

Early profiles of Pleasant as one of the few female anchors in the area present her as smart, ambitious, and quotable. In one 1970 profile, her portrait appears over a subtitle that reads "Hard-boiled, or soft?" Is it common to compare people to eggs? Asking for us. She proved herself the former by commenting on the "new" feminism movement growing in the United States. "I am in general agreement with the goals of much of the feminist movement, as I believe most women are. I do feel that women should be given equal treatment at all levels of society, something they do not always have," she is quoted as saying. "Newsrooms are notoriously Victorian!" We can only imagine what conditions she may have faced there. Something tells us it wasn't the hijinks Mary Richards experienced on the *Mary Tyler Moore Show*. It's kind of bleak that she'd both hint at this and not feel like she could explicitly call out whatever bad treatment she was subjected to directly.

Just like Samantha Parkington and the Victorians to whose culture she compared her newsroom, she also placed an inherent value on femininity that made true equality improbable if not impossible. "I am opposed to the portions of that movement that de-emphasize the basic femininity of women," she explained. "The feminist movement defeats itself when it pounds the table and puts on army boots!" Reporting during the Vietnam War, Pleasant wanted both to be a part of the establishment and also to hold it to account. "We live in a dehumanized world much of which lacks real meaning," Pleasant explained in a comment that still resonates. "Youth is frustrated by hypocrisy they see in the establishment and the world around them in general."

In reporting from this time, Pleasant emerges as a genuine and earnest storyteller who wants to reach people, specifically children, with stories that could inspire. She may not have trended toward exposés on sexism or war, but that is not to say that we can't see the issues of power and politics reflected in writing about her. She would later claim she was inspired in part to invent American Girl because she believed toys marketed toward girls, like Barbies, pushed girls toward adolescence too soon by sexualizing them. It's easy to see where a desire to halt this process and present girls with an identity grounded in something other than looks came from. Articles about her incredible career even at this early stage still insisted on mentioning her appearance, commenting on her "femme face," "blue eyes," or "the slightly protruding upper teeth that give a girl a sexy look." This last phrase makes us sick every time we read it. Even if Pleasant still prized her femininity, she may have objected to its inclusion in articles about her burgeoning entrepreneurship. We know we do! It would be hard to imagine the male CEO of any company described according to the sexiness of his teeth.

In 1972, Pleasant left news and waded into educational products, debuting a phonics program created with J. B. Lippincott and Boston Education Research called *Beginning to Read, Write and Listen*. Originally distributed to over 500,000 kindergarten and first grade children all over the country, the materials are still used in schools today. Pleasant was her father's daughter, articulating a problem and presenting her product as the logical solution. A column that year typified both Pleasant's acumen at sound bites and the penchant of reporters to continue to emphasize the "girl" in "girl boss." "'The average cereal box is more exciting than most grade school textbooks,' declares Pleasant Rowland, a pretty young ex-teacher who dropped out of the school system to try to find a better way of teaching children to read." Can we please profile Pleasant's business without being gross? Sidebar, has anyone explored if Pleasant Rowland is actually the basis for Elle Woods? We wish she'd responded to any of these sexist profiles about her business success with "What? Like it's hard?"

Pleasant's interviews at the time of the launch seemed to encourage a view of herself as a disruptor. "Today's kids have been stimulated by television, magazines, toys—even by clever packaging," she explained, praising new programming like *Sesame Street*. "They come to kindergarten turned on and we proceed to turn them off." Kids could learn letters through new methods and multimedia resources, including cassette tapes, scratch-and-sniff stickers, and books. "Alphabetical order is only necessary for things like filing," Pleasant explained, "and how many five-year-old file clerks have you known?" Clearly Pleasant wasn't with us when we played office as children and forced Ken to file our memos in what we'd retroactively call "equitable divisions of labor."

This was a great moment for Pleasant to enter the chat on how society should influence and teach kids. In the 1980s and long before, conservative groups pointed to "the children" as ammunition to shut down cultural products they deemed inappropriate. In the 1960s, it was American parents who pointed to John Lennon's comments that the Beatles were "bigger than Jesus" as proof the band had the wrong values and was therefore a bad influence on kids. By the '70s, the counterculture, civil unrest, violence on TV, and disco on the radio all constituted just some of the influences that could make kids grow up too soon and with the wrong values. As an avid fan of disco, Mary can in fact attest that some music can make you gay, so perhaps these fears are warranted. By the 1980s, Nancy Reagan was fighting back with her war on drugs and Tipper Gore wanted to slap parental warnings on music.

So much of the conversation was about what kids shouldn't read, watch, or do. Pleasant's girl boss energy trended toward curating good morals in kids through positive influences and innovative approaches (see: imaginatively using scratch-and-sniff stickers to help kids learn to read). She wouldn't call out bad influences. Instead, she'd create a product she knew to be good and sell it like hotcakes, or hot stuff, to paraphrase disco queen Donna Summer.

By 1984, Pleasant was about to experience what Oprah might call her greatest business aha moment, shaping the future of her professional life. But first, she had to go shopping.

Pleasant Learns a Lesson

In 1985, Pleasant created Pleasant Company to produce American Girl dolls, books, and accessories. She was inspired to do this by two experiences she had the previous year. The first was a trip to the cultural mecca of the decade, the mall. Attempting to buy a doll as a gift, she was appalled by the most popular offerings. She once referred to the neon sign of Toys "R" Us as "offensive." As she explained in an interview in 1990, "I have no children . . . But I got to thinking, what if I did have children. What are my choices? Either Barbie or Cabbage Patch Kids."

Before you wind up to reason with Pleasant on this (maybe, like Mary, you, too, had a Cabbage Patch doll you loved), please know her objections to these popular dolls were fierce. She believed Cabbage Patch dolls were "ugly" and Barbie and other toys invited girls to grow up too soon. This fear, of influences that encouraged girls to mature beyond their years, is one we heard several times from people familiar with Pleasant and involved in the development of various American Girl products. It's why, for example, she never wanted her dolls to appear as adults or to be developed physically in any way beyond childhood. Unlike Barbie, who has the physical shape of an idealized thin white adult body, Pleasant would not entertain any notion of dolls for girls who did not appear to be girls themselves. She would also not allow talk of boys or makeup in a world designed for girls too young to care about such things.

This desire not to create a line of dolls that sexualized girls determined some early design choices. Rather than being a line where girls could grow up with the dolls over different ages, like Barbie and Skipper (presumably, Pleasant was also uncomfortable with siblings whose names feel inspired by peanut butter), each American Girl doll is introduced as a nine-year-old, and we travel with them through about a year of their lives. Pleasant could imagine girls growing up with the dolls, and then handing them off to their own daughters. This is a very heteronormative vision of inheritance. However, just like the childless "father of our country," George Washington, who was romanticized as siring a nation, if not biological children, our own "Founding American Girl" was invested in seeing her dolls and stories as an inheritance to pass down. It didn't matter that the dolls didn't age. An American Girl doll could theoretically walk with a girl through her own childhood years and beyond, and then meet her again in her adulthood, ready to play with her children. (Little did Pleasant know that we, two childless thirtysomethings, would be out here talking about these dolls to this day.)

The setting of the original American Girls in different moments in American history is also useful because it allowed Pleasant and the brand that bore her name to place girls in an imagined past and freeze them there. In its early days in the '80s and '90s, Pleasant Company didn't have to navigate stories in which girls dealt with insecurities over not having as much spending money as friends at the mall, or families divided over Reagan-era politics. No American Girl doll weathered wanting to wear a crop top like their cool older sister and trying to sneak out to a New Kids on the Block concert. Pleasant might have found that kind of realness to be, like a neon Toys "R" Us sign, "offensive."

We can't stop imagining what Pleasant was like at the mall. Was she like Elizabeth Taylor in the White Diamonds ad, giving her diamond earring away to a stranger as casually as we place our Dunkin' order? We will never know. We'd love to know what she makes of a more recent historical doll, Courtney Moore, set in 1986 and firmly entrenched in mall culture. Would she be charmed by this nostalgia and want to find her old cassette tapes and boom box, or be triggered by visions of neon toy store signs and Cabbage Patch dolls?

Pleasant took this frustration at the limited doll offerings for children with her on a trip to Colonial Williamsburg that same year where she had what the Baby-Sitters Club might call her "big idea."

Working in educational publishing and research prepared Pleasant to see Williamsburg as an incubator for her next great product to revolutionize how kids learn. She'd recognized the importance of innovations like *Sesame Street* and other interactive ways to reach kids and invite them to learn about all kinds of things. Walking around the museum and seeing interpreters bring history to life, she may have thought, "What if?"

"I was really excited about what I saw," Pleasant later recalled of Colonial Williamsburg. The museum re-creates a revolutionary town and includes costumed interpreters acting out historical characters, tradespeople reproducing crafts from the era, and buildings decorated as they were in the 1770s. "I realized what a wonderful living classroom it was, but I found that none of the written information was for children," she noted.

Pleasant brainstormed that dolls and stories set in the past with girls at the center could inspire both girls' imaginations and their desire to learn. "The idea," explained Rowland, "is that these girls would represent girls growing up in America. To bring the stories alive, I wanted to have the play experience to make the learning alive—to touch, to feel." As she explained in publicity materials reprinted in newspapers across the country, "Books are the heart of the collection, but the dolls are the way the stories are visualized and experienced as little girls act out the stories using the dolls." When quizzed as to which she dreamed up first, the dolls or books, Rowland was adamant: "They came together. I never conceived of one without the other."

Now that she had her big idea, Pleasant set to work to make it a reality. She formed her eponymous Pleasant Company in 1985 and took up offices in downtown Madison, Wisconsin, using her own money to fund her business. We love this confidence! There, she directed a team of authors, including friend and former colleague Valerie Tripp, to produce inspiring and historically accurate stories that put girls in the past.

The books canonically draw on a now familiar formula reminiscent of other children's literature; the main character faces a challenge, has to learn a lesson, and then resolves the crisis neatly by the end of the book. She will make friends along the way and weather storms (sometimes of her own making) with the support of a loving family. Reviewers of the first books compared the early offerings to the Little House books, another series based on a real girl in American history who similarly gets into hijinks and gets out of them with an assist from her family and friends.

The first three dolls launched in 1986, and like Mary, also born that year, their lives are defined by history and a personal sense of drama. Kirsten Larson, a Swedish immigrant who travels to Minnesota and loses a friend along the way (RIP, Marta!) allowed young readers to follow along on an adventure to a seemingly empty frontier, where the Larsons struggle to survive. Kirsten does make an Indigenous friend, but she, like our dreams of ever rebraiding our Kirsten doll's hair to factory standards, quickly disappeared. Kirsten's hardships are many, and the plot points introduce real trauma (hi, grieving friend's death from cholera, never mind seeing a dead body in a cave, stealing from said dead person to help the family survive, etc.). It really does make us wonder what went down in these pitch meetings that *this* is the plotline the crew at Pleasant Company believed would teach young girls essential elements of American character. In some ways, they were trailblazers, as we can't help but believe both Kevin Costner's *Dances with Wolves* and *An American Tail: Fievel Goes West* (from 1990 and 1991, respectively) draw on this origin story.

We'd love to tell you the other characters launched that year had less traumatic storylines, but to paraphrase Mariah Carey, that'd be a fantasy. Samantha Parkington, Edwardian-era suffragist queen and labor organizer, lives in 1904, and we ride along as she hides some orphans in her attic, organizes a labor protest (those who can't do, protest), and explores suffrage by shadowing her soon-to-be aunt, one of the first beards in children's lit. Though she's a child of privilege, she understands the orphan's plight, having lost her parents to a tragic accident as a baby. She is an extremely fancy girl but also very sincere, and the books present a compelling navigation of childhood grief.

In publishing stories of girls facing hardship or tragedy, Pleasant was in part also drawing on tropes in children's literature targeted at girls historically (*A Little Princess, The Secret Garden, Eloise, Madeline,* etc.). In presenting girls facing deaths, grief, and other big emotions, she was also responding to some close-to-home audience testing. Pleasant asked her then eight-year-old niece what she wanted to read about, and she said, "Oh, Aunt Pleasant, orphans." We get it. We, too, lost many an hour reading harrowing stories of girls our age who faced all kinds of tragedy. Sometimes they found themselves in the process. Other times, like when we played the *Oregon Trail* computer game, they tried to ford the river and died.

Last of the original trio, though certainly not least, was living legend Molly McIntire, whose greatest trauma was not getting her way at all times (we get it). As we watch her live through World War II, we worry with her as she awaits the return of her physician father from service overseas in England. In the meantime, she has to battle a housekeeper leaning into ration-chic cuisine (we have been traumatized by turnips ever since) and maneuver her way through a tense casting process to tap-dance as Miss Victory at a fundraising event. Is she the female symbol of the greatest generation Tom Brokaw could not begin to process when he coined the romanticized term for her era in 1998? Possibly. Would we pay to hear Tom Brokaw read the Molly books to us? Absolutely.

Pleasant anticipated the narrative of Brokaw's *The Greatest Generation* by over a decade, but both interpretations of American history lived in the same imaginary (mostly white) universe: They inspired pride in its past and taught life lessons along the way. In thinking this kind of thing was what kids needed, Pleasant may have been aware that their parents grew up living through historical eras defined by the Vietnam War, Watergate, racial unrest, and revolutions, sexual and otherwise. These years provided fewer unequivocal national "wins" in comparison to World War II. As Diana Huss Green, then editor in chief of *Parents' Choice* magazine, said upon the release of the first series, the books "have a value system. Some sense of right and wrong. It's very hard for kids today to learn right from wrong when their parents aren't sure." Pleasant was likely designing a product for girls *and* their parents, those who witnessed government "hypocrisy" in a "dehumanized" world, to recall Pleasant's own words from a 1970 profile. Some early reviews did not universally praise this approach. "In the book world," one early review noted, "there are those who say the books are 'superficial' history and fall short of being great literature and that the books and dolls as yet present only a white face on America's past."

Luckily for Pleasant and company, book reviews don't always reflect market appeal. Pleasant packed her dolls, their books, and all kinds of supplemental accessories and outfits into an iconic catalogue to sell directly to children and their parents, keeping costs down (the dolls still cost $75 each). The response was something akin to Beatlemania or the release of *Red (Taylor's Version)*. In the first four years, Pleasant Company turned a profit of $30 million. The catalogue-driven business was successful immediately and inspired the kind of brand loyalty that only diehards understand.

In July of 1990, the sale of returned or slightly damaged dolls and accessories at Madison Children's Museum drew four thousand parents and children to the event, which raised $124,000 to benefit the museum in two days. Some attendees slept in their cars just to have a chance to buy dolls. That's how big this was. Even more telling is the amount of people who still have these dolls and treasure them, as opposed to, say, the other toy phenoms of the era that inspired a comparable frenzy. If anyone out there still treasures their Furby, we hope you are okay.

Of course, the draw for American Girl was not just the stories, but the whole package. Pleasant and her team obsessed over historical accuracy, and each doll arrived wearing a beautiful outfit from their era. The catalogue included photos of the dolls posed in tableaus from the books: Samantha in a winter scene, Kirsten on her birthday, Molly in a classroom seated at a desk. Everything in the image was for sale: furniture, accessories, and extra outfits. Girls could also buy life-size outfits identical to their dolls', making for immersive, if expensive, play. We still think about Samantha's cape all the time and wonder when the age cutoff is to wear an early-twentieth-century look in a twenty-first-century world as thirty-plus-year-old women.

In a 1990 profile of the brand, Barbara Elleman, editor of *Booklist*, an influential book review journal published by the American Library Association, was asked to explain the immediate popularity of American Girl dolls despite such stinging early criticism. First, she valued American Girl for "having likable heroines" that are "true to their times." The biggest asset to the brand, however, was its pairing of historically accurate books and dolls. "Such a tie-in [with products] is more unusual than one might suppose," she explained. According to Elleman, no one else was taking on historical storytelling at this scale "and of this quality."

After a period of just eighteen months of development (and a lifetime of preparation), Pleasant and the company that bore her name created a means for children to build their own living history museums at home. Girls could learn about history, play with their dolls, and imagine themselves in the past.

Now, having understood some of Pleasant's journey and her genius, we wanted to visit the place that so inspired her. Walking in her footsteps, we set out to appreciate the true measure of her ingenuity by trying to identify what she adapted from Colonial Williamsburg and what she invented herself.

Welcome to Williamsburg

Before we act as surrogate guides through Colonial Williamsburg and reveal the results of our investigation loosely titled "The American Girl Inspiration Tour: A Tripp to Remember," we need to start our story in the hotel restaurant where we found ourselves when we arrived in Virginia one evening in June. We decided to have dinner there mainly because we were lazy and it was past 8:00 p.m. Allison's preferred dinner time is 4:30, so by her internal clock, it was almost midnight. This was a one-room combination bar / restaurant / continental breakfast bar. The breakfast bar was mostly covered so guests could be genuinely surprised by the mini boxes of cereal and orange juice revealed in the morning.

We sat in a booth and waited for our food, talking about what we'd see the next day. Suddenly, Mary stopped to listen closely to the music playing. It sounded sort of like Ed Sheeran, but it was not Ed Sheeran. Without fixating on it, we started talking again only for Allison to stop and point out we were hearing Justin Timberlake's "Mirrors," sung by a person we can only identify as Bustin Jimberfake.

Were we to believe they could not afford the royalties of one former Mouseketeer here? Could this budget chain (which is our brand) not afford the real thing? We felt like we were in the Sims game, which offers clips of real songs presented as indecipherable mumble singing. The resemblance of the covers to the real thing was both uncanny and called more attention to itself than the actual "authentic" tracks. This would prove an omen of things to come on our journey. Hanging out in the hotel hot tub, we started asking questions that would carry us through our Tripp: Would we see American Girl mirrored in Colonial Williamsburg, to paraphrase a song by Bustin Jimberfake? What if we just walked away from this trip with memories but no greater understanding of what makes American Girl so endearing among its fans? And perhaps most importantly, would we ever experience the wonders of not chronically overthinking things?

Our Journey Begins

Approaching Colonial Williamsburg the next day felt like a dream. We'd been to the museum on family vacations as kids, but our memories of it were sort of hazy and mostly about the gift shop(s). For those who, like us, might need a refresher, it's helpful to know some intel on the museum. Like Molly McIntire, who has two birth years (1934 or 1986, depending on your view), Colonial Williamsburg also has an "old" and a "new" history. It is both a colonial city dating back to 1699 and a living museum designed to revive and celebrate the city's colonial origin, founded in 1927. Just as Molly contains layers, so does this museum and its history.

Colonial Williamsburg was the result in part of a late-nineteenth- and early-twentieth-century emphasis on "colonial revival." Starting with the formation of a Ladies' Association to preserve Mount Vernon before the Civil War, organizations like the Association for the Preservation of Virginia Antiquities (now Preservation Virginia), the National Society of the Colonial Dames of America, the Daughters of the American Revolution, and eventually the Daughters of the Confederacy formed to fund "preservation" efforts. In part, this was in response to fears provoked by modernization. What fears? Just take a look at what these groups wanted to preserve and it will tell you a lot about what they valued and what they were reacting against. Early efforts focused on Mount Vernon, Monticello, anything related to Lincoln, places George Washington is alleged to have slept, and a house everyone basically knew was never lived in by Betsy Ross, aka the alleged creator of the American flag design. These interests all reflect a larger turn toward preserving anything related to colonial life, the founders, and reminders of American patriotism and "values." These values trended toward American exceptionalism, democracy, citizenship, and, increasingly, white supremacy.

It's no accident these organizations and the house museums and sites they created popped up in the years also marked by increasing immigration rates, technological advances that changed the look and feel of communities (trolley cars, automobiles, telephone wires, etc.), and fraught racial, labor, and gendered politics. After the war, northern and southern whites found common cause in preserving white supremacy. If you've ever seen photos of the reunion of veterans who fought at Gettysburg, you will see haggard vets in ill-fitting Union and Confederate uniforms shaking hands across a table. They could so easily forget the rift for which they had been willing to give their lives because they could agree on the maintenance of their shared desire to equate civilization with whiteness.

Into this moment stepped Dr. W. A. R. Goodwin, the son of a Confederate veteran and pastor at Williamsburg's Episcopalian Bruton Parish Church. Goodwin wanted to preserve the fading colonial buildings of the town. Did anyone ask this man to empower himself as a one-man preservation society? Unclear. Williamsburg had been the capital of Virginia until 1781, when then governor Thomas Jefferson moved it farther inland to Richmond for safety from British attack. Afterward, Williamsburg entered a decline, with employment available mainly at the college or the nearby Eastern Lunatic Asylum. Goodwin hated to see the town lose its history. He wanted to hold off the encroachment of progress that further erased Williamsburg's once prominent standing, and fought to prevent tearing down colonial buildings and to keep gas stations and other signs of modernity out. Operating on a pastor's income, he knew he'd need a rich donor to make this happen.

John D. Rockefeller Jr., son of the founder of Standard Oil, proved receptive to Goodwin's pitch. He took a tour of the town with Goodwin and was able to appreciate his vision for the future of the town, which was mostly about its past. Rockefeller donated funds to have an architect sketch a plan. He then secretly gave Goodwin funds to buy homes as they became available, believing owners would inflate prices if they knew he was the buyer. By November 22, 1927, he'd committed to the restoration, and by 1928 his involvement became public. That year, Colonial Williamsburg incorporated, and Rockefeller decided to leave most of the restoration to northern architects and experts.

The resulting outdoor living history museum reflects money spent by Rockefeller et al. and the best efforts of Goodwin and others to restore some eighty-eight structures labeled original (including outhouses, sheds, etc.) and rebuild over four hundred others to present an eighteenth-century vision to visitors. In total, 720 mostly nineteenth-century buildings were demolished to make way for what's now called the world's largest outdoor living history museum. The fact that the restored buildings are not immediately distinguishable from the re-created ones is to the credit of designers (who would likely all have HGTV shows today), and part of the challenge of understanding preservation.

The grand effort to both preserve and restore the colonial history of the town must have both captivated and inspired Pleasant. We can imagine she was impressed that the museum went to great lengths to produce this feeling of "being there"; water fountains were hidden in barrels, and lighting that looked candlelit hid signs of electricity. One former guest could be forgiven for asking a guide, in all seriousness, if a particularly friendly squirrel was "mechanical." The cultivation of a refined and curated aesthetic is what some critics have identified as an issue for the museum, describing it as a "Republican Disneyland." Writing in the *New York Review of Books*, Ada Louise Huxtable critiqued the museum's approach for "the replacement of reality with selective fantasy."

The same could certainly be said (and has been said) of American Girl. Pleasant was also inspired by a desire to share a patriotic vision of history with children, just like Colonial Williamsburg. The development of these dolls, outfits, accessories, and stories reflects a similar impulse to curate, or choose what to share, and therein lies the common instinct toward "selective fantasy" using history. We set out to see what vision of history we could identify in both, and how this place used storytelling, objects, and play to invite guests into their version of American history. As it turned out, American Girl and Williamsburg had much in common.

Dance, Dance, Revolution:
A Tour of the Governor's Palace

After passing through the modern visitor center, guests are invited to walk across a bridge that appears to be the answer to Cher's question/threat "if I could turn back time." The bridge has a series of plaques that mark descending decades, taking you from the present to the 1770s, the imagined setting of Colonial Williamsburg. Each plaque flags a right or technological advancement that is being stripped away to remind you that you are traveling to a place where things such as "automobiles" do not exist. "1920," one plaque reads, "from this date you accept that women cannot vote." This hit us hard, and not because we'd just transitioned out of AC and back into high humidity. As Cher herself might say, "Words are like weapons, they wound sometimes." Little did we know that we'd learn more about what rights women do and don't have later on our trip.

Entering the town, it is obvious that a major tactic that helps Colonial Williamsburg educate its guests about history is its historic buildings and the objects they house. By walking into mansions, wealthy homes, general stores, trade shops of various kinds, and other buildings, guests can feel as though they are literally walking into the past.

When we came upon the governor's palace, we really thought our chances were high that we'd encounter one Felicity Merriman. After all, the palace figures significantly in the books. It's the site of the children's ball she attends at the end of the series, wearing an iconic blue gown and escorted by her frenemy/crush Ben. We walked around the gardens, which we discovered were bordered by a canal seemingly to nowhere and serving no purpose (a metaphor?) and returned to wait in line outside the palace for a tour.

Looking up and down the line, we wondered what kind of crowd Colonial Williamsburg gets. We were in line with older white lady friend groups, white families with elementary-school-age children, and a few younger white hetero couples. Right before us in line was a family with a dad wearing camo pants, a camo baseball hat, and a Smokey Bear shirt, which carried the altered slogan "Only you can prevent socialism." It left us wishing he had fully committed to a camo look and was in fact blended in with his surroundings. In a crowd of white people, he did almost disappear.

Blissfully ushered into air-conditioning, we were directed to a room with benches surrounded by images significant to both colonial Williamsburg and Colonial Williamsburg® the living history museum. The juxtaposition of painted portraits of the last royal governors of Virginia colony hanging alongside early photographs of the museum's construction and a portrait of a smiling Eleanor Roosevelt on vacay created a kind of historic TGI Fridays aesthetic that spoke to us.

A very nice guide with a tricorner hat ushered us into the mansion through a dramatic entryway. We stepped through a doorway and saw row after row of guns. The entryway was lined with muskets, which surely offered an exercise in intimidation and a practical storehouse for weapons that could be used against the governor if they fell into the wrong hands. After our guide pointed us to the powder room (small room where enslaved people would powder guests' wigs), we followed him into the ballroom.

Here was where things turned tragic. Our host told us to "line up boys on one side, girls on the other." Already we were nervous, as we do not like forced fun or binaries. Our guide then painted a picture of the balls that took place in this truly impressive room. The walls were covered with portraits of British monarchs of the period, and the room was decorated with candelabras that allowed you to imagine dramatic dance-offs.

Being in the ballroom, which was decorated as it would have been in the 1770s, felt like walking into the Felicity books. For the first time that day (but not the last), we felt like we were in Felicity's world and could easily imagine the ball she attended. The ability to visit a physical place so closely resembling the one rendered in the books made the fictional world of Felicity Merriman feel so real.

Our host called our attention to a harpsichord in the room, noting that it was the only original piece in the place. Earlier, he'd explained that this building had a storied history. It was the governor's palace, then a patriot hospital during the American Revolution, and then it burned down (RIP). The building we were standing in was a replica, a reconstruction made possible by the discovery of the original blueprints and illustrations. So, if the building was a reproduction, what did it matter if this harpsichord was original?

Before we had time to contemplate that to any kind of conclusion, he told us our tour was at an end and we'd be ushered out the back door (which honestly felt right to us; we were wearing jean shorts and were clearly underdressed for the room). However, before we left, he was going to teach us how to minuet, or curtsy, as if this act could make up for our other cultural faux pas.

"Look at the boy or girl opposite you," he instructed, "minuet, and say 'How do you do?'" In a feeling of true dread, Mary realized she was standing opposite Smokey the Anti-Socialist Dad. Leave it to Colonial Williamsburg to take us right back to our middle-school-dance-anxiety days. That exercise did help us appreciate the politics of etiquette and comportment culture that meant so much to elites in the time; so much relied on the body, posture, and performance. On the other hand, being asked to bow to someone with whom you likely have nothing in common is, as Avril Lavigne might say, "complicated." Closing her eyes, Mary did what was less a minuet and more a full-body cringe. Turns out T-shirts may help prevent socialism, but they can't prevent firsthand embarrassment at historic sites. With a quick pivot, we were able to move on through the gardens (which are gorgeous).

Back out on the street, we talked about the emphasis on the harpsichord as the only original piece in the room. Did it really matter what was real or reproduced in the palace? The emphasis on authenticity was something we noticed throughout our days at the museum. Was this emphasis on how authentic things were to convince us their museum was a "real" presentation of the past? Did that actually matter?

What impressed us the most about our brief time in this mansion (we sound like *Bachelor* contestants) is how easy it was to imagine ourselves back in that time simply by standing in a place designed to appear that way. Whether the furniture was real didn't stop our imaginations from spinning out visions of what a ball might have actually looked like in 1774. Seeing some clothing in portraits on the walls and remembering Felicity's iconic look allowed us to guess what women might have worn, what food may have been served, and how music would sound in this space. A candelabra gave us brief *Phantom of the Opera* flashbacks, but still, we were in it. We were clearly not the only ones who so quickly moved to a sense of wonder on our brief walk through the palace. This effect—the ability to build a world and invite guests in—is something at which Colonial Williamsburg excels.

Pleasant learned worldbuilding here and used it to great success in American Girl. Thinking about Felicity's ball, we remembered the ways her books built anticipation to attend a children's ball in the palace inspired by this space. It's not hard to imagine the wonder she might have felt arriving at a place like this, even coming from a family of some means. The catalogue helped girls like us reenact the anticipation she must have felt about attending by offering her blue gown for sale both for dolls and for girls. Fans could also buy Felicity's own "Fashion Doll" dressed for the ball, which came with a royal invitation. Not unlike the harpsichord and trappings of the mansion, the line between real and fake mattered little compared to the feeling these things offered in transporting kids back into the past.

The chance to take part in activities grounded in the past seemed essential to the sense of place the museum created. Pleasant adapted this when she created American Girl. Although the writing around the museum may have been geared toward adults when she was there, she likely saw activities that invited kids to attempt different trades, try household tasks, or learn about the colonial government. These kinds of interactions through play can make a huge impact on kids.

We later spoke with a listener named Lindsey Wood who now works at the museum, which she described as a kind of full-circle moment. When she was a child visiting on vacation with her family, she wandered into a demonstration of a drop spindle (picture an early version of a spinning wheel). The woman running the demonstration showed her how to work it and invited her to try it herself. She remembers the woman saying, "You're doing really well! You're a natural!" which encouraged her. She felt like history was something she could be good at because this adult made her feel like she could be. This, combined with the books, dolls, and accessories of American Girl, inspired her imagination to picture what life was like in the eighteenth century for girls her age. This is exactly the kind of moment Pleasant hoped to create, and it's easy to see how Colonial Williamsburg helped inspire it.

Living (with) History: Stories We Tell About Our Shared Past

Perhaps the greatest influence of Williamsburg on Pleasant and the brand that bore her name was the ways it taught history through storytelling. In its earliest years, it focused on communicating patriotism. We can see Pleasant being into this on arrival as she visited the same year Lee Greenwood's "God Bless the U.S.A." hit the airwaves and was used by Ronald Reagan in his bid for reelection. Whatever her politics, Pleasant was one of many who believed that some of society's ills lay in a post-1970s cynicism that created what she called a "sour" world, or what MTV's *Daria* might call a "sick, sad world."

In the World War II era, Colonial Williamsburg was more explicit in its commitment to patriotic storytelling. Molly would have felt right at home in Williamsburg, as ties to the presidents were front and center and provided the kind of content that would help her get an A on her President's Day report on George Washington. Iconically, her partner on said project insisted on dressing up as George and posing dramatically as Molly pointed out key dates on a timeline. This child's report card may have read "maybe she's born with it, maybe she's a future living history interpreter." In that era, patriotism was a key to interpretation. In one telling anecdote from the period, a G.I. is alleged to have stood before a portrait of George Washington and said, "You got it for us and we mean to keep it." When Rockefeller was later told of this exchange, it reportedly left him teary-eyed. We wish we could tell you this entire exchange left us what Whitney Houston might call "so emotional." Alas, every time we are confronted with praise of George Washington, we react like friends who are told someone they love has a crush on a mediocre man, to which we can only respond incredulously, "Him!??"

The interpretation of the museum shifted through the years from overt patriotism and an admiration for colonial architecture and craft to include issues of race, power, and economic self-interest by the 1980s. This may have been inspired by a broader turn in history to tell more inclusive stories that felt less like propaganda and more like investigative reports into the truth of the past.

The most influential element of this storytelling on Pleasant was the notion that you could communicate the story of an age through one person's experiences. Colonial Williamsburg typically shows a film in its visitor center that embodies this kind of storytelling. The film was shown daily at the park for sixty-three years, making it the longest-running motion picture in American history. Called *Williamsburg: The Story of a Patriot,* or, as we call it, *American Boy,* it follows a fictional Virginian planter, James Fry, as he begins his first term as a representative in the assembly in Williamsburg and witnesses the lead-up to the colonies' declaration of independence. We didn't get the chance to see it in person due to a Covid-related interruption in screenings, but we watched it on YouTube and it is worth a viewing.

By following James through the days and weeks leading up to the colony declaring independence, we get a sense of the issues driving the debate among representatives and the human cost. It's not hard to imagine how Pleasant could have walked away from this and believed one girl could be a stand-in for the histories of the frontier, the Civil War, World War II, the Gilded Age, and the Revolutionary War.

A Williamsburg innovation that Pleasant also adapted into American Girl was the use of first-person storytelling to humanize the past. By 1977, the museum evolved beyond offering tours of its spaces and included "living history" interpretation. The museum recruited and extensively trained actors to "be" actual historic figures or composite characters based on extensive research. They would be relied upon not just to repeat a script, but rather to improvise how that person might have behaved in real time, responding to interactions with guests from the future.

This is an area where we part ways in terms of what we can personally handle. Allison has performed as a mill girl both in person and on film, and

Mary is still struggling to offer a convincing living history performance of "woman living in the 2020s." A few years ago, we went on a murder mystery train ride that featured actors performing as '20s-era Gilded Age elites. Over the course of a few hours, we laughed, we cried, and we solved a crime (we solved a murder, and all we can remember about it now is that he confessed when we told him we knew he wore the wrong tuxedo jacket for the dinner hour). We will never forget how convincing the actors were as insufferable rich people whose manners and class outshone ours. Their talent was especially admirable considering we met them after they pulled into the train station lot in a used Corolla that itself appeared "historic." Watching them pile out of the car in costume jewelry and evening wear is a juxtaposition we'll never forget, and we respect them to this day. (Please note we arrived to this performance in a used Saturn, so we are not judging these icons of dinner theater.) Throughout that experience (and generally), Allison wanted to join the performance, while Mary wanted to hide under the table whenever it seemed like the performers would approach us to volunteer.

This was the respective energy with which we engaged the living history interpreters at Colonial Williamsburg. We passed George Washington in the street, had a quick confab with the Marquis de Lafayette during which he remained on horseback the entire time (is this what Kacey Musgraves meant by "high horse"?), and saw an advertisement for a Q&A featuring Martha Washington that we could not resist. This exchange demonstrated the ways that living history can make history feel immediate (a person in the past is talking to YOU). It also became apparent that this storytelling approach only works if the audience is game to be in on this fantasy and to sidestep any sources of potential discomfort.

In the outdoor theater where we were about to hear from Martha, we felt a sense of excitement (Allison), fear (Mary), and anticipation (both of us). It felt both fun and surreal to see a young Martha Washington hold forth and answer any questions thrown at her. It reminded us of that college-life reality of having friends in improv groups who beg you to come to their shows, where they riff on "wild" suggestions thrown out by the crowd. Had we played this on this day, the suggestions might have been "Love story! Humidity! Happy marriage?" The crowd was very interested in her marriage to George, and Martha cracked wise about their relationship as if they were like any married couple in the crowd. She seemed prepared for any question thrown at her and answered in the kind of nonregional dialect that would be familiar to Katharine Hepburn or other stars from the golden age of Hollywood.

This approach can be very playful and fun. We can see a direct link between this kind of first-person storytelling and American Girl books. Reading any of the books leaves us with the feeling that we are not only living through these moments with Samantha or Kirsten or Molly but are also privy to their internal thoughts, which their families and friends are not. Are we insane for thinking we were the *only* ones who really "got" Molly because we'd read her thoughts and felt like we were riding along with a simpatico, potentially sociopathic, queen? Don't answer that. All we know is that this approach creates a real sense of intimacy, which makes it useful in drawing people into a topic that can feel distant, like history.

It's one thing to imagine someone in the past speaking directly to you through the pages of a book. It's quite another to have it literally play out live and in person. The performance of living history at a place like Williamsburg hinges on the audience playing along with the fantasy and not getting out of pocket with their questions. This is where the wheels come off for us. Do you think if you really talked to someone in the past, they would be on the same page with you, and vice versa? This is a storytelling style that relies on a certain level of etiquette. It's usually like an opposite of MTV's *The Real World,* where things never stop being polite so they can start getting real. If they *were* real, wouldn't it occur to someone from the present to ask Martha anything about claiming ownership over so many people? Or how the wealth she brought to her marriage affected the power dynamics between husband and wife? Spill the tea, ma'am! For Martha, might she want to ask something of the crowd? Perhaps how the refinement of eighteenth-century fashions devolved to a sea of cargo shorts before her very eyes?

This emphasis on politeness between performer and guests was evident throughout our tour and clearly influenced the kind of storytelling and interpretation available at the museum that seemed to rely on fantasy. Specifically, this form of storytelling appeared to privilege the comfort of the almost entirely white audience. This tension between a dedication to authenticity and the reality of wanting to attract a mostly white clientele influenced a vital question that absolutely impacted the development of American Girl. How do you tell stories about difficult things in history? Whose comfort do you privilege in the telling, and to what end?

Both the museum's and American Girl's treatment of slavery demonstrates these challenges.

How to Avoid a Vortex to Hell

One night in Williamsburg, we attended a ghost tour. For years, Williamsburg wouldn't offer them, thinking such flights of imagination might affect its dedication to authenticity. After all, if you offer ghost tours *and* sell magnets of a cartoon Ben Franklin and his BFFs, how can anyone take you seriously? (Said magnet is now on Mary's fridge.) However, the popularity of ghost tours offered by other vendors in town pushed Colonial Williamsburg to create its own official tours. Historians Tiya Miles and others have noted the ways ghost tours offer stories of slavery, suffering, and violence for profit at the expense of the dead. Other writers have similarly examined tours of abandoned asylums, showing how they present disability as a spectacle and source of entertainment. In the South in particular, such ghost tours can offer spaces to romanticize white Civil War dead and further perpetuate "the Lost Cause."

Gathering around lit torches in the pouring rain, our tour group was here for a good time, not a long time. A little girl dressed exclusively in *Moana* gear asked, "Why are we doing this?" and immediately became our leader. In front of the Peyton Randolph House, owned by a revolutionary-era lawyer and the owner of over twenty enslaved people, our guide described the experiences of a medium who'd previously taken the tour. She explained that the medium felt a lot of "dark energy" near the house and believed it was actually a vortex to hell. The only way to escape said vortex, she claimed, was to avoid it. Standing in the center of said vortex, being pelted with rain, our leader, the *Moana* stan, spoke for the group when she offered a barely credulous "Huh?"

We were similarly confused, but the idea of escaping a vortex to hell by avoiding it became a kind of metaphor for us about the challenges of talking about difficult subjects in history. You can escape the vortex (difficult or awkward subjects) so long as you consciously avoid it. We saw this play out at the Wythe House, where we thought a lot about the direct impact of erasure and avoidance on storytelling in early American Girl books.

In the 1770s, George Wythe was known as an eminent judge, law professor, and learned man. His home is one of the nicest you can tour in Williamsburg. When we waited in line, two women of color (the only Black guides we saw that day) corralled the mostly white guests outside and gave us CliffsNotes on George Wythe to prepare us for what we'd see inside. He'd married a woman of standing whose father built them this home, where George entertained former students and friends, including Thomas Jefferson. Importantly, the guides hit us with the statistic that half of the population in Williamsburg in this time was Black, either free or enslaved. They also told us that when we entered the house, we could explore the first floor on our own. We'd see some of his scientific instruments set up in his study, and it would look as though he had just stepped away.

As we walked through the rooms of the first floor, everything was as they said. The geometric-patterned wallpaper they'd flagged as a reproduction from the original vendor was vibrant and seemed to suit the space. After touring the first floor, we went outside to the garden, where we saw one of the Black interpreters from before waiting to answer questions. She was standing facing the back of the house, and we could look over her shoulder and see various outbuildings and slave quarters. We stopped to listen just as she was speaking to an older white woman about the Wythe family. In reference to slavery, she said, "It's important we speak about these injustices because they still exist all over the world." This was the first time someone we'd met in our tours connected the histories we were seeing in Williamsburg with issues in our own time. We were not just experiencing Williamsburg in a vacuum, after all, but living through a moment when Black Lives Matter protests forced our nation to reevaluate the statues honoring Confederate leaders just an hour away in Richmond and across the country.

Through much of its history, Williamsburg did not directly address the history of slavery. Mary Wiseman, a founder of the living history interpretation program that trains guides to improvise and interpret the lives of real and composite historical characters, remembers that time well. She started as a guide in the 1970s and recalls how adept she became at walking backward as she offered tours through town. She'd taken the job as a then professor's wife, and the hours were convenient as her youngest child started school. The training was arduous and required days-long deep dives into history. "We went to class five days a week from September to March," she explained, reflecting on her training. "We had to know every building in town, how to interpret the architecture, the collections inside the buildings, we had to know every craft."

Yet, she recalls looking back, slavery was both present and uninterrogated. "When I was taking tours around Colonial Williamsburg, every kitchen was open and there were Black ladies interpreting in the kitchen wearing a costume, but we never mentioned slavery, not one mention the whole time that we were taking tourists around."

This changed in the late 1970s with the incorporation of discussions of slavery into exhibits and tours. A living history program that included Rex Ellis, associate director for curatorial affairs at the Smithsonian's National Museum of African American History and Culture; Christy Coleman, executive director of the Jamestown-Yorktown Foundation; and other leaders in public history trained Black interpreters to perform as enslaved historical figures. These efforts, Wiseman and others argue, dramatically improved Williamsburg's representation of slavery and of people of color in the museum from the 1980s forward.

Prior to this, Black figures were visible in these spaces but not invited to speak about their histories or show the trauma and violence of life as an enslaved person. As one study of Colonial Williamsburg also argued, the choice to decorate a slave quarter with selected items emphasizing the domesticity of the enslaved cook invited trainees to view an interpretation created by staff as historical facts, facts that in this case softened the violence and degradation of enslaved experiences through the presentation of relatively comfortable accommodations.

We can see the influence of this kind of interpretive choice in the depiction of Rose, the woman enslaved by Felicity Merriman's family, described as a "cook and maidservant" in *Felicity Learns a Lesson*. Living in Williamsburg in 1774, Felicity Merriman inhabits a household with two enslaved people, Rose and Marcus, "the man who helps Mr. Merriman at home and at the store." The books emphasize Rose's domestic work with its apparent comfort, not her lack of freedom and its impact on her life. This is particularly striking when we consider Felicity spends her entire series obsessed with freeing a mistreated horse whom she names Penny aka Independence while never considering whether Rose deserves the same.

What was going on in the '90s that we thought this was okay? Did it help matters that Felicity had a free Black friend so we'd get that she enslaved people but was not racist? It seems like a polite framing for white readers of her series while also acknowledging the reality that any "authentic" depiction of Williamsburg in this period would have to include slavery in the frame. Would it not have been more authentic in a series that prided itself on its accuracy to delve deeper into Rose's life or at least show some of the household labor from her perspective?

Black interpreters at Colonial Williamsburg also questioned the citation of "authenticity" as the reason why certain histories remained unexplored in these spaces. The largely white staff of the Wythe House, they claimed in a 1990s study, cited a lack of historical evidence for why they would not speak about possible sexual abuse committed by George Wythe against the women he enslaved. A devotion to "authenticity" in this case allows the legitimization of silence. Archives were not designed to record such history, so claiming the evidence doesn't support it while fully knowing why such evidence doesn't exist allows the continued erasure or foreclosing of such histories.

At Colonial Williamsburg, fantasy is useful in allowing interpreters and guests to imagine themselves into the past. However, a comparable leap of imagination to picture sexual violence or other uncomfortable realities necessitates a reversion to what's provable and "authentic" to preserve an interpretation of history that's comfortable for mostly white guests. We saw this desire to comfort white guests firsthand while standing in the gardens of Wythe House. A Black interpreter explained that we all need to learn about slavery because racial injustice still exists in our world. Taking a beat and perhaps noting the discomfort of the white woman to whom she was speaking, she quickly added, "But I'm a Christian, and I believe in peace and love." The woman to whom she was speaking nodded vigorously at this pivot to an apparent common cause.

Being able to explore a physical space with slave quarters, like the refined home of George Wythe, invited guests to engage with a loaded historical moment. The question for us as we walked on was what kind of engagement Colonial Williamsburg was prepared for guests to have. Did they want the public to come to this house and breeze through, seeing only the wallpaper and beautiful objects owned by George Wythe? What was the purpose of these scenes from history? Or of history itself? Was it something that allowed people to fetishize the past, or something that helped explain the present?

The instinct to comfort white guests at any moment they may feel uncomfortable or complicit in histories of slavery may be one born of self-preservation. As we heard Margarette Joyner, an actor-interpreter who performs as an enslaved woman named Succordia, say during a talk about her work at the museum, "You'd be surprised what some white people feel comfortable saying to your face."

The choice of how to tell stories about history also reveals the tensions of being both an educational organization and a business. When forced to prioritize the needs of a business (accommodating guests and making them comfortable) or of education (forcing guests to confront a long history of white supremacy), employees may feel pressured to privilege the needs of the business first. As we'll see, Pleasant Company took a similar approach to historical interpretation in its early years.

Have You Seen This Horse Girl?

We had done a lot of hard work on this trip so far. We'd taken in elements from the museum that clearly inspired Pleasant: the use of many kinds of storytelling, material objects, and activities to interest people in the past. We sweated through all our clothes. We went on a ghost tour in the pouring rain and got soaking wet, only to find we forgot where we parked our car.

By day two, we were ready for some retail therapy. We stopped into a general store on a main drag to pretend we were visiting the Merrimans' store. Along with some little kids, we were drawn by the sight of toys in the window, including dolls. Imagine our shock when we went inside only to discover that this was not Felicity Merriman, but an imposter. Actually, two imposters.

We learned that Felicity Merriman has not been in residence for some years. Instead, Williamsburg now sells two suspiciously American Girl–like dolls, each accompanied by a book that recounts their lives in Williamsburg. Sound familiar? Each is based on an actual girl who grew up in town during the revolutionary era. We see you, Williamsburg! Some might call this progress, using real historical figures unlike the completely fictional Felicity. Did the youths around us understand we were upset that Felicity had been replaced? No. Did it impress us that they now center the story of real girls who lived in Williamsburg? Absolutely not. Are we haters from the old school who refuse to be reasoned with on this topic? Without question.

We were in our feelings, specifically rage, confusion, and lots of nostalgia. Some of these feelings were appropriate. History sites usually like to inspire feelings of nostalgia for aspects of the past while also celebrating the progress of the present. It keeps you curious about the past and appreciative of life today. We get it. Maybe for people in product development at Colonial Williamsburg, offering dolls with books based on real historical figures feels like a refreshing innovation. After all, Felicity Merriman debuted in fall 1991, and some might call her vintage or even dated. To this we can only say, Felicity had her problems, but she is OUR problem.

As we walked to our rented Corolla after another day at the museum, we knew the bridge to the past that we needed to feel whole. We'd seen what inspired Pleasant to create American Girl, but we wanted to explore how she innovated on the museum's offerings to create something unique and special. To do this, we had to revisit the making of Felicity Merriman.

Making Felicity

"I was actually present when Felicity Merriman was born," Mary Wiseman explained. At seventy-six years young, Mary had only recently concluded an illustrious career in living history by retiring as Martha Washington at Mount Vernon. She'd spent decades before that working at Colonial Williamsburg. There, she acted and interpreted Martha Washington and served as the head of the character department, where she was integral to creating programming for children, women, and Black history. By the end of her career, she worked among women who'd grown up loving Felicity and who were somewhat awed by Mary's involvement in the development of the doll and her story.

Because of her decades-long work at the museum and direct involvement in developing Felicity, Mary seemed like the perfect person to explain how Pleasant took something she loved (Williamsburg) and made it uniquely her own. Mary was called into the office of Vice President Dennis O'Toole one morning in the late 1980s and introduced to Pleasant Rowland. Pleasant explained the nature of her company and her desire to work with Williamsburg to create a doll based on the revolution and living in the town. Having launched her first three dolls, she wanted to create a character who lived in Williamsburg.

The vice president handed Pleasant off to Mary and they became fast friends. Such good friends in fact that Pleasant revealed a personal connection she had to the museum that explains in part her devotion to it. "Sitting in the back of the Williamsburg Inn," Mary recalled, Pleasant tried to explain her love for Williamsburg. "She thought," Mary repeated, "'Well, I really believe it's because my parents honeymooned here . . . And I think I was conceived here.'"

This revelation caught us off guard and sent our own Mary spiraling as she recalled the time her friend Tanya told her she may have been conceived on Halloween considering her birthday (July 31). Does the place and time of your conception predict (or doom) your future professional path? Asking for Mary, who is now considering a career change after discovering M. Night Shyamalan is also a Leo.

While Mary Wiseman was not conceived at the museum, she did bring some of its now foundational elements to life. In the late '70s, she was part of the earliest actor-interpreter training program at the museum ("I majored in theater and gave a dramatic tour," she noted). She'd been a force at the museum and wanted to put women in the story at Williamsburg, much like Pleasant. She told us about a meeting she organized to bring women together to commit to creating Women's History Month programming every year. She'd reserved a fancy conference room for the occasion in a building mostly used by the administration. "I remember the door was slightly open that first meeting, and one of the senior vice presidents peeked his head in the door. And he couldn't think of any other reason, poor man, why all women would be sitting there at this table," she recalled. "He looked in and he said, 'Oh, are you gals having a baby shower?'" We didn't follow up on this but sincerely hope they responded, "WHO ASKED YOU?"

Her own experiences in these kinds of environments is what in part led her to develop such respect for Pleasant and the company that bore her name. In the same years she met and worked with Pleasant, a group of anthropologists received permission to study Colonial Williamsburg with full access to staff meetings, training, etc. The resulting book, *The New History in an Old Museum*, recounted its shifts from colonial revival to patriotism to so-called social history, and the challenges of running an educational enterprise that was also a business. A female researcher with the project told Mary privately that had she been alive in the 1690s, she'd have been tried as a witch.

By this point, Mary was divorced, in her forties, and had the energy and ability to make a real impact on the organization. That made her a threat to men in the administration, the researcher explained. While we don't know if Mary would identify as a feminist, like Pleasant, she had to navigate an industry mostly led by men. Though Pleasant began her career reluctant to call herself a feminist, she created and ran a company as a woman who employed women to create dolls and books to empower girls, a trajectory that inspired other women like us about what might be possible. Mary was among them. She was so enamored of Pleasant that she suggested she'd be a great candidate to lead Colonial Williamsburg when the head of the museum retired (Pleasant declined).

Her respect for Pleasant drew on experiences working with her and members of her company. That day when she was called in to work on the development of Felicity, she had never heard of American Girl. Pleasant Company was already a huge success, producing millions in profit a year, unbeknownst to Mary as a woman whose children were grown and who was then expecting her first grandchild. Mary also likely missed this cultural development as she lives so much of her life in the eighteenth century. Even in our conversations, she would casually slip into eighteenth-century expressions. She doesn't do email, and with that in mind, it's understandable she missed the iconic catalogue spreads on Samantha, Molly, and Kirsten. Can we also say that the sign of true wisdom is a person who just declares they "don't do email"?

In their first meeting, Pleasant explained her vision for the brand. "Pleasant was really a teacher at heart," Mary explained, "and she developed the idea of the stories from the past to help encourage students to want to know more."

Remembering all the times she'd seen girls walk around the museum hugging their American Girl dolls, Mary also repeated the comparison to Barbie we'd heard before. "She wanted also to extend the girlhood a little longer to put off the wanting-to-look-like-Barbie phase and to give the girls a chance to have a best friend who was not the pubescent type of Barbie."

Most importantly, Mary realized she could work with Pleasant because they both so valued storytelling as a way to bring people into the past. "I think there's no question everything is a story. I spent forty-five years in character interpretation. When you make history personal, people take it in and take it to heart. And that was really her first step, her first real incentive to make history come alive."

Pleasant and her company were obsessed with accuracy, and to make sure the doll reflected the times both in appearance and in her story, Pleasant explained that she'd be sending staff members to the museum to shadow interpreters and work with the curatorial department to get every detail right. This is how Mary met Valerie Tripp. Previously, Valerie had contributed books to the Samantha series and written all the Molly books (we can never forget this fact). Valerie shadowed Mary for a few days and, as we learned, incorporated several details from Mary's interpretation into the books.

At that time, Mary was the artistic director for the character program and the manager of women's history. This was in the years prior to her work as Martha Washington. She'd created and acted different characters, but decided she'd create a new character for a program she was running for girls. "I had a group of young ladies, the teenage girls who would come in, and they would work and research with me, and then we'd put on programs together at holiday time and others," she described. "I called them the young ladies of accomplishment." Working in the Benjamin Powell House, an original house in the historic area filled with reproduction furniture, she would sit with them and take tea in the parlor. She decided for this program she'd create and perform a new character, a deportment teacher, Ms. Manderly. "I would gather the girls together and give them their lessons in deportment and tea," she remembered.

With Mary's charm and eighteenth-century knowledge, we could easily imagine her teaching Felicity the polite way to decline tea during the boycott by overturning her empty cup on its saucer and saying, "I shall take no tea." Why did she choose "Manderly"? we wondered. "I'm always reluctant to confess this part of the story," Mary explained, "but the idea for Ms. Manderly's name came from the fact that I'd seen *Rebecca* the night before I met with the girls for the first time, and when she said '[Last night I dreamt I went to] Manderley again,' I thought, well, that's a great name." It feels iconic that Mary based the name of a deportment teacher on a romantic psychological thriller with queer vibes that ends in an act of arson, aka an act of which Ms. Manderly would disapprove.

Assisting Mary was a young woman who had just graduated from Berkeley named Michelle Cude. Now a professor in the Middle, Secondary, and Mathematics Education department at James Madison University, Michelle compared her discovery of and love for Colonial Williamsburg to our generation's love of American Girl. For her, growing up in California, it had felt like a big deal to vacation there at twelve. She was enamored of the guides and actor-interpreters and blown away by the scale of their knowledge. It helped her to realize a career in history might be possible. She was so impressed that she'd found the head of HR on this first trip and asked how she might work there herself someday. Later, in college, she'd done a study-away program that let her work at Williamsburg and returned after graduation. She hoped to get some experience as a museum professional before becoming a teacher.

Her first job after college was as part of a research team putting together interpretations on life in an eighteenth-century family. She also took harpsichord lessons and would occasionally perform for the public. While she loved the work, she was presenting as a guide from the twentieth century. This was fine at first, but then she met Mary Wiseman, who would stop by the house in character leading tours. Michelle discovered, as we learned ourselves, there was something about Mary.

She went to Mary's office one day and asked how she could get into character interpretation. Mary took her under her wing and became a mentor and close friend, and had Michelle help her with the young-ladies-of-accomplishment program. It's easy to imagine how teen girls would find Michelle extremely cool. She was a young adult who must have seemed very hip in the way women in their early twenties do to girls in their teens. She rocked an eighteenth-century look and styled her red hair in sausage curls. Mary's work was well known by then, and prominent figures often came by to see her. This explains in some part why Michelle does not remember her first meeting with Valerie Tripp. Although Michelle has no memory of this meeting, the sight of Michelle and her red hair made an impact on Valerie Tripp. She used Michelle as the inspiration for Felicity Merriman's iconic red hair and overall aesthetic.

We asked Michelle what it was like to be the basis of the Felicity Merriman doll. Did she own a horse named Penny? (No.) Is there a statue of her at Colonial Williamsburg? (No.) Did she name either of her daughters Felicity? (Also no.) Mostly, Michelle has the coolest two truths and a lie ready to go at all times. In practice, Michelle got to observe how assiduous Pleasant Company was about getting details right. For example, an expert from Pleasant Company wanted to get the colors of her freckles right, and she remembers them holding up color swatches to her face to attempt a true color match. (Felicity would ultimately not have her freckles. Kit Kittredge was the first girl to have them when released in 2000.)

Michelle has fond memories of working with Valerie Tripp, a refrain we heard from several people who worked with her. For a few days, Val (a nickname we use as her aspiring friends) shadowed her and then had a photographer follow her around in her eighteenth-century costume. She wanted to make sure that the illustrations showed Felicity with the correct eighteenth-century posture period clothing would create. When the books came out, Michelle recalls, she was impressed that Felicity wore stays.

Pleasant Company and their entire team—from Pleasant to Valerie Tripp to the team developing costumes and accessories—wanted every detail to be perfect and accurate. One day, we are told, Valerie walked by a shop window and saw an eighteenth-century doll in a beautiful blue gown in the window. Working with the costume department, Pleasant Company developed a comparable iconic blue ball gown for Felicity.

As Valerie developed the story arcs and sent along drafts of the books, she'd frequently call Mary and others and consult them on various details, asking, "Would this happen?" The only thing about which they strongly disagreed was what to name the new American Girl. "Felicity is a very New England name," Mary reminded us. "It did not appear much in Virginia." Most girls' names from that period derived from nicknames. Common names from the period included Molly for Mary, Dolly for Dorothy, and Patsy for Martha. Despite these suggestions of more historically accurate names, Pleasant Company went with "Felicity," and the rest is history.

Despite the brand's attention to detail and accuracy, which you would think would impress the administration at Colonial Williamsburg, one marketing executive spoke out against the partnership. In *The New History in an Old Museum*, a marketing vice president was quoted saying "he worried that the foundation had sacrificed 'credibility for profit,' because those customers, however loyal, would associate the place with 'a doll, a fake person, a person who never lived.' In becoming too closely associated with 'a total fantasy,' Colonial Williamsburg had, he emphasized, potentially 'compromised' its 'mission.'" The anthropologists wondered if his issue was just that American Girl would get to use the museum to promote a doll that Colonial Williamsburg could itself produce and profit from entirely. As we learned, that is in fact what they're doing now.

What's harsh about this marketing executive's assessment of American Girl and their collaboration is that it completely erases the real efforts at authenticity that Pleasant and her company had in common with the museum. It also completely missed what made American Girl unique. We shared this published quote with Mary, who strongly disagreed with it, saying the executive failed to appreciate Pleasant's insights about children and what they needed to feel special.

Pleasant brought her passion for education, authenticity, and children's advocacy to her work along with her business savvy. This was not just a new business venture, either, Mary reminded us, but a very personal project. For example, Pleasant is the face of the brand. We don't mean figuratively. No, as Mary explained, the face of American Girl dolls is literally modeled on Pleasant's face. There is something about this that is both very Mount Rushmore of her and deeply revelatory. She is invested enough to put not just her name on this company, but her image. Imagine if Mark Zuckerberg put his own face all over Facebook. Consider that such branding choices are both ego trips *and* signs of someone's willingness to be so closely associated with their products.

Mary also described design choices Pleasant and her team made to encourage children to connect with the dolls. Physically, the dolls were designed to be huggable. We love that, but also want to know what that research process looks like. That level of intention shows how well Pleasant understood how kids would interact with the dolls. They would not live on a shelf, but be played with, dragged on adventures, and, as the friends she hoped they'd be, hugged.

When it came to balancing historical accuracy versus storytelling, Pleasant Company always privileged a quality story to inspire girls. This explains in part why they chose not to base Felicity on a real girl who lived in Williamsburg, as they didn't want this story to be confined to actual experiences. This would limit the potential for one girl to hit so many greatest-hit moments of her historical era *and* moments of what we'll call "things girls love." How else do we get the tea party throwdown *and* horse girl magic that is Valerie Tripp's Felicity stories?

We learned a bit about Valerie's process from a true archival treasure. In 1991, Pleasant Company hosted a Felicity launch event at Colonial Williamsburg that attracted thousands of children and families. A woman who attended the event as a girl put together a YouTube video recounting her experience from the distance of adulthood. The first thing that captured our attention was the grainy video quality of '90s tape as we saw a sea of girls walking around Williamsburg in a wide shot. The narrator notes that upon arrival these girls received a mobcap of their very own along with a copy of *Meet Felicity*. She describes the absolute thrill and adrenaline rush of being there and of seeing the new doll Felicity behind museum glass, ready to debut to the world. She read *Meet Felicity* that night and the next day got the chance to talk to Valerie Tripp in a Q&A *and* see a play acting out scenes from Felicity's life at a tea party where Ms. Manderly herself taught the girls how to take their tea. Girls swarmed Mary throughout the weekend. "It's the closest I ever came to being a rock star. I couldn't go to the bathroom. I was mobbed by the kids!" she gleefully remembered.

The portion of the video showing clips of Valerie's Q&A and her introduction to the play at the tea party are revealing. First, a girl asks Valerie about her process of creating an American Girl book. Valerie responds in ways that feel both candid and relatable. "I really like doing the research, getting all the information about Williamsburg in 1774 and 1775," Val explains. "Then a day comes where I have to really sit down and start writing.

"Now," Val says, pivoting in a move that made her 1,000 percent likable then as now, "that day usually doesn't feel like too much fun. That feels like hard work. Probably all of you in school are asked to write reports or even just a paragraph, and maybe you do what I do, which is you sort of put it off because it really doesn't feel like fun." We love a procrastinating queen.

Later, she gave attendees a window into her inspiration for Felicity's narrative as a young girl who wants independence (for herself and her horse) at the moment the colonies seek it. "Felicity wanted to be independent," we learn, "and like the colony, she was going to have to learn that independence doesn't come easily, it has to be earned, and with independence comes responsibility for yourself and for your world." This "girl stands in for nation" vibe drew on the tradition of *Little House on the Prairie* and other series. A through line of these books is an assumption that the nation is defined by whiteness, privilege, and a very specific vision of womanhood.

On our show, we've called out some choices in the Felicity books we think are tough to sit with now. Felicity desperately wants to free her horse, but not any of the people her family enslaves. She lives in a world with slavery and white supremacy, but has a Black friend to show she's not racist. This kind of multiculturalism imposed on the past that "doesn't see race" shows the brand's commitment to historical accuracy: not to the 1770s, but to the 1990s. What kid from that time doesn't have a memory of a multicultural fair in which every nation was represented as equal with every other? This flattening of difference and erasure of racism is a comfort mostly to white people and a very '90s trend we wish would leave us (that, and acid-wash jeans, tbh). We'd love to see what Valerie would make of Felicity's life and choices with the context of our own Black Lives Matter movement.

As Michelle Cude noted, the Little House books were special to her growing up, and appreciating the regrettable aspects now doesn't diminish what they meant to her, but rather invites a more mature reading. We have found that for ourselves with the early American Girl books. A rereading now has asked us to question what erasures the brand supported as white girls of privilege, and how we might use that awareness to tell different stories of our own histories, national and otherwise, as adults. Michelle suggested Val may write different versions of those books if she wrote today, reflecting our own culture and its contested values. We wonder what that would look like.

Would Felicity be rebellious and call out how contradictory it was for patriots like her dad to refer to themselves as slaves to England when they themselves enslaved? Could she channel her horse girl energy into being a messenger for a revolutionary-era spy ring? Better still, what if she were Rose's daughter, a girl with knowledge of the stakes of revolution who can call out its contradictions and demonstrate the realities of being excluded from its rewards? Maybe she'd be written today as a loyalist who becomes a caricature for the pitfalls of unquestioning devotion to monarchy and privilege. After all, wouldn't we love to see a main character who isn't necessarily meant to be read as a hero? This would really hit a nerve with Americans obsessed with the Royal Family, *Downton Abbey*, and every example of privilege we literally fought a revolution to distance ourselves from. We also write this as people who have seen every episode of *Downton Abbey* and *The Crown*. We contain multitudes and won't explain ourselves!

Sadly, we'll never get to see how Colonial Williamsburg might interpret Felicity now. Mary describes Pleasant's decision to part ways with the museum as entirely gracious after Colonial Williamsburg's leadership changed hands and corporate took umbrage at AG wanting to film videos in front of some of the museum's buildings. According to Mary, management felt that the museum was just being used by American Girl to promote its own products. Instead of helping to sell American Girl dolls, they ultimately decided to create their own dolls based on actual girls who lived in the town. Colonial Williamsburg continued to offer some Felicity-related programming, but these days, the only Felicitys you'll see in Colonial Williamsburg are the dolls ushered around the museum by young children themselves dressed like Felicity.

Trying on Italian Hats: Or, Why We Still Need American Girl

Before we leave Colonial Williamsburg behind in our journey to explore the world of AG fandom, we wanted to emphasize the biggest innovation to historic storytelling that Pleasant made to the model we saw at the museum. She put girls in the center of the story, or as Bikini Kill might say "all the girls to the front!" We can't overstate how important this is, especially if we take a broader view and think of putting all kids at the center of books and toys designed for them.

On our last day there, we took a tour of the colonial capitol building in Colonial Williamsburg. We were taken into the reconstructed capitol by a tour guide whom we would like to leave as anonymous as possible for

#LegalPurposes. Please take this moment to picture anyone in your life who appreciates making others small so they can feel big.

This individual took us first to the General Court, where we sat on hard wooden benches and got a stern talking-to. He told us there was a lot of misinformation in the world, and he was going to put a stop to it. Big swing, John Doe. He decided to teach us by asking us leading questions and acting exasperated when we couldn't provide the intended answer quickly enough. "You might be called to testify as a witness and come up here to testify at the stand. WHAT'S THAT CALLED?" Everyone was sitting up straight now. School was in session and we were failing. "Taking the stand?" someone weakly offered. "Yes!" he said, already tired. Suddenly we were bonded to the other people on our tour: some random newlyweds, families with young kids, and an older couple who seemed extremely into his exasperation. They became the students who wanted to win the approval of the hard-nosed teacher. We were hiding in the back wondering if he could take our citizenship rights if we failed his test. He was teaching by Socratic method, and we felt like we were living the answer to the question "Have you ever wanted the thrill of being in law school with literally none of the perks?"

He took things to an even more intense place by asking us who had voting rights in colonial Williamsburg. The room offered some wild guesses. The confusion pleased him. "NO ONE. VOTING IS NOT A RIGHT!" We felt like we'd run into that guy you meet in college who reads the Wikipedia page for the Declaration of Independence and then promptly lectures you on the ways the plot of *National Treasure* is impossible. Nothing made sense, and somehow his ultimate point was that we were idiots. Our fave moment in the court was when he tried to paint a picture of the people most excluded from the colonial legal system. In a move that surprised no one, the victim he imagined looked a lot like him. He let us know that he himself could not vote in colonial Williamsburg even though he's a landowner because he's Catholic. We all sat pondering this in silence.

At that moment, we were at that point of sitting in air-conditioning after walking around in devil heat when your skin is clammy and takes on a chill. Our bodies were trying to tell us a story, and we refused to listen. Tour Guide John Doe then took us to the House of Burgesses, where things escalated. At that point we wished we had Pleasant's phone number, or really that of any adult who might come pick us up. He continued with his misinformation theme, but this time took on women's rights. We were scared. "What rights did men have that women didn't have?" he asked. At that moment, we tried to exercise our rights to sink into our own bodies. This proved unsuccessful. Some brave tour guests made guesses, all in vain. "NONE!" he gleefully told us. Allison took a secret selfie of us at that moment, presumably for authorities if we were taken out by this tour. He told us a bit about coverture, or the idea that a man's legal identity covered that of his wife. Her property became his upon marriage, etc. And this is where things get really bleak.

He wanted to make the point that men were responsible for their wives, which was a kind of burden for them. He did this by pointing to a woman in the crowd there with her husband and kids, including a girl who looked to be about American Girl age (eight years old). He pointed at the mother and said, "If you were my wife and you bought many Italian hats and couldn't pay the bill, which one of us is going to debtors' prison?" The daughter answered, "The woman?" With no hesitation he told her she was wrong. While we could get into wondering about the choice of this example as a kind of out-of-pocket thought experiment, our own attention was caught by the little girl. After she'd sat up straight in her chair to venture an answer, her posture had totally changed. Being told no and not brought into whatever game we were playing in the name of education, she had deflated into herself. It was heartbreaking to see.

It's obvious how much kids want to be part of something like this if they aren't humiliated in the process or made to feel less than, or unintelligent. That same presumption applies to everyone. But here, in this place, after trying to follow Pleasant's path through the museum, we saw something she may have seen herself, that children need their own stories and their own spaces to be invited into history and to learning. Inclusive children's programming does exist at the museum, but we were on a general tour, which seemed concerned only with adults. And what did our John Doe get out of this? To feel like the smartest guy in the room?

We decided to fight for our right to party and/or leave and hit the exit. We tried to imagine what that girl would take from the tour. New knowledge on coverture, voting rights, or Italian hats? Or the feeling of being wrong and not meant for a conversation among adults? Back out in the street and walking through the rain, we couldn't help but imagine how Pleasant would have met that moment—how she would have considered not only the value of stories and play in bringing kids into the past, but also the need to do so with kindness.

Pleasant Company: Our Brand Is Memories

The entire time we were at Williamsburg, we tried to conjure Pleasant herself as a guide we might find on a tour (vortex to hell notwithstanding). Walking around and taking in the excellent tours from guides and actor-interpreters we met and reading about what the museum was like during her visit in the '80s, we could guess at the kind of interpretation she saw and adapted into her own work. What proved more elusive was Pleasant's own personal journey. What did this place mean to her? Yes, it inspired her to create a line of products that put girls at the center of the story, but was there something else?

The closest we got to answering this question, and perhaps the most telling moment we could find, was in the YouTube video shared by a now adult attendee.

After the girls arrived with loved ones, put on their mobcaps, and clutched their *Meet Felicity* books, they gathered for the tea party and a play. There, Pleasant Rowland welcomed them with a speech that proved deeply personal. She opened by reminding them that this place inspired it all. Recalling her vacation years earlier, she explained, "It was . . . in this very place that the idea of the American Girls collection was born. Here is where I dreamed up the idea of a group of nine-year-old heroines who would teach girls of today about history." She elaborated by revealing something of the scale of her ambitions for the brand, noting she wanted to offer girls "the history of our wonderful country and also . . . the history of themselves, of the experiences of girlhood that have lasted for hundreds of years, experiences of family and friendship, and feeling that have linked mother to daughter for generations." Here was a vision of girlhood that seemed timeless.

She offered an experience of her own childhood that demonstrated how she hoped girls would interact with her creation. "I remember the experience of getting lost in a good book, spending hours flung across my bed absorbed in a wonderful story," she said. "I hope the American Girls books have provided just such an experience for all of you. Years from now you may not remember the details of these stories, but I assure you, you will remember the experience of loving the American Girls and being absorbed in their life and times."

Watching this for the first time gave us chills, and we had to pause the video. This is exactly what happened for us. When we started the podcast, we had no memory of the Felicity books. We had definitely read and remembered loving the Felicity books as children. Yet, as adults, we genuinely believed she was a servant who worked for John Adams, lived in Boston, and was somehow involved in the patriot cause. Needless to say, we were wrong.

The conclusion of Pleasant's speech is what really got to us and is perhaps the most personal narrative of Pleasant's life we've heard, sentimental or not. She told everyone in attendance about a special day she had with her mother as a child, not unlike the day the girls in front of her were having. When she was eight or nine years old, her mother took her to the Chicago Symphony as a treat. "It was just the two of us," she explained, "which made it very special because usually we did everything with my sisters, but that day just Mom and I went downtown to the city." Together, Pleasant and her mother wore their Sunday best and attended the concert, where Pleasant delighted in hearing "Beautiful Dreamer" performed.

In her account of the special outing, what really mattered most was the connection she felt to her mother. "We walked down Michigan Avenue hand in hand, squeezing our own private code," she recalled. "Mom squeezed my hand three times—it meant 'I love you'—and I squeezed back four; it meant 'I love you too.'" Pleasant ended her remarks by directly connecting her own cherished childhood memory with the Felicity event. "Perhaps sometime while you're here in Williamsburg, you can try squeezing that private code, and someday you may do it with your own little girl," she imagined. "Maybe you will even bring her back to Williamsburg years from now and share with her the same happy time that you are having here with your mother or grandmother or aunt. That is how the happy experiences of girlhood are kept alive in our memories, and in our lives, generation after generation."

In sharing something so personal and suggesting girls there that day might have a similar experience, Pleasant makes us wonder if what she's selling is really about history at all. Yes, it's important to learn about the past and to empower girls by putting them at the center of the story. However, it also seems like what really matters to Pleasant is creating occasions for memory making while learning. She notably doesn't share why she thinks the American Revolution is so important, or any of the historical connections that she could easily make between Williamsburg and Felicity. Instead, she talks about a special time with her mom that made her feel valued and loved.

Thinking of her very personal story reminds us of something Mary Wiseman said to us—that she wished American Girl existed when she was a girl. She wanted to have a reason to play in an eighteenth-century dress, and to receive the message her parents would send by buying it for her. "It would say 'we buy in' quite literally to the world you're in. We love it, and that you're loving it, too," Mary explained. Of course, all of this presumes that parents have the funds for the pricey merch to back up the good intentions all parents of AG-obsessed children likely have. However, it also supports a generational element of American Girl, that it be shared between parent/child or grandparent/child. Contrived or not, the secret code Pleasant shared with her mom, squeezing each other's hands to exchange "I love yous," demonstrates the exchange she hoped the brand and its products could foster between girls and the grown-ups who loved them. Rather than squeezing secret messages, they could read books together or play with dolls. This could become a ritual that could be passed down, incorporating American Girl into not just girlhood, but a girl's life cycle, and continuing with her daughter and granddaughter.

Such a pattern would keep the same values circulating among every girl in the family, no matter the climate of the era in which a girl received her dolls. This generational cycle sustained the timeless connection between mother and daughter that defined girlhood for Pleasant "across hundreds of years." A return to traditional girlhood that didn't rush girls to be like Barbie and kept them connected to the women in their lives was needed now more than ever, Pleasant argued. "I created it at a time when the world has somehow grown too sour and cynical," Pleasant concluded. "I am so gratified to know that you and thousands like you appreciate the American Girls collection and have come from so far across our country to reaffirm its values."

By launching Felicity at Williamsburg, Pleasant articulated the ideas she so valued in the nation and so wanted to preserve in girls. The image of Felicity enshrined behind museum glass embodied the fulfillment of Pleasant's original moment of inspiration at Williamsburg with her entrepreneurial genius. She'd been able to create a brand that packaged elements of the museum—the use of narrative and material culture to teach about the past—and sold it as a means by which girls could create their own living history museums in their bedrooms for a hefty price.

The intimacy of her talk, the sharing of such a personal story—more personal than she usually shared in interviews or public addresses—tells us something else about her vision for her work. Pleasant not only wanted to preserve and commodify the past, she wanted to encourage and sell memory making. She had a grander vision than just interesting girls in history by putting them at the center. Her genius lay in articulating a vision of girlhood she could shape through her company, a vision that would influence how girls saw themselves, the kind of play that helped them create themselves *and* memories along the way.

So many YouTubers / influencers / content creators repeat a famous line at times attributed to Maya Angelou about people never remembering what you say, only how you make them feel. This kind of invitation to sincerity could easily be ridiculed as something utilized by influencer culture or businesses to engage sentimental messaging for profit under the guise of authenticity.

While we are right to meet any invitation to feel for feelings' sake as sus, Pleasant's words get us every single time. In part it's because her ambitions succeeded. We used the stories and the dolls to learn about history and ourselves through play. We had goofy productions at home performed with imagined eighteenth-century speech and colonial dress. Mary read the books and magazine before bed with her mom and brothers while Allison made clothes for her dolls with her mom. It's notable to us that when we started the podcast, we had almost no memory of the plotlines of *any* of the books. While we sincerely treasured the impact the books and dolls had on us, it clearly wasn't the content that lingered through the years. What stayed with us were the memories we made. Pleasant was right.

Though the brand would continue to release historic characters such as Addy Walker (1993), Josefina Montoya (1997), and Kit Kittredge (2000), in the years after her initial introduction of dolls set in history, Pleasant expanded her brand to feature dolls, activities, and clothes that spoke to girls and their needs in the present. The brand gave us a magazine to help navigate friendship, school, and all the facets of life in the '90s. It gave us *The Care and Keeping of You* to help us figure out how our bodies were changing and how we might be in healthy relationship to them. Pleasant built her name on history but made her empire by developing a lifestyle brand that educated women our age on health, beauty, friendship, and more. We're not saying

Pleasant was the origin of Goop culture, but we're not *not* saying that. And just like Gwyneth's, the lifestyle advice culture she created came with a price. The question for us then as now was: Could we afford to buy what Pleasant Company was selling?

And in a question we wish we'd submitted to the Help! section of the *American Girl* magazine, considering how awkward it felt to be a youth in the '90s, could we afford not to?

Top Tips for Visiting a Historic Site Like Us

Bring some of your own snacks to power through the day. Enjoy an over-priced beverage (from really any time period) and bask in the knowledge that you are *living history.*

- Play one of our favorite games on a guided tour: "Is this tour about the history of this place or the history of this tour guide?"
- Buy yourself a treat in the gift shop. Life is too short not to buy a print, scarf, or other random object you may never use again.
- Ask lots of questions! Maybe too many questions.
- Find a Shaker connection. Not finding a Shaker connection? Look harder!
- Bring a doll or beloved object if you feel so inclined. Don't be embarrassed about taking photographs with or without that doll as you wish.

CHAPTER 3

Surprise, It's a Lifestyle Brand

*In which Pleasant builds a brand, and we wonder if we might
be the American Girls of Today. Mining our personal treasures,
we explore the magazine,* The Care and Keeping of You,
and other products designed to help us navigate the '90s.

American Girl grew into something much bigger, and much more ambitious, during our formative years. During our childhoods, Pleasant Company stopped being an educational toy maker and turned into a full-blown lifestyle brand. No longer limiting herself or her company to products based in the past, Pleasant expanded her empire to create a brand that could support all facets of girls' lives. As one newspaper in the '90s reported, "Rowland repeatedly says she's not in the doll business or the direct mail business, but in the 'girls business,' particularly helping and encouraging girls between the vulnerable, often-overlooked ages between 7 and 12."

In a letter to girls at the front of the Fall 1996 catalogue, she wrote that the mission of American Girl was "to provide girls with beautiful books, dolls, and pastimes that celebrate the experience of growing up as an American girl." After all we discovered on our foray to Colonial Williamsburg, it may surprise you to learn how quickly the brand pivoted away from the past to the present. To truly get in the American Girl business, Pleasant and company knew they had to expand to meet girls where they were at. To do this, American Girl broadened its scope.

From 1992 forward, American Girl rolled out a line of books to meet the modern needs of girls, developed a line of dolls that looked like girls today, and launched its iconic *American Girl* magazine. We'd love to travel to a fun place to explore this important piece of American Girl Culture, but the place we actually needed to visit was freezing, crowded, and completely disorganized. Yes, we're talking about our parents' attics and basements. We're pulling out all the stops (and all of our American Girl merch) as brand ambassadors (unpaid and unendorsed) to take you back in time.

Expanding the Portfolio of Pastimes

Before we get into what Pleasant could teach us about life in the '90s, it's important to recall that the merch Pleasant Company designed for modern girls drew a lot on the secret sauce that made the historic girls and their accessories so popular. At the start of the decade, the brand released cookbooks, craft books, and more based on the historic characters, allowing girls to participate in what some educators would call "active learning," and our parents might call "That's enough, now!" These products, grouped initially into something called Portfolio of Pastimes, launched in 1990 and initially offered subscribers activities based on the original three characters. By 1994, fans could buy kits—including cookbooks, theater kits, paper dolls, and DIY craft kits—for their favorite doll without a subscription. This lineup now included the first three characters, Samantha, Molly, and Kirsten, along with the two more recent additions, Felicity (1991) and Addy (1993). This play in the past created just the kind of memory making that Pleasant knew was the real power behind her brand. The success of these lines was an important transitional move to offering more products for girls "today," even if remembering them now is a challenge for fans.

In January 2022, a self-described "very serious writer" named Carrie Wittmer, from Brooklyn, New York, reflected on the origins of a beloved soup recipe. In a tweet, she explained that "for years I went around telling people that my mom had the best potato soup recipe until I found out that it was the potato soup recipe from Kirsten the American Girl doll's cookbook." As it turns out, Carrie's mom did have "the best" recipes. They just happened to have been tried and tested by the Pleasant Company Publications focus groups first.

Kirsten's Cook Book, the source of this treasured soup recipe, was from one of the Pastimes kits filled with "activities from the past for girls of today." For just $22.95, you, too, could learn to make dinner Kirsten-style, and a whole lot more. This cookbook would also teach you basic facts about her time period ("There were no supermarkets in 1854") and how to make a killer Swedish meatball.

The Pastimes kits offered multiple points of immersion into each American Girl's world.

Being totally devoted to your doll was one thing. As a budding Kirsten, Samantha, or Molly, you could easily go broke just buying all of those dolls and their growing ensemble of outfits. But the Pastimes kits told you there was more to learn. They also gave you permission to go into their stories on an even deeper level.

For some girls, knowing that Kirsten made her family St. Lucia's buns in *Kirsten's Surprise* was an interesting story—memorable, in part, because her parents seemed okay with her playing with fire. There was another subset of Pleasant Company catalogue subscribers who wanted, or needed, much more. They read *Kirsten's Surprise* as an invitation to have your own St. Lucia's Day and to re-create that moment with a doll or . . . yourself. This might mean making your doll balance a tray of hot treats. Or finding a wreath and a set of candles to complete the full St. Lucia's look. If girls wanted to live in the worlds of these books, Pleasant Company was happy to provide the recipe, craft outline, or anything else they might want to order.

When Felicity and Addy were added to the team of historical dolls, elements from their stories were used for the same kind of individual kits, just on a faster timeline. Whereas Kirsten preceded her cookbook, other historical characters of the 1990s, including Addy, were made in tandem with their accessory and publication lines.

Based on what we know about American Girl and Colonial Williamsburg, the creation of Felicity felt pretty inevitable. Addy Walker, a Black girl who self-liberated during the Civil War, was the first American Girl of color whose life was comparatively defined by challenges and triumph over huge adversity. Her books, and especially *Meet Addy*, have many difficult moments as Addy confronts racism and white supremacy. While some Black fans of Addy embraced her appearance as a sign of welcome representation, many could not engage her doll or books because of the choice to ground her story in the trauma of slavery and racism. Addy's doll and accessories are especially fraught considering her positioning early in her series as herself a commodity in the slave economy. Perhaps because of this, Addy was written to have some tender scenes amidst her family's struggles, but these too became opportunities for product development.

In one of the most poignant chapters in *Addy Learns a Lesson*, Addy bakes cookies with her mother. By this time, Addy and her mother are newly resettled in Philadelphia. After starting to learn to read, Addy teaches Momma the word "love" while baking, molding the words from dough. In a series that centered the first Black American Girl amidst a traumatic liberation narrative, this moment of connection and joy resonates. For fans who wanted to make those cookies themselves, the brand offered *Addy's Cook Book*. Every girl had a cookbook fans could buy and use to re-create memorable meals or treats from the books, however different a doll's relationship to wealth, privilege, or commodification might be. It also collapsed the foreignness of the past for modern fans who wanted to feel kindship with favorite characters with whom they could share common activities.

In 1989, Pleasant addressed her customers in a letter printed in the catalogue. She explained that she wanted girls to know about the lives of people "who lived long ago" and to "see that some things about growing up have changed, while others—like families, friends, and feelings—haven't changed at all." This desire to have girls make connections with people from other times was really a hallmark of the company into the early 1990s. Pleasant didn't want to see girls hanging out at the mall. She wanted to see them learning "old-fashioned" and "traditional" games, or writing in a diary because that is what girls had done in the past.

When these elaborate cookbooks and other kits came out in 1994, we were just starting to stir brownie mix from prepackaged boxes. A lot of the cooking was too advanced for us, but we did fall for some of the other stuff. Allison especially loved the American Girl trading cards and the American Girl Games set, which included "Get in the Scrap." This game was a nod to Molly's time spent scrimping for the war effort. It was not exactly a ticket to popularity, but it did mean you had an awareness of austerity measures long before you could even get a bank account.

We chose not to party like it was 1854, or 1864, or any of these other eras. That would probably be a disappointment to Pleasant, who would want to see girls learning that potato soup recipe and putting it to use. In the back of *Kirsten's Cook Book*, young girls were given directions on how to "plan a pioneer party," Kirsten-style. This essentially meant having people over to cook in the form of a "winter baking bee," or "fall apple bee." If that didn't work out, you were told to get dramatic. This meant a pivot to performing *Home Is Where the Heart Is*, a play about Kirsten's trip to the United States and, we would argue, her growing crush on her teacher, Miss Winston.

As adults, we have proudly performed *Home Is Where the Heart Is*. It has held up a lot better than you think when you are willing to engage a queer reading. We do have our limits, though, and we have not gone and will not go to a "pioneer party." First, we're not open to party activities that feel like chores, like peeling potatoes. Far more importantly, settler colonialism is not a theme anyone should want to pull from the past. From what we have been told, beyond chatter on Twitter, Kirsten's soup recipe has held up. But the idea of encouraging girls to "play" like pioneers for the afternoon has not aged well.

This change in attitudes became apparent when American Girl rereleased the Kirsten doll in 2021. A lot of adult fans were thrilled—this was their chance to get a new Kirsten! Instead of begging someone else to help you with a mail order, it was now possible to just get the things you wanted! To hype up the doll, the company's website had a "create your own" shirt option. One design tied to Kirsten had a cabin and the words "Settlers Gonna Settle." Was this a meme-ification of western dispossession?

When Kirsten came out, her tagline was: "A pioneer girl of strength and spirit who settles on the frontier." You can read entire books about problems with just about every word in that sentence, starting with "frontier." Kirsten was designed to teach girls about the "strong" values of immigrants who "settled" the West. Pleasant Company chose to talk about immigration only in the form of a white girl whose family takes over "empty" "frontier" lands, which were in fact Indigenous homelands.

In response to complaints from consumers, the "Settlers" design was taken down. At least some of the people who had attended "pioneer parties" as kids had grown up, gotten more information, and rejected the idea that "pioneer" play could still be regarded as cute. Pleasant Company's marketing materials told us that "by reading these books, you'll learn what growing up was like in times past." Asking a little girl to play "like a pioneer" in the suburbs had very little to do with learning about midwestern history. Telling girls (who could afford it) that the past was theirs to claim was also a way of gatekeeping, and of sanitizing the past.

We know that a lot of people took their American Girl play very seriously. Yet even the people who are really devoted to American Girl in theory don't remember much about the actual stories or content. We are exhibits A and M for this phenomenon. This is partially why a grown person could claim to still love Kirsten while easily forgetting some of the more cringe aspects of her product development. As the soup tweet reminds us, it is possible to care deeply about a product, story, or recipe and to forget where it came from in the first place.

In addition to digging out our old stage notes on the Felicity play, scores of "old-fashioned" craft kits, and other American Girl historical products, we have also wondered about other lessons the brand was trying to teach us. Pleasant wanted her mostly middle-class consumers to feel empowered to learn all about girls who had lived in totally different times. What did her products have to say about living in the 1990s?

Selling Friendship and Blue Jeans: Modern Life in the American Girl Catalogue

When we were in graduate school, we got to hear Toni Morrison speak about her life and career. At one point, she noted she could recall the changes in her life as an American based on how Americans were defined on the news. In an interview with the *Guardian* in 2015, Morrison put it this way: "When I was a young girl we were called citizens—American citizens. We were second-class citizens, but that was the word. In the 50s and 60s they started calling us consumers. So we did—consume. Now they don't use those words any more—it's the American taxpayer and those are different attitudes."

American Girl products have certainly taught us lessons about citizenship, including the kind of second-class citizenship Morrison experienced as a Black person in the United States. More often, though, Pleasant Company's mission was to show us how to buy something to solve an issue happening with *us*, instead of a problem in society. Don't know how to host a bowling-themed birthday party? Here's a guide. Don't know how to deal with emerging acne? Please see the relevant section of *The Care and Keeping of You*. Can't understand why Grandma goes off about the disrespect of Ben Affleck's opus *Pearl Harbor*? Here are the Molly books or, later, the Nanea books set in Hawaii during the same time.

Lots of people who make things for kids want people to believe they really care. So what made this company any different? The American Girl lifestyle books and kits came from a place of wanting to empower girls. This meant actually listening to what girls had to say. Staffers made this real for some

American Girl consumers by using over-the-top active listening in their catalogues, books, and other branded content, constantly affirming girls and their needs as valid. "They talk to us, and we listen," American Girl explained of its relationship with girls in its Holiday 1997 catalogue. This conversational approach establishes "a bond of trust with American girls."

We learned about the value of self-esteem from our parents and from underpaid gym teachers at school. But American Girl really wanted to hammer it home that other adults cared about our well-being, too. As the Fall 1996 catalogue reminded us, "At Pleasant Company, we think being an American Girl is great; something to stand up and shout about. Something to celebrate! On each and every page of this catalogue, you'll see it's true. Everything we do is a celebration of you!" It may be Mary's Leo-ness speaking here, but it always feels good to feel like someone is paying attention to you. This may also be cult talk; we can't be sure. In a 2003 article on the brand's communication style called "Everything We Do Is a Celebration of You!: Pleasant Company Constructs American Girlhood," communication scholars Carolina Acosta-Alzuru and Elizabeth P. Lester Roushanzamir argue that the brand's direct address to girls and offers to solve their problems with products was purposeful. We believe it, and a review of the catalogues shows just that.

It is rumored that top pop stars of today listen to what fans are talking about on forums to get ideas for future projects. American Girl did this, too, or that is at least how they would frame new product rollouts. Since so many girls had questions about their lives, Pleasant Company responded with a magazine and book after book with practical bits of advice. They also started making dolls that could serve as helpful mirrors for life in the 1990s: the American Girl of Today. When these dolls first came out, American Girl explained the idea was driven by demands from girls themselves. "Girls told us they wanted us to help them address the challenges of growing up in the 90s. The American Girl of Today line [. . .] was our answer."

What challenges faced us all in 1995? you might ask. Here's some Cliffs-Notes: OJ was on trial, Selena had been murdered, and the macarena emerged as a party addiction for which even the D.A.R.E. program posed no cure. While other girls may or may not have clocked these cultural milestones that rocked our worlds, they were also likely dealing with the pressures of girlhood that the brand presented as timeless: anxieties about making friends, navigating school, the quirks of family life, etc.

American Girl wanted to be there for all girls, in theory, but really, this was a call-and-response relationship with a high price for entry. In the Fall 1997 catalogue, one article told of a modern-day middle school tragedy: "Lately, girls have been telling us they're bored with their well-worn jeans and baggy sweatshirts. We heard their message loud and clear! Our response? A great new batch of American Girl Gear for back-to-school." Why be "bored" with your wardrobe when you could just enter this community of consumption?

American Girl also used the language of friendship to get us on the hook for even more stuff. Some catalogue copy invited us to imagine the things they sold as our friends. "These true-blue denims are friendly and familiar," the Holiday 1998 catalogue explained. "They feel just right—like the start of a great friendship!" We would never think to compare the fit of a new friendship to well-worn jeans, but we are now questioning if this was the inspiration for the 2001 classic *The Sisterhood of the Traveling Pants*.

Linking elements of a girl's life (friendship) to buying things is nothing new. Anyone who grew up playing Mall Madness remembers the shared thrill of playing a game with friends that tested how good you were at buying things. (For those with no Mall Madness experience, just recall going to an actual mall.) We also grew up playing games like *Oregon Trail*, which asked us to wager how much we'd spend on clothes, food, supplies, etc. and then set us off to most likely die of dysentery. Teaching kids to value and practice consumption through play is not news, but doing so in the spirit of pushing girls to treasure family, friends, and self as values did feel unique to American Girl and the 1980s and '90s.

Does something become less cool if your parents think it's cool? We're not sure, since we've been on a thirty-plus-years-long tragically uncool streak. If you read any brand language from the period, American Girl hit hard on its values (family, friendship, self) and suggested parents were as much buying those for their kids as they were buying a doll or book. The catalogues routinely included testimonials to this point. The holiday catalogue from 1998 included this endorsement: "Thank you for being a company that obviously cares enough about our children to offer them not only an entertaining experience, but also an education in our past, traditions, and values." Every time we read "traditions" in the catalogue, we hear it to the tune of the *Fiddler on the Roof* classic. Would Bette Midler be open to reprising her role in an American Girl catalogue–themed adaptation? "Your product line reinforces so many of the things I hope to teach my daughter—a love of reading, a passion for history, a rich imagination, and an appreciation for cultural diversity," another parent praised. Our parents never invested this much responsibility in a single toy we owned. Imagine expecting a Game Boy to do this kind of work. An "appreciation for cultural diversity" also sounds like a very nice white parent thing to say. It gives Mary flashbacks to when she had to appear in an almost entirely white Martin Luther King Jr. remembrance event as part of Black History Month at her school. Nothing says diversity like a very well-intentioned but extremely out-of-pocket reading of King's works by mostly white kids.

We've spoken to parents who love the brand's offerings for all of these reasons. Michelle aka Model Felicity told us she loved sharing Felicity and Kirsten dolls with her daughters along with the books because of the brand's strong values. It's a joy to offer such fun stories and sources of play to girls who learn how to love themselves, how to be good friends, and how to value family along the way. To the parent who allegedly wrote, "Molly's more than a doll—she somehow embodies the best of childhood" in the Spring 1997 catalogue, we can offer both praise and questions. We can easily recall Molly's Tracy Flick–like drive to be the tap-dancing Miss Victory as the star of a fundraiser. We have revisited her books and are asking ourselves hard questions about how and why we identify so much with the pure chaos of

Molly, and if our parents would refer to those aspirations as the best of childhood, but we digress.

The feeling of these parental testimonials with the repeated (and we mean repeated) emphasis on the "values" of American Girl give the suggestion that this content was safe and would train us to be good citizens who make good choices. A focus on these "values" kept us from growing up too fast and falling prey to the good-girls-gone-bad lifestyles our parents were taught to fear by all the culture warriors of the '80s and '90s. We went to school learning how to say no to drugs, "We're too young for this" to cassingles bearing "parental advisory" stickers, and "Absolutely, yes" to anything bearing the magenta profile of Pleasant Company.

This emphasis on family values has led some to suggest American Girl—specifically the lifestyle books and activities we're going to get into here—is not cool. Some have questioned whether girls in the '90s/2000s really valued the stuff of American Girl, or if it was just the wishful thinking of middle-class parents who wanted to empower their daughters with inspiring products. Picture your dad awkwardly handing you a *Care and Keeping of You* book on your birthday while saying, "Your future's so bright, I need sunglasses to look at it!" Or your favorite aunt, flummoxed as to what to bring to your D.A.R.E. graduation, handing you a copy of *Help!* the advice book with the look of a nervous magician wondering, "Is this your card?"

As world's coolest former teen / author / actor Tavi Gevinson wrote in her first Editor's Letter of *Rookie*, an online magazine for teens (much beloved and missed by us non-teens), "I don't have the answers. *Rookie* is not your guide to Being a Teen." Seeking a useful uncool example of what *Rookie* was not, she offered, "It is not a pamphlet on How to Be a Young Woman. (If it were, it would be published by American Girl and your aunt would've given it to you in the fifth grade.)" Maybe this is a slam about products aimed at girls younger than *Rookie*'s audience (American Girl is allegedly for girls ages seven through twelve), or it's a callout of didactic girls' culture offered under the guise of empowerment. We get it. American Girl is not the cool brand of girlhood that's going to make you a zine about capitalism, talk about owning your power, and then convince you to try going vegan. American Girl is both affirming values-centered stuff that can help you be just like all the other girls *and* a space for many to figure out how to be their own brand of American Girl.

"For more than a decade," the Fall 1997 catalogue explained, "we've been the company that American girls trust. When they speak, we listen, because we believe that what they say is important." But what were girls saying? Where could we speak back to Pleasant & Co. to let them know our thoughts, feelings, and fears about owning too many stuffed animals (and would our other animals get jealous if we add more?)?

The answer was *American Girl* magazine.

The *American Girl* Magazine

In 1992, American Girl gave the world the gift of the *American Girl* magazine. Unlike the historic books, which hoped to reach girls through stories of relatable characters, the magazine was designed to speak directly to us and our lives in the 1990s.

From 1992 to 2019, this magazine served up feel-good content for girls just trying to figure it all out. It emerged at a moment when kids had a wider range of magazines to choose from than kids might find today. It lived on our nightstands alongside *Highlights* (iconic), *Cricket* (introduced in 1973 by editor Marianne Carus, who called it "*The New Yorker* for Children," and *Nickelodeon* magazine, which began its life with distribution via Pizza Huts in 1990 before wide distribution in 1993. Nothing feels more opposite "*New Yorker* for Children" than "distributed by Pizza Hut."

In the movie *13 Going on 30*, Jennifer Garner's character pitches a redesign for her magazine that refreshes its cynical/sexy branding to something more wholesome. Standing in front of a photo spread of happy white teens at an imagined homecoming game, she suggests a magazine that celebrates "your best friend's big sister." This sweet pivot is reminiscent of the tone of *American Girl* magazine, minus any attention to dating. Unlike in *Tiger Beat* or *Cosmo Girl*, readers of *American Girl* magazine in the '90s/2000s would not find lyrics to their favorite boy band's hit songs or Q&As with celebrity crushes for you to memorize and weaponize at school and slumber parties. Instead, the subjects were the very girls whose slumber parties you might attend. What scared them? What did they think it meant to be a good friend? Exactly how *do* you plan the slumber party of the social season? This was the province of *American Girl* magazine.

American Girl magazine was the only offering to speak directly to girls, and unlike other now defunct teen mags like *Cosmo Girl* or *Bop*, it was purposefully not like all the other girls. It consciously did not discuss dating or makeup. The magazine was aimed at girls aged seven through twelve and, like the broader brand, did not want to rush girls to grow up too soon. This magazine was so pure it still ran with a Valentine's Day theme with no mention of crushes. It also didn't run any ads. Like Disney Channel movies of the same era, the only product placements were for the company making the stuff. We did not see rail-thin people on the cover, and we were not told to diet week after week. This makes it different from almost any other magazine we can think of.

Every child for whom this magazine mattered can close their eyes and recall a typical issue: a girl who looked like us (a normie) on the cover holding a baseball bat or flower, maybe wearing a cowboy hat and smiling at some source of joy just off camera. Notably, they were not exclusively white girls, as the magazine foregrounded diversity in ways that predated other fare from American Girl. Inside, we'd find reliable features designed to frame a conversation between readers and the brand. Each bimonthly issue printed letters from girls, stories submitted by girls, crafts to make at home, cartoons, games—including *Giggle Gang* and later *Amelia's Notebook*—and guides to plan themed birthday parties and celebrations.

It covered all facets of life—from school to family to friendship and everything in between—and exemplified the brand's pivot to support girls in the present by offering representations of themselves. Even the cover girls were profiled in initial issues, further emphasizing that they lived lives not unlike readers and were approachable. This was yet another difference between the magazine and other fare aimed at girls and teens. Sure, we'd love to think we could be like Julia Stiles or other celebs from the era, but honestly who among us could simultaneously star in Shakespeare remakes *and* offer a monologue/poem on black combat boots with equal gravitas in yet another Shakespeare remake? Not us.

If girls were hungry for history-related content, they had an early reminder of where the brand began. In a paper-doll feature initially called "Grandmother, Mother & Me," the magazine highlighted a real American Girl and the women in her family history. Girls could submit their own family photos and information on women from whom they were directly descended. Aunts were explicitly excluded, and to that we say, Sorry to aunts everywhere.

These paper dolls directly positioned girls in a long line stretching back to their moms, grandmothers, and beyond. One reader even traced her family back to the Middle Ages and submitted an ancestor's name from that time.

Readers could tear out an insert featuring a paper doll with the girl's illustrated image, often depicting her wearing a favorite outfit. Her paper doll collection would also include outfits copying clothing worn by the girl's relatives in submitted family photos. Researchers would reimagine outfits for relatives for whom girls had no photographs. The backs of the outfits featured the family photos on which the outfits were based and information on each woman's life story. Readers could also tear out a mini book for their dolls.

From the beginning, the paper dolls feature allowed the brand to present the diverse histories of their readers, offering greater representation among its paper dolls than its actual historic or contemporary dolls. This mattered to readers like Courtney Price, famous in our minds as *American Girl* magazine's first paper doll, published in the November/December 1992 issue. Courtney may be the only subject of the paper doll feature to be recruited and not self-nominated to the magazine. A child model who loved figure skating, Courtney was deep in her own American Girl phase at the time. Growing up in Detroit, Courtney described herself at that age as "girly" and a "nerd" who loved having a book club with friends at school.

Courtney was also a big American Girl fan and, of the three original girls then available, identified as a Molly. (We did not pay her to say this.) Like us, Courtney viewed Molly as a bridge to her grandmother's time and experiences and loved her stories. An editor at the magazine described the new paper doll feature to Courtney's cousin, a friend from college, and asked if she knew of any girls who might be appropriate. Courtney remembers receiving a letter in the mail describing the project and asking if she'd be interested. Feeling like she'd received a golden ticket, she described this moment as a "Willy Wonka experience."

The process, which involved sending family photos with research on matrilineal histories, presented a connecting point for Courtney and her mother, who happened to be the family's genealogist. "I think for my mom it was big, because she had done all this history, and to see it displayed in a way that honored my ancestors, and our heritage, was a big moment for her," she explained. Courtney's doll feature includes her mother and grandmother, and traces her family's origins back to her enslaved great-great-grandmother Celie, and an "unknown" matriarch dated to 1792 and described as "from Ghana, West Africa. No one today knows her name." The acknowledgment of this ancestor creates a moment of real representation for Courtney and her family, and reminds readers that though all may be paper dolls, not all can recover names of ancestors that were never recorded in archives that didn't value them.

Courtney herself still remembers how special she felt as a result of the brand's attention to her life and the quality of her paper doll. Continuing her "Willy Wonka experience," she was invited to visit American Girl headquarters in Wisconsin and offered swag. In an age before the internet, the proofs were snail-mailed to her house for her approval. All these years later, she does still treasure her paper dolls. When they were published in the magazine, she marveled at the final product and still remembers how proud she felt to share them with her parents and friends. Opening the magazine, readers would see her doll wearing one of her favorite figure skating outfits, surrounded by clothing that told the stories of her ancestors' lives.

As an adult now working in public health, she has fond memories of American Girl and the conversations about books and dolls she had with friends. She continues to treasure the lessons in friendship she learned then, and still uses American Girl to connect with others. Her dolls live online still in fan blogs. Seeing herself on an informal fan archive even inspired Courtney to connect with another former paper doll subject. She wanted to know if they'd both had a positive experience becoming paper dolls, and thankfully, they had.

Courtney's story made us wonder: What would our own paper dolls look like? Would the magazine okay a denim-on-denim aesthetic? Asking for Mary—Allison would never be caught in jeans as a signature look. Imagining our female ancestors and their iconic looks really sends us on a journey. How would Mary's grandma Fluffy want to be depicted? What era of her life and associated looks would she choose for herself? A dress and beehive hair as she rocked in the '50s? Or her iconic aviator shades, wide-collared shirt, and blazer pantsuit from the '70s? Mary would ask which captured Fluffy's "essence," but she remembers the era when the Herbal Essences shampoo ads were featuring women having what we'll call an "experience" washing their hair, which inspired a call from Fluffy saying only, "Mary, please promise me you'll never use that shampoo. That's how babies are made." For anyone reading this and wondering about truth in advertising, we don't think this is strictly true.

Allison's mom, Donna, is a nurse, and it would be great to feature that history in the story of Allison's family. We can imagine how cool it would be for girls to see her story and imagine themselves pursuing a similar path. Allison didn't get the chance to know her grandmothers as well, so it's fun to think how family photos would have been powerful to bring them to life in the pages of the magazine.

By taking time to learn about Courtney and her family's history, *American Girl* made her feel seen and heard. This same intention to make girls feel valued guided much of the magazine's content. A feature called Heart to Heart, itself a phrase suggesting intimate girl talk, collected letters from other girls like us offered in response to themes like "Best Friends" or "Bragging." Here, girls formed their own consciousness-raising group, offering one- or two-sentence hot takes in response to prompts such as "What's the difference between bragging and being proud of yourself? What can you do when you're with a bragger?" Here, girls set the tone for all the content that followed, leading with 100 percent sincerity and genuine vulnerability. "My feelings get hurt when I hear someone bragging because it makes me feel like I'm not special," one nine-year-old shared. "Don't brag. It's a drag!" While the sign-off gives us big-time D.A.R.E. PSA "there's no hope with dope" slam poetry vibes, the message is sincere. Imagine being this vulnerable at any age.

In a Heart to Heart that asked whether girls should have one best friend or lots of good friends, one reader offered this earnest response: "I had a really good friend. We became so close we both agreed we were best friends. Then I saw her wearing half of a best friend's necklace, and I didn't have the other half!" Everyone reading this can probably think of some childhood hurt stemming from early experiments in friendship.

What is fascinating and retrospectively amazing about the magazine is that it gave girls the space to talk about the anxieties and triumphs of growing up in their own words. It also did so without making them the subject of a joke or shaming them. Other magazines for slightly older girls offered features on how to apply makeup or get a crush to like you, or collected "I was so embarrassed" stories. So much of this content was about navigating life to please someone else or normalizing feeling shame.

By comparison, the *American Girl* magazine presented a range of feature stories on "ordinary" girls and celebrated that as their norm. Focusing on the values of family, friends, and identity, the magazine profiled a wide range of experiences, including those of an Indigenous girl sharing her experiences of powwows and the importance of dancing to her family and culture; an aspiring dog-show trainer and her ambitions to go pro someday; a Mormon girl going on a re-created pioneer trail to learn about her heritage; and a soccer player training for big games. In the earliest years of the magazine, these articles often appeared alongside short stories featuring American Girl dolls, indicating by proximity that these girls' lives held similar value and meaning. Later, top children's authors also contributed short stories that ran alongside stories submitted by readers themselves. In the design and its content, the magazine did the work of empowering readers.

We do have to note that one such story featured a fight between friends that we don't necessarily think left us feeling empowered. In the story in question, two girls living next door to each other are lifelong friends. One wants to spread her friendship wings and bring new friends into the fold, which threatens her first neighbor friend. To teach her a lesson, to scare her (and us), or for a reason we truly can't understand, this friend decides to steal her friend's pet guinea pig and hide it in her own garage. There, said guinea pig dies. Somehow the funeral for this pet reunites them (briefly), but it would appear the victim is hoping to get away from this emerging sociopath ASAP. We're still rocked by this story and would love for someone to tell us how premeditated pet theft teaches us about friendship. As of this writing, Nicole Kidman has not bought the film rights to this work, but we are awaiting a press release to that effect.

Eyebrow-raising short stories aside, this approach of empowering readers was met with immediate success. The brand reported in 1995 that in just two years, the magazine accrued 500,000 subscribers. This success was due in large part to this girl-centered approach, Aubre Andrus, a former associate editor at *American Girl* magazine, explained. Working at the magazine from 2006 to 2009, Aubre was one of the first employees at *American Girl* to have grown up with the brand's products. She was raised in Chicago and first saw the magazine at an art store when she was in fifth or sixth grade. She'd had a Kirsten doll and loved the books and catalogue, and fell especially hard for the magazine.

She liked that it didn't tend to "age up" as other magazines for girls did, and it was something she and her younger sister loved. When she noticed the magazine reprinted a story from an earlier issue, she realized actual people made the magazine and that she could have prevented this repeat. "Why didn't they call me?" she remembers thinking. Big same, Aubre.

Flash forward to her college years at the University of Wisconsin–Madison and Aubre was preparing to graduate with no job when she saw a posting for an internship at American Girl. She arrived at her interview with a letter she'd written to American Girl with her sister years before suggesting a line of camping-related accessories and the company's response. We love this power move. She got the internship and eventually landed a job as an assistant and then associate lifestyle editor, working on activities, party planning, and other fun spreads. Aubre lived our dream, and her memories of it do not disappoint.

An average day might see her at her desk writing, in the test kitchen, brainstorming in the "creativity room," or out buying forty size 10 bathing suits for a photo shoot. The group was constantly planning content for issues months ahead and truly scrambled to come up with content like brand-new holiday games to play with friends or a fully realized doll birthday party plan.

What Aubre remembers treasuring about the magazine was that it had the quickest turnaround of American Girl products, and it was the most accessible. A subscription would run you $19.99/year for six issues as opposed to the much bigger ticket price of dolls and accessories. "I was really proud to work for a part of the company that was affordable and accessible to all girls," Aubre explained. If she told someone she worked at *American Girl*, she'd get one of two responses. Either "Oh my God! I love American Girl!" or "I couldn't afford that but I always wanted one."

The focus on accessibility and inclusion came from the top at *American Girl* magazine, where editors would flag illustrations that didn't reflect girls of different races or feature and normalize disability. Aubre remembers an editor one time pushing back on her suggestion to do a story on planning a snow day party because "not all girls live in a snowy climate." The direction of content came not from editors, but from the girls themselves. Aubre credits the "direct communication with our readers" as one of the greatest assets of the magazine. They took direction from girls and tested every recipe, party plan, and activity with area girls in focus groups before it reached the magazine.

No other part of the company heard from girls every day, as the magazine did, Aubre noted. Girls wrote in all the time, offering drawings, letters, and poems. One girl shared a poem called "Life Is like Opening a Barbie," Aubre remembered fondly, which featured the iconic line "it is hard, but in the end it is always worth it." It's not hard to see why the poem was treasured by magazine staff, even if American Girl dolls are allegedly the anti-Barbie.

A majority of the mail they received included requests for advice, which were collected and answered in the Help! section of the magazine. Of the 10,000 letters the magazine received for each issue, 1,500 were for the Help! column. There, you can see how timeless girlhood is in the kinds of issues girls discuss, whether problems with sibling rivalry, friends, or the awkwardness of growing up. "When I'm at my friend's house, I act like a little angel," one girl wrote, "but when I'm at home I'm a little devil! What should I do?" She signed this confession in the form of advice letter "Dr. Jekyll and Ms. Hyde." We are prepared to pitch this to HBO Max.

One girl, identifying herself only as "Cringe!" asked, "All of [a] sudden, I seem to think my parents are really embarrassing. When I say, 'Can you please not do that, it's embarrassing,' they take it as an insult." It's fun to imagine the parent who had to mail this in on behalf of the writer and if they, too, waited desperately for a response.

Aubre recalls the editor in chief responding to girls' requests for help and taking it very seriously. While some letters were somewhat playful, asking how to know when you've bought too many My Little Ponies (the limit does not exist), or how to tactfully tell a friend they talk about Jonathan Taylor Thomas too much (fair), some questions got at the timeless issues of girlhood.

As Aubre described to us, though, the brand never gave them a definition of girlhood to use as a model for what did and did not fit the magazine's profile; the letters they received helped them navigate that terrain and added to the feeling of timelessness Pleasant and others used to refer to adolescence. So many girls wanted advice on how to deal with siblings or parents who didn't make them feel seen. Others wanted advice on how to live with divorced parents or how to deal with feelings of wanting new friends or losing old friends.

When Mary was growing up, the magazine was her favorite American Girl product short of the historical character books. Before bed, she'd read the magazine's Help! questions out loud to her mom as part of a game they'd play. They'd take turns reading a question, and the other would guess what advice the writer would receive. Without fail, her two brothers would join and take their own places at the end of her bed. They approached American Girl fare as if they were anthropologists embedding themselves in a foreign group of which they were deeply suspicious. "We're just here doing research," they'd seem to say with eye rolls and huffs at the questions girls asked. However, without fail, they'd play the game and end up talking about the issues that mattered most to these girls (and to us). Did Mary clock at that time that her brother also liked to talk too much about JTT? No. Did she ask herself deep questions about why she didn't care at all about JTT? Also no. However, just like the contents of the magazine itself, there is real value not in having all the answers but in simply making space for the questions and conversation.

Education scholars Pamela Bettis and Natalie Adams have argued that "ideal girlhood . . . is constantly being rewritten" based on the needs of each moment and societal context. *American Girl* magazine is one such place where you can see girls working out the awkwardness of growing up in the '90s and early 2000s (in addition to our now deleted AIM Buddy Chat archives and LimeWire downloads). Here, and often not in the magazines geared to slightly older girls, we found a place that took the plight of girlhood seriously. Not all of us could imagine ourselves as Melissa Joan Hart in *Clarissa Explains It All*, a Nickelodeon show in which MJH spoke directly to camera with a confidence we found aspirational. Issues of girlhood might feel timeless, but some of the questions girls asked were very of their time, and there we met the limits of the magazine.

As Aubre told us, the magazine wasn't always sure how to respond when girls wrote in about millennial hot topics, and not the timeless stuff of sibling rivalries, friendship, and family. For example, editors were really thrown by girls writing in about wanting cell phones. How do you know when you are old enough to handle a brick of a cell phone that will weigh down your backpack and change your social life? Adults still grappling with car phones did not have easy answers. How young is too young to raise a Tamagotchi? This is a question truly no one can answer. Could we be trusted with our own AOL Instant Messenger account? This one we *will* answer: absolutely not. The amount of truly cringeworthy uses of song lyrics in our AIM Buddy List Away Messages is a shock to recall even now. We're sure these were questions editors didn't imagine they'd have to answer when the magazine began in the early '90s.

American Girl as a brand was slow to adapt to the increasing role of the internet in our lives. They offered surface-level advice, like one feature on the ins and outs of the internet that warned us to stay out of chat rooms when we were "on-line," not that we listened. It offered a glossary of helpful internet terms, and seeing the literal meaning of "lol" spelled out as "laugh out loud" truly makes us feel ancient. We can still remember debates over whether it meant "lots of love" and the fears over using it to send mixed signals to friends or foes on AIM.

We grew up with the internet, and were perhaps the first and last generation of girls who had to explain it to our parents, who struggled to supervise technology they didn't fully understand. Without spaces like *American Girl* magazine or the later much-loved *Rookie*, where do girls (adolescent and teenage) turn now? Parents debate what age is appropriate to give kids cell phones or how much screen time is healthy, etc. We are not parents, so these issues exist to us in theory only, but we do wonder where girls find a safe sounding board and community now that magazines like *American Girl* don't exist.

Data leaked from Instagram in 2021 confirmed how toxic a space it is for teenage girls. The platform is well aware of this fact, though it has done little to mitigate its most harmful effects on body image, anxiety, and depression. This makes us even more nostalgic for spaces (print and otherwise) that empower girls and offer support they won't get elsewhere, especially in their teenage years. It makes us wish there were still someone answering the Help! column who could help parents (and us) navigate this today.

The American Girl of Today

While the brand was slow to figure out that girls wanted to be extremely online, they did broaden their scope beyond the magazine to offer more dolls and resources for the modern girl. In the Fall 1996 catalogue, they described the Girl of Today and her accessories and explained, "Letters urged us to expand our vision from the past to the present . . . *Our response* is an entirely new collection—The American Girl of Today."

Whereas the early dolls all lived in another time, and preferably a year that ended in four, this girl was born, well, probably around the same time as the average millennial customer and fan. This was a doll that did not have to be sweet, or sour, or even historical. Her main quality of note? She would be made in our image, so long as we could choose a similar-enough look from a chart of twenty faces. Arriving without the baggage of the colonial era, settler colonialism, or even Edwardian orphan drama, she was simply an American Girl of Today.

Looking back, the launch of this line was a defining moment in American Girl's evolution as a doll-making brand. For a decade, the people behind American Girl had worked meticulously to research and present stories about girls in history. The marketing materials were filled with girls dressed like their dolls, living their best history nerd lives. In the glossy photographs, kids with perfectly coiffed hair could be found in meadows and fancy parlors sitting with a doll and a book perched right on their laps. There was a lot of material that you could "play with," so to speak, when it came to a character like Felicity.

Yet, much like the universe, American Girl was and is always expanding. The canonical story for a character like Addy had a lot of layers, but it was also set within a six-book arc. With these new products, the backstory was totally up to you. These girls lived in the here and now, and could be molded, quite literally, into who you'd like them to be. Looking back, this is both fascinating and daunting. Did we even know who *we* were in 1995?

The short answer is no, we didn't. The longer answer includes our confession that we sadly did not own any of these dolls, but we were super intrigued by them. We can also relate to the impulse to want to get something that helps you figure out who you are or who you might become. When these dolls were becoming popular among our age set, other people in our lives were staying up late, watching prime-time television, and asking themselves deep questions such as "Am I a Monica, or a Phoebe?" Or they were simply opting for a hair appointment to get "the Rachel." Some of us were also taking direct action to get new haircuts in our own bathrooms, but that's not really a childhood hobby we can recommend. All of us grasp for some kind of shorthand for identity, and we can tell you that's a process that doesn't end even when you stop buying tween apparel, if you ever stop.

Buying and to some degree designing your own American Girl of Today was a way to get a handle on your changing self. Through a few order forms, this was your chance to have American Girl make something for you, like you. No need to imagine yourself or anyone else in the past—with the check of a few boxes, you could commission a doll that would live in your timeline and be a kind of mini-mirror. Along with all of her great outfits and chances for dress-up, you'd even be invited, and trained, to write her story out for yourself.

When the doll selections were limited to historical dolls, part of the allure of joining the American Girl fandom was knowing that you were connecting to other lovers of the same characters. After all, you needed some shared knowledge to go to something like a Felicity tea. How else could you determine whether you were a loyalist at age nine? This pivot meant that you could stay attached to American Girl *and* ditch the history books. No need to visit a place like Colonial Williamsburg; your life was the backdrop and perfect setting for this doll's story.

This shift toward contemporary life meant that you could participate in the growing world of American Girl just by being yourself, and showing up with a kind of doll avatar. For those who may have been weary, a line in the catalogues marketing these dolls assures you: "She's just like you. You're a part of history, too!" Forget Felicity and her contributions to history, this was your time! This catalogue snippet perfectly encapsulates the brand's pivot from focusing on interesting girls in the past to framing their fans as important people whose stories matter as history makers themselves.

All of the American Girl of Today dolls had seriously detailed and fashionable accompaniments. The first dolls launched under this label came dressed in a special outfit primed just for 1995. This means magenta leggings paired with a matching tee under an oversized white button-down shirt, a denim vest, plain black flats, and a scrunchie. While these dolls cost $82, they do come with a cool hat, a pendant, and a total of $3 in play money. From conception, learning to be a consumer is critical for dolls. Late 1990s dolls in this line were even trendier. They came with a red vinyl jumper and a matching beret. Another iconic set of attire included a multicolored fleece jacket, accented with up to ten Grin Pins. One look that we've especially taken to is the purple varsity jacket looks (no sport-playing needed). These girls wear cargo pants, bucket hats, and all sorts of gear that would shockingly make a comeback with Gen Z. Sometimes, peering into these catalogue pages years later is less like a walk down memory lane and more like a highlight reel of recent fashions.

If you're worried these dolls are too focused on their looks, have no fear. Did we mention this doll is literary? In addition to a library card, she has an *American Girl* magazine (Never! Stop! Promoting!). If you thought the historical books were preparing you for a life of meta-analysis when each doll received a doll within her *Surprise* story, buckle up. This doll crafted in your image also comes with a stencil kit and "six blank books" designed just for this girl's story. Not sure where to even begin? No fear, a *Writer's Guide* has been included.

In terms of storytelling, the possibilities were limitless for these dolls. But the actual manufacturing process did have some constraints. From the start, buyers had twenty face options to choose from, labeled GT1–GT20 (Girl of Today 1–20). These options included different skin, hair, and eye colors. In the presentation of these dolls, race and ethnicity are not mentioned. The skin options are "dark" or "light," and the hair choices are "textured" or not textured. Some girls have bangs, others do not. All have two visible and pearly white teeth gently poking out from a smile. There are no variations in body size. There is an option to buy crutches and a wheelchair for dolls with mobility issues, an early and rare gesture toward disability.

If you want to feel a deep and disturbing existential crisis, pull up this "GT" chart from the American Girl archives. Looking at the neat rows of options feels like peering at a weird lineup book or yearbook you were not supposed to see as an adult. If that doesn't help, imagine being asked to watch a game of Guess Who? being put on by a eugenics think tank. While this might seem like an outlandish way to view these catalogue pages, social scientists have long known that how we respond to dolls and toys says a lot about the world around us. Offering children a twenty-photograph spread of face and hair types to choose from is not a neutral or simple act in a culture with deeply racialized beauty standards.

Almost exactly fifty years earlier, Doctors Kenneth and Mamie Clark asked children to pick out dolls to play with and then watched what they did. They found that the Black children in the study preferred to play with white dolls. More recent re-creations of the study, including one in 2021, have found that, unfortunately, little has changed in how children respond to dolls of the same or different races. Researcher Toni Denese Sturdivant, PhD, watched how Black children treated Black dolls and saw the same kind of rejection witnessed a half century prior. White supremacy is still prevalent in the doll aisle, in other words.

Offering a wider range of dolls meant that more children could see themselves in what they could buy from American Girl, but the mere existence of dolls with a variety of skin colors and backstories is not enough. This was a way of expanding representation, certainly, but the lineup of faces without any further context is a bit baffling. During this same period, girls of color were rarely, if ever, featured on the covers of other American Girl catalogues or books, with the magazine proving an important exception. All of the girls who were on the cover were usually "ordinary" girls, and not models, but they all still fit a thin body type.

When we were first introduced to these dolls, debates over the ethics of cloning, and not-so-distant fears of the collapse of, well, everything with Y2K were commonplace. Picking out a doll that could look like you probably feels insubstantial compared to the large social issues of the mid-to-late 1990s. But it was emblematic of a moment when the social fabric was, in fact, fraying, and it is telling that one of the answers provided to young girls was simply to look for another version of themselves to play with.

Given the prevalence of the discourse of "race-blindness" in this time, offering this kind of customizable doll was a way to sidestep discussions of difference. Consumers looking for more context for modern dolls of any race other than white would have to dig deeper into their pocket. Even when American Girl created a problem, they were also quick to offer another costly solution. Additional accessories could provide a deeper story for your doll, particularly for the holiday season. While all of these girls mingled at school during the day, and had fun at group sleepovers, during winter break, the family customs that set them apart would come to the fore.

On a recurring Season's Greetings! page of the catalogue, consumers could choose from a series of special outfits. These included a Kwanzaa outfit, a violin recital outfit, a Hanukkah outfit, a Chinese New Year outfit, or a ballerina costume. Forgive us for wondering how all of these really fit together, except as a kind of 1990s gesture toward diversity without any probing about culture, faith, or inequalities. To be clear, there is nothing in the catalogue about Blackness or the origins of an event such as Chinese New Year. This is nothing more and nothing less than a display of costumes, of special clothing to be worn. Who would be wearing these clothes in real life, and what the clothes might mean to them, is left entirely up to the consumer to discover.

For another brand, this kind of superficial inclusion of different holidays might not be so glaring. However, think back just a few years earlier to the extensive research undertaken to make Felicity's holiday gathering accurate, or to show the deep roots of Kirsten's St. Lucia's Day offering. As a contrast, the American Girl of Today line included vague and limited gestures toward multiculturalism that seemed only to further confuse what they were trying to do or who they were trying to reach.

Today, there are far more products that address the myriad ways that American Girl fans celebrate holidays. There are also conflicts within the fandom about the appropriateness of selling "costumes" that are important to a culture or a faith group for the sake of dressing a doll up. We talked about this on our show with guest Colette Denali Montoya, a member of the Pueblo of Isleta and a descendant of the Pueblo of San Felipe, who noted the hurt caused by white collectors who dress up their dolls in Indigenous clothing without thought or understanding of the culture they're attempting to replicate.

American Girl would morph and change this line of dolls many times in the years to come. One year into its launch, the line would be renamed American Girl Today. A decade later, it would be called Just Like You. My American Girl would be the next rebrand, followed by Truly Me. None of these labels should be confused with the Create Your Own line (we'd love to know why they rebranded so often). Unlike Truly Me, which allows girls to choose from a selection of doll types to find one that most resembles them, Create Your Own is entirely customizable. These dolls, which let customers select every aspect of the custom-made doll, from face shape to hair to freckles to outfit, run about twice the cost of an average historical doll ($200 versus $82).

The vibe in the late 1990s American Girl catalogues suggests that all the dolls are for girls who think for themselves and make their own path in life. This is entirely in keeping with the brand's focus on developing yourself. But to really, truly get something individual—to really get a doll with a distinct style or "personality" (we are kind of too scared to really understand what that means)—you'd have to pony up extra money. You'd also have to spend the time building a profile and to know exactly what you're looking for. The act of curating a version of yourself defined by accessories and a customizable face in some ways anticipated the skills we'd have to develop curating online presences of ourselves just a few years after this. How do you pick which traits to highlight? Which clothes or outfits to distill your personality? What accessories to hold so people know you're deep? Think back to your first Facebook profile pic, Instagram post, or tweet. What portrait does it offer of you then, and who are you now?

Thankfully, American Girl did have other tools we could use to develop our emerging selves that didn't require a willingness to be part of a eugenics experiment. These accessories would cost far less than the locker or sleepover bundles offered for the contemporary dolls. They would slide easily onto any bookcase or fit into almost any backpack. They were somehow colorful and discreet at the same time. These literary guides to modern life would prove vital for many readers, and it all started with *The Care and Keeping of You*.

The American Girl "Bible"

At the same time that American Girl announced the launch of the American Girl of Today in September 1995, it also debuted the American Girl Library. According to the brand's PR, the success of the magazine proved "there is a real need for fun, contemporary reading for girls. With this line, our purpose is to provide books that are both entertaining and informative." The first books in this series offered activities and games for girls, but in 1998 they offered what came to be a treasured guide to health called *The Care and Keeping of You*.

This compact, easy-to-read book was pitched to young people at an in-between age of seven through twelve. *The Care and Keeping of You* was nothing less than a guide on how to get through life when you were dealing with zits, a new level of consciousness, and the looming threat of puberty. In January 2019, Emily Nussbaum, Pulitzer Prize–winning writer at the *New Yorker*, asked this question on Twitter: "If you were elected to political office and you weren't allowed to swear in on a religious text, what book would you use?" One of the viral responses came from @AmandaJagg, who wrote: "The American Girl Doll Book 'The Care and Keeping of YOU.'" It is no great surprise that many people still call this book their own kind of Bible.

The Care and Keeping of You opens with an imaginary letter from "Growing Up." They write to American Girl, explaining that "growing up is becoming a big and important issue." The writer adds, "I feel like it's too personal to talk to an adult about. Please help me." The opposite page includes a reply, a beautiful preface to the book. The "Letter to You" explains, "The head-to-toe advice in this book will give you the words to start a conversation with your parents or other adults you trust." The letter acknowledges how hard it can be to find "the right words to use" when asking a hard question.

Like *Our Bodies, Ourselves*, the foundational women's health book created by the Boston Women's Health Book Collective in 1970 to empower women with knowledge about their own health and bodies, *The Care and Keeping of You* is similarly structured to offer girls a wide range of information. In just one hundred pages, *Care and Keeping* really does cover a staggering number of topics. It is fairly comprehensive in terms of anatomy, and features sections called "Heads Up!" (ears, eyes, mouth, braces, acne, etc.), "Reach!" (hands, underarms, breasts, bras, etc.), "Belly Zone" (food, nutrition, eating disorders, etc.), "Big Changes" (legs, feet, fitness, rest, sleep toubles, etc.), and "The Girl Inside" (your feelings, the whole you).

Despite this range, it somehow strikes just the right balance in reminding readers they're more than the sum of their parts. After telling girls *they* are the bosses of their own bodies, a small cartoon of a girl watching a television reminds them, "Most images of women you see on TV just aren't realistic. Look around. *Real* women's bodies look like your mom's, your teacher's, your next-door neighbor's." This book does not promise to solve any one of your problems, but it does at least provide a starting point.

How does a brand focused on dolls and history pivot to health empowerment? It starts with a great idea and a kind of "corporate conscious raising meeting" reminiscent of the makings of *Our Bodies, Ourselves* (whose authors were decidedly not corporate). The cover offers an iconic illustration of girls in bath towels, not unlike a Go-Go's album cover, and seems to purposely decenter the names of its author, Valorie Lee Schaefer, and illustrators.

Schaefer began working with Pleasant Company back in 1989 as a copywriter on a range of products and in multiple departments. Yet unlike another certain Valerie, she's not as well known within the fandom, or among readers in general. In a 2018 article appearing in *Mashable*, Schaefer revisited the project and its production process in an interview with reporter Morgan Sung. According to Schaefer, Rowland was inspired by a newspaper article on puberty. As she recalled to Sung, Rowland had "been on some airplane and there was an article in the *Times* on the early onset of puberty. And she ripped the page out, and she put a sticky note on it for Michelle [Watkins, the editor of the book], and wrote, 'WE NEED TO DO SOMETHING ABOUT THIS NOW.'" What's with the urgency, Pleasant? Did she just then learn about puberty? Periods? We're honestly impressed with the serious work she got done on a plane. When we fly, we mainline movies we'll forget about immediately upon landing.

Schaefer and her team were striving for the book to feel as though it came from "your cool aunt." (We can feel Tavi nodding at this.) This created a tone that balanced great authority with some sense of chill confidence. It wasn't like the awkward movies we'd watch in health class that carried basic info with a shaming morality, or glossy tampon commercials that told you everything but how to use the product. By candidly offering information and reassurance, the book found a broad audience and went through multiple editions that reached millions of readers.

Part of the value of packaging this information (including how to insert a tampon, with helpful illustrations) is that it allows readers to explore questions they may be embarrassed to ask adults in private. Many people have reported that the book filled important gaps when adults did not or would not have conversations about puberty with them. Brenna, a self-identified Samantha and Scorpio, wishes she still had her own Samantha doll. She recalls being handed an American Girl book at a formative moment. When she first got her period, Brenna recalls, "My mom figured it out," and slid the slim "book and a pad under the bathroom door." Adding, in a detail perhaps many mothers and daughters can relate to, "we never spoke about it."

This private means of learning about your body was important, especially if you had little other access to comparable information or your parents didn't know how to have these kinds of conversations with you. During this liminal time of web development, many people would not have had any kind of privacy on a computer, especially at a young age. If you got your hands on this book, though, you didn't need to ask someone how to shave your legs. That was something you could read about and choose to do—or not. On an early page of the book, readers are even reminded that "your body is yours and *yours alone*. You have the right to protect it and keep it private from anyone . . ." The focus is on developing the reader's sense of comfort with the topics, and her own changing body.

This kind of private affirmation is exactly what proved so powerful to readers and remains a point of pride to the team that worked on the book, even decades later. We got a chance to talk to one of the designers who had a major role in making this book. Ingrid Hess was still a young woman herself when she was working for a design firm called Kym Abrams in Chicago. They'd been contracted to work for Pleasant Company, which itself was a big deal. When we asked Hess about this book, she told us details about the process and tried to convey the feeling of being part of something that would become so big. Finally, Allison came out and asked: Did she know—did all of them know—that it was special? Hess nodded her head vigorously. "When we were making it, we all knew that we were making something really special that really mattered."

We're living in a time of '90s nostalgia that has made the style and culture of the period cool again. While that impulse helped make our show and this book possible, it has also generated conversations about what has and hasn't aged well. *Friends*, for example, is having a renaissance although some have noted the gay panic of some of its plotlines carries the danger of normalizing homophobia. Comparably, women who grew up on *The Care and Keeping of You* have spoken out on their wariness to pass it on to their own children, noting its limitations on a range of subjects. In March 2021, Leah Campbell wrote an essay for *Scary Mommy* called "Why You Shouldn't Give Your Kid the Book 'The Care and Keeping of You.'" She explains that upon reread, "the whole book felt outdated, heteronormative, and not at all body positive to me." Looking for additional counsel, she started clicking around and "when I started looking through the reviews, I realized I wasn't the only one." She concludes, "I had to believe there was something better out there."

Campbell's reaction to *Care and Keeping* all of these years later is filtered, in part, by the fact that she was looking at it as a guide for her child. People who do hold this book in high esteem now seem to only remember what they have chosen to remember, and like us, frankly, have forgotten the rest. This selective memory affected fans of *Our Bodies, Ourselves*, too. Many forget that early editions invited readers to use astrology to make health decisions.

Health books reflect an understanding of the years that produce them, and times change. The book *is* heteronormative. People have also criticized the language on eating disorders and body acceptance. There is little in the way of celebrating different body types and shapes, and the concept of a "crush" in this book has long been limited to what a girl might feel for a boy. As Schaefer told Morgan Sung in 2018, she felt that shortcoming in her own family, acknowledging the limitations of that kind of language for her own daughter, who identifies as gay.

These and other products also presumed all readers identified as girls. While many people think of this book as the text that taught them how to use a tampon, a newer version today might address people with periods, as opposed to girls getting their first menses. This explains why articles that circulate on the web about *Care and Keeping* books frequently have conversations about transphobia in the comments sections, and why critics like Campbell remain uncomfortable with handing this kind of guide over to a growing tween today.

This awareness of issues like inclusivity and accessibility was not lost on illustrator Ingrid Hess. While the book was still a work in progress, Hess had her own reservations about *Care and Keeping*. On the one hand, she was deeply proud of what she and her colleagues had done. On the other hand, she knew that not all girls or kids in general had access to this material. Since she worked on projects outside of just this book, Hess was well aware that this stuff was not cheap. During our talk, she acknowledged, "We were putting out quality products, and it was expensive to produce." Still, she remembers pushing, as often as possible, for more books and guides that would be affordable.

For years, Hess and her colleagues at the firm wanted to make something for American Girl that would only cost one dollar. They thought about all different kinds of book designs and pitches but never quite got down to a true "buck a book." American Girl *did* agree to make the Backpack Books collection. These books were $1.95 palm-size guides that were easy to collect because of their size and the price.

Even if you were rocking a tiny backpack in the 1990s, you could manage a stack of Backpack Books. Small, square, and with a ring in the top left corner, they could easily hook onto any key chain or backpack, and focused on a single topic. Trying to take better photos? Grab *Say Cheese* and stick it in your backpack. Want to tell better jokes? Perhaps *Gigglets* will get the job done. Knowing how to work barrettes, become a babysitter, and make popcorn are just a few of the other topics in this collection. Importantly, each of these books invited girls to learn something with the goal of connecting with other people their age. Yes, you'd learn how to take better pictures, but you would also learn how to stage a photoshoot with friends. Looking at these books now, we could use a few refreshers. You are never too old to figure out how to best coordinate your hair clips and find your angles.

A major through line in the books and products American Girl offered definitely was forging a healthy relationship with yourself, but we can also appreciate the products it developed that really emphasized and valued the importance of friendship.

Pen Pals, Fan Clubs, and Friendship

It's surprising how little friendship gets discussed even today, considering how vital a relationship it is across a person's life. *Big Friendship: How We Keep Each Other Close*, an exploration of friendship by friends/podcasters/ writers Aminatou Sow and Ann Friedman, is a notable example of books that take friendship seriously as formative nonromantic relationships. We aren't the first to bemoan the lack of serious treatment of friendship in our culture and talk frequently on our show about the importance of these relationships and their challenges.

Many have written to us about the struggle to make friends as adults, for example, and the few outlets that offer meaningful advice or solutions. Facebook famously suggests connections with everyone from a person you met once at a conference to your childhood bully turned MLM influencer spon-queen as potential "friends." In 2016, Bumble launched Bumble BFF to help people not satisfied by Facebook friendships connect with potential real friends. Part of the reason we may know to feel the absence of real attention to friendship is because we had it as girls. In the American Girl universe, friendship is a key part of every book series and is encouraged as a focus of play with dolls. Significantly, American Girl created opportunities for IRL friendships via its fan club and pen pal programs.

American Girl was invested in connecting pen pals early on. In the '90s, they did this through the fan club, a club we'd still love to join. For just $24.95 a year, girls got a sense of belonging with an organization that otherwise looked on paper like a mail-order business. The biz transformed itself into American Girl Nation via the fan club by offering a considerable collection of swag. Girls could store their ID card in a Velcro wallet with pride; try their hand at designing clothes for American Girl characters using an American Girl Wardrobe Flip-Book; read the *American Girl News*, published six times a year; record their reflections in reading journals; hang a poster of the original five dolls on their bedroom wall; wear a members-only charm bracelet and baseball cap to school; and work through the club handbook.

The American Girls Club Handbook was similar in a lot of ways to the early craft kits and other historical doll offshoots like *Kirsten's Cook Book*. But this handbook had a lot more range. Through it, members would get super practical life skills like "how to make a colonial mobcap, weave a daisy wreath, and make petit fours." With each completed activity, you got a sticker to put in the all-important PastPort. "Once your PastPort is full," the catalogue explained, "you'll have earned the rank of American Girls Historian™." This, readers learned, was "a title reserved for those club members who are American Girl experts." Finally, a club that COULD handle us! Sidebar, would we have gotten PhDs had we known this was an option all along? Asking for the years of our lives we won't get back.

All of these signs of membership were things we could enjoy solo (hat, bracelet, news), or we could invite friends to join us in working through the Flip-Book or handbook. (We presume this is true if said friends are also members. We'll assume AG Club is like Fight Club and should live in our minds with Y2K and other things we don't talk about.)

Significantly, the club encouraged girls to connect with one another through its included pen pal program. "Do you want to share secrets and compare notes with a girl who loves the American Girls as much as you do?" the catalogue asked, defining friendship as a common love for American Girls and, amazingly, the willingness to share secrets with a relative stranger. Girls were encouraged to request a name and address to start corresponding.

This pen pal program flourished in the magazine, where friends were invited to write in and celebrate their connections. "My favorite Beanie Baby, Inch the Caterpillar, is pen pals with my friend Brooke Eberle's Beanie Baby, Pinky the Flamingo," a twelve-year-old girl named Kirby shared. "They write about what they do all day, like having play picnics." We love the image of two girls communicating through much-loved Beanie Babies. Also, let's take a moment of silence for the grown-ups out there who still have their personal wealth tied up in their Beanie Baby collections.

The charm of American Girl was not only connecting girls as friends as part of their business model, but that they made space for girls to share about the friendships that mattered to them, to work out friendship drama (see Help! in the magazine), *and* to suggest how pen pals in particular might keep their snail-mail friendships going. One 1998 issue of the magazine had a section called the Write Stuff that invited girls to "M.A.I.L." or "make another interesting letter." You could do this by sending gifts that fit in an envelope (self-portrait, drawing of your room, poems, stationery) or inviting your friends from home to write a note for inclusion in the letter.

Two friends, Nathan and Mindy, shared that they wrote a short story together by trading it back and forth for the other to continue. Similarly, the magazine suggested girls could send a notebook back and forth with shared messages or even incorporate what they called "email hail," or early emojis typed with your keyboard, such as :) . These shared experiences from real girls and boys and the suggestions of the magazine's editors all provided children with ideas about how to nurture friendships, whether via mail or IRL. Friendship could be conversations about American Girl characters or "secrets," as the catalogue described, but it could also be shared silliness, creativity, and descriptions of their daily lives. These examples demonstrated the brand's overall suggestion that we take our friendships (and ourselves) seriously, and that we be willing to sustain our friendships through letters and other gestures of support.

We have made our own contributions to the idea of sustaining friendship though snail mail. In over a decade of knowing each other, we have never lived in the same state. Sending each other funny postcards and letters has been a staple of our friendship to bridge this distance. One of our favorite things to do is send each other postcards from a historic site written by a historic person from that place (yes, we are big-time nerds). We have written to each other as Shaker women, Mary Todd Lincoln, Alva Vanderbilt, and countless others. Our notes often take a pretty big artistic license with what we imagine these people might be comfortable saying. For example, it would surprise you how often we imagine people in the past saying "no scrubs." Mary's fridge still displays a custom birthday message Allison made of an illustration of Nathaniel Hawthorne with a note reading "Here's hoping your birthday is worthy of a Scarlet letter."

In 2004, the American Girl pen pal program moved online and was just as effective in connecting fans. Looking back, we can see that for women of our generation, it was an early space for a now common phenomenon. As a tweet by @rebirthcanal put it, "a new type of relationship first experienced by my generation is 'girl I've been friends with online for 20 years.'" Helen Schultz, self-described on Twitter as "feminist person and general delight," who works in New York City, immediately tagged her online friend, Elisabeth Montanaro, an actress in Orange County. Helen and Elisabeth have been friends for almost twenty years after their parents signed them up for the online pen pal program in 2004. All these years later, both of them note that this platform encouraged parents to make sure the connections their girls made were safe. Before anyone could call themselves "chronically online," the internet really did feel like a strange and new place.

Both women grew up treasuring the brand and its dolls, books, and accessories. One Christmas morning, Helen received a Molly doll and the single ". . . Baby One More Time" under the tree. What an iconic pairing that truly screams "I'm not a girl, not yet a woman." Like many women our age, Helen remembers holidays being "all American Girl," recalling, "it was an all-consuming thing." For Elisabeth, American Girl was a similar object of devotion. She still keeps her dolls at her parents' house, where they have been cherished through the years. Significantly, the brand and its products are not the only thing she cherishes from her time absorbed by American Girl. "I just cherish my friendship so much with Helen," she said. "It's irreplaceable . . . and rare."

Like the pen pals who came before them, they bonded over shared interests, activities, and traits. Though they lived miles apart, Elisabeth and Helen both felt "nerdy" and loved to write. Soon, they began to write for each other, something they both treasured. Elisabeth "was really yearning for a friend that had that same mindset and the same interests," she explained. Thankfully, Helen "couldn't have been more of a match made in heaven." In addition to weekly emails, the two got to know each other through virtual meetups playing *Toontown*, a Disney game.

Even though American Girl shut down the pen pal program in 2006, their friendship has endured. Their lasting bond has left them with an appreciation for each other and a wish that comparable programs encouraged the formation of similar bonds. "I think we really hit the lotto with our friendship and how we met," Elisabeth noted, "and I wish that they would bring back American Girl clubs."

Through its pen pal programs, American Girl (and Pleasant) built mutual aid and solidarity into the culture of the brand by both encouraging and monetizing friendship (we see you, pen pal kits). These, along with the activity and craft kits, party-planning stories in the magazine, and other content designed to be consumed and shared with friends encouraged girls to create and value connections with one another. These relationships could sustain us through the dark times of the '90s and early 2000s, defined in part by their increased social isolation (thanks, internet!), culture war debates about the threat of *everything* to the family and "the children," and an increasingly destabilized environment and national political scene.

One of the most reassuring things about this period, and American Girl's lifestyle offerings for modern girls in particular, is the fact that it affirmed something you might have suspected, deep down. Almost no one really knew what they were doing. Everyone was trying to figure out how to be around other people, whether how to pop a zit correctly or how to be a good friend. American Girl products like these were not asking you to take on any major world issues or to tackle any crises. These were not "girl guides" that taught you about impeachment. But they were texts that imagined girls and women strong enough to support one another through something as serious as what happened to Monica Lewinsky, an event that seemed to play relentlessly in the background of one of our formative years.

Grin Pins might not change the world, but maybe if wearing them gave you a boost, *you* just might. It would take two decades or more for American Girl to deal with topics such as racism and sexism in a more direct way in their contemporary materials. For the most part, we learned through American Girl to situate those problems in the past, through characters such as Addy. Yet we were also given *just enough* confidence and self-awareness through some of these tools that we wondered what kind of change we could effect once we came into our own. It's as Pleasant wrote in a letter to parents in the back of a 1995 catalogue: "We firmly believe that the girls we inspire today will become the women who make the difference tomorrow."

Thank God we still had Pleasant running things at American Girl! What a role model! She gave us a lifestyle, and her leadership would help us maintain it. Through her letters in catalogues and mailings, she was the ultimate pen pal.

Are You There, Pleasant?
It's Us, Grown Women with Attachment Issues

Okay, if you're not familiar with the history of American Girl, we've set you up for some heartbreak here. To soften or increase the blow (depending on your view), please imagine Lilith Fair's own Sarah McLachlan singing "I Will Remember You" as you read the next passage.

In June 1998, Mattel, Inc. announced it was paying $700 million for Pleasant Company. Since 1986, Pleasant Company had $287 million in sales and sold more than four million dolls. Pleasant Rowland was its largest shareholder by far, and the deal would make her what we might call "Samantha Parkington rich." Congratulating Pleasant, a reporter recast the sale as an example of a familiar story, the fulfillment of the American dream: "Maybe the American dream now is to get a megabucks buyout of your start-up company. And Pleasant Rowland is one of the first women to pull it off so successfully."

Confusingly, what began as a celebration of Pleasant's achievements by a female reporter in the *Chicago Tribune* devolved into language more reminiscent of the world of Barbie than the empowered, desexed world of American Girl. "Will she be happy in a corporate marriage to Mattel? Can she really protect Kirsten, Felicity and the American Girls of Today when Mattel becomes their corporate father?" We're starting to wonder if the reporter was working out some of her own stuff here. That, or she was workshopping the plot of a *Jane Eyre* adaptation we'll skip. It's perhaps unsurprising that reporters attempting to understand and write about Pleasant had not evolved too far from the first pieces on her in the 1970s that remarked on her eyes and good looks. The reporter closed by addressing Pleasant's doll "children": "Molly, Addy, Samantha and the others have survived wars and fires and slavery and the death of parents," she warned. "Let's hope they can survive Barbie." We're proud of us for surviving this write-up.

Mattel's ownership would change the brand in many ways. Pleasant Company would become "American Girl" and by the year 2000 include physical stores featuring merch, a café, and, in some cities, a stage show. News outlets reported Pleasant would stay with Mattel in some capacity and advise on her brand, but Pleasant had other ideas. According to several former Pleasant Company employees, Pleasant gathered all her employees in front of the company headquarters around oak trees that served as a common gathering space. There, she gave a speech about what it all meant to her, thanked everyone, and then walked off into the sunset (and toward the parking lot), never to return. We'd love to know what her staff made of this. Now employees of Mattel, did they just give themselves the rest of the day off? Buy a Barbie as some kind of protest?

Photo credit: Ann Mahoney

You might think cohosting a doll podcast means you've had a lifelong love of dolls. This is one of only two existing childhood photos of Mary with a doll—a Barbie, or as Pleasant might call her, "a bad influence."

Photo credit: Donna Horrocks

This Molly is actually not much of a sports fan. Nonetheless, she chose to strike a pose and have this backward-ball-cap moment; maybe there are just some secrets a doll will never tell.

Photo credit: Helder Mira, Trinity College Office of Communications and Marketing

Getting a guided tour of New York's American Girl store included a stop by the doll clinic and the hair salon. Needless to say, these luxuries did not exist when we were deep in our childhoods.

Photo credit: Helder Mira, Trinity College Office of Communications and Marketing

There are not many places in the world where you can celebrate the things you love *and* find out if your aging doll has a condition called "silver eye."

Photo credit: Helder Mira, Trinity College Office of Communications and Marketing

Just two Mollys casually having tea at the American Girl store.

Photo credit and doll styling: Stefanie Ryan, or @agdollcleaning on Instagram

There is no greater tribute than being rendered in doll form, especially when the scene makes us seem cooler than real life might suggest. Part of what we love about this is that the scene mirrors our own way of appreciating American Girl; everything is in the details. Listener Stefanie has Allison holding a mini Molly (of course), with Mary writing down seltzer-fueled notes on Kirsten that mimic the classic run through American history that is Billy Joel's "We Didn't Start the Fire" (which, of course, is a thing Kirsten could never say).

Photo credit: Pamela Landau Connolly

Here we see listener Margot doing what we might call performance art and what she called a Halloween costume as both Molly *and* the *Meet Molly* book, along with her sister, who is dressed as Samantha. How two sisters coexist when they identify as Molly and Samantha respectively is a mystery. If we are what we read, Margot is an icon.

Photo credit: Gwendolyn Brown

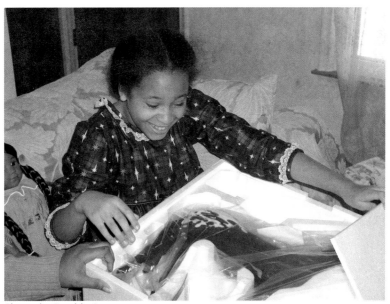

Photo credit: Gwendolyn Brown

Everyone fortunate enough to receive gifts of American Girl dolls
or books knows the expression of pure joy on Kayla's face. Kayla is now
an author who shares her love of history with a new generation.

Photo credit: Lindsey Wood

Photo credit: Lindsey Wood

Lindsey Wood brings a whole new meaning to the phrase "dress for the job you want." Here she is as a childhood Felicity, maybe around the same age she describes visiting Colonial Williamsburg. Little did she know she'd grow up to work at Colonial Williamsburg herself, wearing a dress reminiscent of Felicity's iconic ball gown.

Photo credit: Allison Horrocks

Colonial Williamsburg cut formal ties with American Girl, and now offers their own dolls with accompanying books for sale. These dolls are based on actual people and yet still feel like a fraud. On our visit, we encountered this doll. Though she is practicing appropriate Covid protocol, we don't know her story and we refused to ask. If you're not trying to liberate a horse, why are you even at this living history museum?

Photo credit: Mary Mahoney

Just a photo of two adult women who've been yelled at by a man about
Italian hats and voting. Sure, didn't know that came with the price of our
ticket, but in the words of an '80s classic, we . . . had . . . the time of our lives.

The Care & Keeping of

YOU

★ American Girl™

The Body Book for Girls

Photo credit: Mary Mahoney

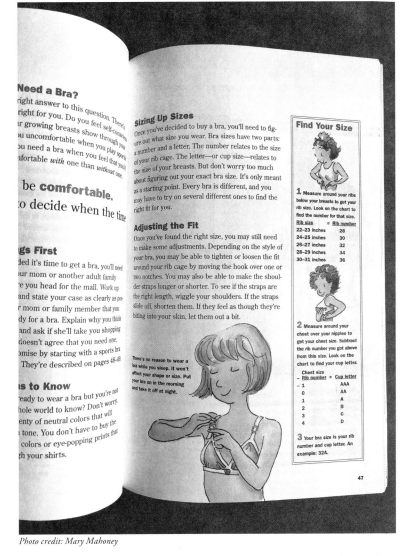

Need a Bra?

right answer to this question. There's
right for you. Do you feel self-conscious
r growing breasts show through your
u uncomfortable when you play sports
u need a bra when you feel that you'd
nfortable *with* one than *without one.*

be comfortable.
o decide when the time

gs First

ded it's time to get a bra, you'll need
ur mom or another adult family
'e you head for the mall. Work up
and state your case as clearly as pos-
r mom or family member that you
dy for a bra. Explain why you think
and ask if she'll take you shopping
doesn't agree that you need one.
omise by starting with a sports bra
They're described on pages 48-49.

s to Know

eady to wear a bra but you're not
hole world to know? Don't worry!
enty of neutral colors that will
tone. You don't have to buy the
colors or eye-popping prints that
h your shirts.

Sizing Up Sizes

Once you've decided to buy a bra, you'll need to figure out what size you wear. Bra sizes have two parts:
a number and a letter. The number relates to the size
of your rib cage. The letter—or cup size—relates to
the size of your breasts. But don't worry too much
about figuring out your exact bra size. It's only meant
as a starting point. Every bra is different, and you
may have to try on several different ones to find the
right fit for you.

Adjusting the Fit

Once you've found the right size, you may still need
to make some adjustments. Depending on the style of
your bra, you may be able to tighten or loosen the fit
around your rib cage by moving the hook over one or
two notches. You may also be able to make the shoulder straps longer or shorter. To see if the straps are
the right length, wiggle your shoulders. If the straps
slide off, shorten them. If they feel as though they're
biting into your skin, let them out a bit.

There's no reason to wear a
bra while you sleep. It won't
affect your shape or size. Put
your bra on in the morning
and take it off at night.

Find Your Size

1 Measure around your ribs
below your breasts to get your
rib size. Look on the chart to
find the number for that size.

Rib size	= Rib number
22–23 inches	28
24–25 inches	30
26–27 inches	32
28–29 inches	34
30–31 inches	36

2 Measure around your
chest over your nipples to
get your chest size. Subtract
the rib number you got above
from this size. Look on the
chart to find your cup letter.

Chest size – Rib number	= Cup letter
– 1	AAA
0	AA
1	A
2	B
3	C
4	D

3 Your bra size is your rib
number and cup letter. An
example: 32A.

47

Photo credit: Mary Mahoney

Not since Oprah decided to "revolutionize" how women understood
bra size on an iconic episode of her eponymous show has the public
consciousness been so shaped by one source on the topic of women's
health. The prospect of puberty is scary enough, but the thought
of facing it without this book was absolutely terrifying.

THIS AIN'T A TEA PARTY.

Photo credit: Mary Mahoney

To paraphrase the Talking Heads, the 2004 *Samantha: An American Girl
Holiday* movie let us know that being a rich girl in the Edwardian period
was neither disco nor tea party. Following our labor activist queen, this
adaptation took us on a journey of grief and activism, and asked us
to imagine what it would be like if Mia Farrow was our grandma.

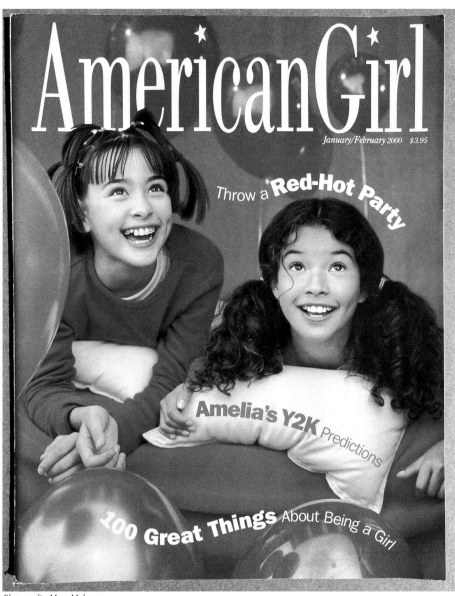

Photo credit: Mary Mahoney

American Girl magazine offered advice, stories, games, and fun for its readers. Here you can see some typical offerings, ranging from a listicle of reasons why it's great to be a girl to "Y2K Predictions" from Melissa Moss's Amelia's Notebook. Someone please take us back to the days when Y2K was a legitimate concern.

Heart to Heart
Best Friends

Is it better to have one *best* friend or lots of good friends? These girls share their thoughts about friends.

 It's good to have a best friend. Everyone needs someone to giggle with under the covers and to pass notes to. Best friends fight, but best friends also patch things up.

Merrily McFegan
Age 12, Massachusetts

 I had a really good friend. We became so close we both agreed we were best friends. Then I saw her wearing half of a best friends necklace, and I didn't have the other half! I was upset. It's better to have a group of friends because people can change their minds about being best friends.

Ann Robinson
Age 11, Virginia

 I hate when a friend asks me who my best friend is in front of my other friends. I just say, "I like you all the same." It makes everyone smile, and I mean it!

Kelly Boyles
Age 11, Texas

 If you have a bunch of friends you'll have more than two ears to listen to your problems, and more than one mouth to give you advice!

Genny Szymanski
Age 11, Alaska

 I think you can have lots of good friends, but you can only have one *best* friend.

Sarah Bumgarner
Age 10, North Carolina

 My best friend and I have a lot in common. We take dancing together, we have the same middle name, and we both have dogs. But there are also a few things that we don't have in common. It's nice to like similar things, but our differences are what keep our friendship interesting!

Jade Hicks
Age 12, Missouri

 A best nd is someo you can always k to. I have a lot of good fri ds, and each one has a little place in my heart, but my best friend has a slightly larger place!

Rebecca Castine
Age 9, Massachusetts

Photo credit: Mary Mahoney

The Heart to Heart section of the magazine asked girls to sound off on a common question affecting their lives. Here girls weigh in on the question of "best friends." This often extremely primal space in the magazine not only made readers feel less alone around vulnerable topics, but also centered girls' voices as worthy sources of advice.

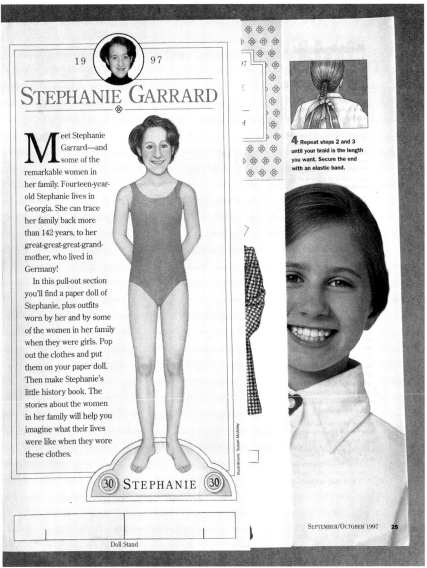

Photo credit: Mary Mahoney

Stephanie's paper doll takes us back to her great-great-great-grandmother living in early nineteenth-century Germany. Seeing outfits from different moments in time and history, readers can follow the story of the women in Stephanie's family *and* get a sense of fashion history at the same time. It's too bad our great-grand-children won't get the chance to immortalize us for our millennial fashions. Who wouldn't want to be enshrined in paper-doll form wearing bootcut jeans?

Photo credit: Mary Mahoney

This 2005 adaptation of the Felicity books, a Julia Roberts–produced gem, offered lines like this that ring as true today when spoken by haters at the Met Gala as they did in 1774 when delivered by a baby-faced Shailene Woodley.

After her dramatic exit, Pleasant stayed in the Madison, Wisconsin, community and has used her wealth to fund libraries, hospitals, and a series of cultural organizations. Tellingly, like the industrialists whose history playground at Williamsburg inspired her at the start, she also started to buy and renovate buildings in Aurora, New York, home of her alma mater, Wells College, to restore it to an imagined past of her design. We would try our hands at this, too, but we lack the money, time, and inclination to engineer an experiment in eugenics by architecture. For budgetary purposes, we may just rewatch episodes of *Gilmore Girls* and revisit Stars Hollow, Connecticut.

Pleasant may have walked off into the proverbial sunset, but we're still here. She gave us the dolls, books, lifestyle brand of today, and so much more. What did we do with it?

We want to explore what we all did with the world Pleasant made. We've learned from our community that everyone's relationship with the brand is unique, and we want to explore what it meant to play with American Girl dolls and books in the '90s from other perspectives than our own. We're also aware that not *everyone* wants to make a podcast, and that there are in fact other ways of reinterpreting a love for American Girl from the vantage of adulthood beyond audio interspersed with ads for meal kits. We're going to get into that, too. But first, we want to invite you to a playdate.

Questions We Still Want Answered . . .

People who worked for American Girl received lots of letters from young fans.

If we were to pick up our pens and pull out our beautiful AG stationery, here are some topics we might want to bring up in a letter to executives:

- Who was in charge of Coconut the dog, and why is their backstory so inconsistent?
- What kinds of plays got left on the cutting room floor? Did you

ever imagine a Kirsten theatrical production with the ghost of Marta, her deceased friend, playing a leading role?

- Where is the capital of American Girl Nation, and do we need an up-to-date passport to gain entry? Please consider this our application for ambassadorship also.
- When is it time to retire your varsity-style American Girl jacket?
- Why did you make mini Grin Pins? Weren't the actual Grin Pins tiny enough?
- This one is personal, but how did Allison's shipment of Felicity's Winter Entertainments get so lost more than twenty-five years ago? Her lantern, top, and fire screen seem to have gotten waylaid. Can we get a tracking code? We will wait.

CHAPTER 4

Happy Birthday to Us!
The Gift of American Girl

In which we explore our childhood obsessions with the catalogue, dolls, dressing up, and birthday parties with other millennial fans.

In 2020, the National Museum of American History at the Smithsonian debuted an exhibit called *Girlhood: (It's Complicated)*. In copy that could have been ripped from Avril Lavigne's teenage diary, the museum's exhibit text set the tone for what followed: "The history of girlhood is not what people think; it is complicated." Before you respond in true Avril style, "Uh-huh, life's like this," let's dive deeper. "Young women are often told that girls are 'made of sugar and spice and everything nice.' What is learned from history is that girls are made of stronger stuff. They have changed history."

We love an exhibit about girls making history. Yet this description leaves some questions. Is the complication of girlhood that people think we're "sweet," but we're really "strong"? What is the stronger stuff we're made of? Can Kelly Clarkson tell us?

Mary traveled to the Smithsonian, where she explored the items in the exhibit and was filled with wonder at their collections. They had Helen Keller's watch, a '50s poodle skirt on which a teen had embroidered scenes from her Minnesota town, zines, and all kinds of great historical objects. She was in awe. It arranged explorations of girlhood across American history in themes it labeled story sections: "Education (being schooled)," "Wellness (body talk)," "Work (hey, where's my girlhood?)," "Fashion (remix)."

It was fascinating (and tragic) to see recurring themes of girls' minds, bodies, time, and lives being controlled through various forms of discipline. Mary saw displays on the ways girls were controlled in school through dress codes and limitations on what was appropriate for them to study, for example. An illustration showing young farmworkers also acknowledged that for some, school was a luxury out of reach. However powerful it was (and it was), she left feeling something was missing from "the story" of girlhood in the exhibit. She wanted to jump up on a table and hold a sign over her head, Sally Field as Norma Rae–style. Instead of "protest," she'd write a single question: What ever happened to fun? Didn't Cyndi Lauper sing something about that in an episode of *Pop-Up Video* on VH1? (We won't get into the wrinkle of a man writing that song.)

Admittedly, the exhibit's emphasis was on how girls shaped culture and history against real barriers. "We argue . . . that girls, like suffragists, used their voices to make a difference," curators noted in the first exhibit label. But what about the goofy, fun, silly, weird stuff girls get up to? How did they play in the distant past, or in our own lifetimes? What did friends do for fun? Not to mention toys: There was not one single American Girl doll on display. No Beanie Babies, slap bracelets, or Skip-Its in sight. The only American Girl product on display was *The Care and Keeping of You* in a section on conduct and advice books that included a sign asking "Why do we give girls so much advice?" We're not sure, but we may look for the answer at the bottom of what some men on the internet have called the "Well, actually."

We cannot fault the Smithsonian. They fell prey to a trap we learned in school; the quickest way to rob something of fun is to study it or call it "educational." That's what's so special and cool about American Girl. Pleasant really did want to teach us things, and she even called her dolls and books educational toys. But instead of hiding what we owned in the backs of our closets, only to be taken out for display when Grandma visited (sorry,

Grandma! We did really love those multiplication table flash cards), we *loved* American Girl and everything it threw at us.

While Pleasant had very high-minded intentions for us, she had no control over what we'd make of the brand's books, dolls, and other products. Could Pleasant or any adult know the chaos of a '90s/2000s girl's imaginary life? Where you could find yourself swept up in a game of Pogs one moment, then caught up in a Beanie Baby trade, only to lose yourself in a complicated historical drama of your own design starring your American Girl doll and a coerced sibling? Probably not. And that's just some of our own experiences. We are just two women for whom American Girl mattered as a source of joy, imagination, and play. There are so many others, and so many ways to be a fan.

On Mary's way out of the Smithsonian exhibit on girlhood, she noticed a label that described as its inspiration "magazines and zines—how girls have been spoken to and how girls talk back." This reminded her of the episode of *The Bachelorette* where discarded contestants are invited to return and share their perspective in an episode called "Men Tell All," which she genuinely believed was called "Men Talk Back" for an embarrassing amount of time. Since we started our show, we've invited listeners to "talk back" to us and share their experiences with American Girl. We've heard stories about playing with the dolls, loving the books, making doll clothes with loved ones, and staging epic American Girl birthday parties.

The fourth book in the traditional six-book American Girl arc is typically the birthday book. In those books, the American Girl faces a challenge only to be rewarded with a birthday celebration and a gift (typically a doll). Birthdays are a moment of unapologetic celebration for no real achievement. Leos love them (just ask Mary). We want to treat you like it's your birthday and gift you stories we've gathered from our community of listeners and delve into what playing with American Girl was like for our generation of fans (women, nonbinary folx, and men). We'll play with dolls, make doll clothes with loved ones, read books, stage plays, write newspapers, and party like it's 1854. So much of who we are as people was formed through play as kids. We wanted to explore what playing with American Girl meant for a generation of people, and how it lingers in our memories as some of the best days of childhood and formative moments for who we would become as adults.

The Only Gift Guide We Need: The American Girl Catalogue

To this day, if you wanted to buy us a gift, the American Girl catalogue would be a great place to start. We're forever grateful Pleasant didn't bring her dolls to Toys "R" Us #RIP, instead giving us the gift of the catalogues. We're also sending up a prayer that the post office never goes bankrupt, because we can't imagine a world where these aren't showing up at our doors.

In the press rollouts of American Girl, Pleasant described the catalogue as a means of keeping costs low. Costs were a concern from the beginning—both keeping them down and justifying the expense of everything AG. Selling through direct mail kept costs down by 30 percent, Pleasant explained. She wanted to keep the price within reach of kids who wanted to play with the dolls, rather than collectors who wanted them only for display. With such consideration to keep costs down, Pleasant took umbrage at any talk of her dolls costing too much. Buying Kirsten with her first book cost $68 that first year, she acknowledged, "but lots of people spent $80 last year for a talking teddy bear that likely stopped talking a few months after Christmas." Teddy Ruxpin deserves this shade! Honestly, after Mary played a Janet Jackson tape in her brother's Teddy Ruxpin, she was anything but in #control.

But we're more interested here in what children made of her catalogue, and not the business savvy behind it. The earliest fans of AG could easily relate to Pleasant's "my feelings cannot be contained" energy. When Pleasant was going on her media tour, newspapers printed profiles of the brand with information on where to write to obtain the hallowed catalogue. One newspaper failed to include the contact info and had to print the address in the next edition in response to the outpouring of letters they'd received. These young readers were about to find out something we know all too well: the only thing better than owning something from American Girl was dreaming about buying something from the American Girl catalogue.

Women of our generation can conjure an almost religious devotion to it. With senses fully engaged, our listeners echo our own experiences, recalling the exhilaration of receiving it in the mail, the feeling of turning the pages. Did you skip to your favorite character's section first? (Molly, obviously.) Did you want clothes for yourself so that you could match your doll? When we got the catalogue in the mail, we re-created our own interpretation of *2 Fast 2 Furious*, flipping through pages with the recklessness of Vin Diesel behind the wheel. We'd make lists of everything we'd buy if we lived on Samantha Parkington's budget. Even knowing we'd never get everything on the list, the cultivation of that desire into a wish list brought its own kind of thrill.

We weren't alone. In talking to other people our age about American Girl, we found a lot of fans who felt the same. "I remember vividly the day that the catalogue arrived," one listener shared with us. "My two sisters, and my mother[,] would sit around the kitchen table, going page by page." Especially in a pre-internet age, many referred to the catalogue as "window shopping for children," which feels right. We couldn't drive ourselves to the mall or other favorite '90s haunts to buy toys (#RIP New England gems Ames and Caldor). We *could* sit at home and amuse ourselves for hours with this catalogue. It offered highly compartmentalized and curated goods. Each section contained a dizzying amount of historically accurate accessories and furniture in addition to the dolls themselves and their "we'd probably not die for this but we'd think about it" wardrobes.

The catalogues also featured models our age wearing girl-size versions of the dolls' outfits that were the stuff dreams were made of. As the brand progressed, the back end of the catalogue contained spin-off products, including the Girl of Today dolls, Bitty Babies, etc. This was beyond aspirational content, and multiple listeners have shared that the catalogue helped to inspire their entry into fashion or museum fields, as they so closely resembled exhibit catalogues.

Preowned catalogues on the internet market today—even the ones labeled as "very good condition"—are filled with circles and annotations. This tells you something, and not just about the honesty of online retailers.

Sadly, none of our well-worn examples have survived into the present. The catalogue could bring the thrill of window-shopping right into our homes. One listener described falling asleep with the page opened to the Samantha doll section so her "parents would see when they came to turn out the light," noting, "it totally worked for Annie in *Father of the Bride*!" We love a hero who knows when to flex the right references. Who could forget Annie (Ms. Kimberly Williams-Paisley) falling asleep holding an issue of *Bride* magazine opened to an article on how to have an uber-budget wedding to guilt her dad (Steve Martin) into bankrolling the wedding of her dreams? It worked out for this listener, too, and she got Samantha for her birthday that year.

Another listener had an experience many can relate to: She salivated over the accessories. She still identifies as a Samantha. "I used to dream about having life-size versions of all of her things," she explained. "I can remember being especially obsessed with the white porcelain pitcher and matching bowl meant to be kept on her bedside table. To me, there could be nothing more glamorous than washing one's face before bed using gold-trimmed pottery and a lacy towel. And her bedding! White with pink bows! How could my quilt compare? And why were my clothes kept in a boring closet instead of a trunk with leather detailing?" It's wild to imagine that now the adult version of this is salivating over a bed from the Pottery Barn catalogue (which we still can't afford) or watching Open Door videos from *Architectural Digest*. At least we can be comforted by the knowledge that, like the doll of the same name, Kirsten Dunst also owns a trunk from Sweden (a detail we learned from her Open Door tour).

How could our lives compare with the girls' we saw in the catalogue? We would ask ourselves this as a kind of reflex because of the apparent luxury of a Samantha tableaux, but that wasn't all. There was something about the aesthetics of each doll that felt so desirable. Our own lives could not compare.

Sure, we had cassette players and eventually CD Walkmans, but who actually believed that was somehow better (if less expensive) than Molly's doll-size 1940s radio? Some things are just iconic. Looking back, as we examined these pages, we were learning something about how girls came into their own at an age when we were starting to figure some of this out for ourselves, too.

American Girl merchandise, even just experienced in the pages of a catalogue, invited readers to imagine a different life. What would it be like to live on the prairie like Kirsten and attend a one-room schoolhouse? The fabrics in Felicity's wardrobe were so beautiful it almost hurt to imagine getting to wear them. What a comedown for Felicity to wear her blue ball gown against '80s and '90s décor. She truly deserved better than a landscape of pastels and acid-wash jeans. The lush sets of the catalogues presented a vision that could only compete with what we saw when we closed our eyes as our parents read us the books. Is this what the past looked like? Some girls who asked this have spent their adult lives answering this question far better than we can, but how wonderful, in a way, that we are all still weighing it.

These catalogues invited us into the stories and became a story themselves. One listener recalled treating her catalogues almost as storybooks. Her father read her American Girl books before bed when she was growing up. However, "on days when we got a new AG catalogue in the mail, I would demand he read the descriptive blurbs from the catalogue instead." This is the same listener who dreamed of Samantha's bedside porcelain pitcher and matching bowl, so of course she knew where to direct her dad's attention first. "Dad, read me 'Samantha's Bedroom'!" she remembers saying.

For some listeners, it was hard to live in the story of the catalogue without also noticing the price tag. The catalogue offered a means to accessorize a fictionalized version of the past that had its own barriers: e.g., time machines don't exist (that we know of). One aspect of the catalogue that did accurately mirror the time periods it portrayed was the reality of class differences and issues of privilege. For many, to have the only doll that looked like you be a self-liberated formerly enslaved person sent some complicated and off-putting messages. For others, the catalogue represented other kinds of inequities. One listener shared that her next-door neighbor had a Kirsten doll that she never let her play with, for example. She did, however, let her see the catalogue. This anecdote reminds us that *Mean Girls* was definitely based on real phenomena.

For another listener, she couldn't separate the wonder of the catalogue from the reality of an $82 price for a Kirsten doll. She admitted she had no idea what her family's financial situation was but guessed that that was a lot of money for anyone (correct). She talked herself out of wanting the eighteen-inch doll for Christmas, trying to talk herself into wanting the mini version of the doll instead. Imagine her surprise when she received the full-size doll on Christmas morning.

This makes us wonder if American Girl was an entry to early conversations about money, that topic so many don't want to discuss. Though many of these books deal with moments of want, or challenges within a family, somehow someone always pulls off a great event, no matter the obstacles. But this obviously is not always the case in real life. We've heard from listeners who had frank conversations with parents about money, in some cases some of the earliest conversations about the limits of their family's budgets, when they asked for a doll for Christmas or a birthday and learned it wasn't possible. Others wished for dolls and books and clothes from the catalogue with no sense of whether their parents could afford it or not, in some ways showing their privilege by their distance from concerns over money. Still others appreciated their parents' efforts to get them American Girl dolls secondhand and to hack accessories that looked like the products offered in the catalogue.

One such listener, who fell asleep dreaming of Samantha with her catalogue opened to Samantha's items, did get a new-to-her Samantha doll, but a secondhand one. Her shrewd mom got an entire bag of thrifted Samantha clothes *and* altered a trunk from Walmart to house them that closely resembled the much-more-expensive trunk sold in the catalogue. The act of generosity on the part of her mom to create the trunk and curate this collection of Samantha gear is the memory that holds the most value from the distance of adulthood. As this listener described, "It really is a shame that American Girl was and is still so inaccessible to the masses, but I am so lucky to have a creative mom."

This story also reveals how effective American Girl had become at promoting its products. Precisely because some of these toys were hard to get, girls would push their parents to read from *a catalogue* as if it were a Dickens novel. They would travel to budget stores and make their own Victorian-era luxury item. We wanted everything in the catalogue because it was beautiful, because our friends wanted it, and because we all liked playing with the dolls and everything that made up their worlds.

Let's Play Dolls

The memory of receiving a doll at a birthday or holiday is one that many women our age have enshrined in their own peak nostalgia hall of fame. One listener, Laura Colon, offered perhaps the most sensory memory of what it felt like to receive a doll as a gift. "I remember coming home from school and seeing a big box in the dining room," she recalled. "I kept eyeing it through dinner and the Pound Puppy party my brother and I had for our toys. I finally got up the nerve to ask[,] and it was for me! I opened it slowly and PINK STYROFOAM came out. I dug around and there was the burgundy box with a real ribbon," she remembered. Inside, she discovered "a lovely doll that looked just like one of my aunt's historical Victorian dolls. I just stared at this beautiful doll who was mine! I asked my mother if she had a name, and she said, 'Yes, Samantha' and held out the book to me." Her aunt generously gifted her Samantha and some of her accessories, and the moment of just opening the box has lived forever in her mind.

"This is one of my core memories," Laura recalled. "I can remember the dark night outside our kitchen windows, my baby sister sitting in my mother's lap, my brother playing nearby. I can even smell her, that lovely new-doll smell that I now associate with Christmas." Hallmark is not brave enough to make this kind of Christmas romance film, of the intense devotion a child can have for a doll. Only the Tyra Banks / Lindsay Lohan 2000 epic *Life-Size* came close, imagining Tyra as a doll come to life at Lindsey Lohan's request due to some kind of science we can only refer to as "Jurassic Park for dolls." All we know is the earnest love and sensory connection to a childhood toy is something to which most can probably relate and that lives frozen in our own minds like the mosquito trapped in amber that made those dinosaurs.

Dolls could be a source of solo play, and many girls who grew up as the only child or the only girl in their family found a cherished friend to play with in their dolls. One woman grew up with three much older brothers and was homeschooled, so she explained, "My American Girl dolls were my best friends. I loved them like the sisters I wanted so badly." They played with her as friends and seemed almost alive to her somehow, a feeling she ascribes to the fact that she "may have seen *Toy Story* one too many times." Girl, same.

Allison also had older siblings, and her dolls allowed her to play out any imaginative scenario she dreamed up with willing participants. She, like Samantha, got to teach her dolls in school and took them on all kinds of adventures. When a real-life friend came over to play and believed this meant she could pick the activity as the guest, Allison had to let her know that no, she was still in charge. With dolls, she ran into no such difficulty in terms of chain of command.

Beyond companionship, dolls invite the kind of imaginative play Pleasant wanted girls to experience. She could not, however, control what kinds of scenarios we would dream up. As listener Holly recalled, "My fondest memories are the intense imaginative games my sister and I played at home. Our doll outfits were all bought at craft fairs[,] and we constructed a home for Kit and Josefina in the cupboard under the basement stairs. In our games, the dolls were siblings[,] and they lived the kind of lawless parent-free lifestyle preteens can only dream of."

Playing with our dolls, we could create a world defined by, in the words of Outback Steakhouse and likely some enlightened thinkers, "no rules, just right." Want to create the set of Sally Jessy Raphael's talk show so you can pretend to be a roving moderator who looks great in red and knows how to get answers? Go for it. Want to use Samantha's beret as a convenient model for Monica Lewinsky's even though you genuinely don't understand why she's on the news? Godspeed. In other words, if we felt confined by a world where we couldn't pretend to live only on rations and hide orphans in our attic out of a burgeoning sense of human rights, we'd make one where we could.

One listener even worked her dog and its chaos into the story she dreamed up for her Molly doll. "My dog chewed my Molly doll's arm," Sivan Piatigorsky-Roth explained, "so I pretended my dolls lived in a postapocalyptic world where they had been ravaged by nuclear war and had to stay in a small bunker for safety while the world burned around them." Makes sense to us! "I feel like in retrospect this could have been an interesting commentary on the melding of the past and the future and the building fear of nuclear warfare post WWII," Sivan said. "But in reality, I think I just wanted to justify her disfigurement."

Sivan's story perfectly encapsulates what is so amazing about kids' imaginations. They know no bounds and accept no limits, including the boring nature of reality. It would be easy (and accurate) to let her dog take the hit for chewing on Molly. How much better a story is it to imagine it's a Cold War horror story playing out on the arm of your favorite doll? It reminds Mary of when her brother dropped a heavy toy truck on his foot, resulting in a nasty cut. When asked what happened by their mom, he wanted to prevent said truck from being taken away, so he tried to cover his tracks by claiming Mary's "Barbie bit me." The case remains unsolved.

There are things that stick with us about how we played long ago because our play really matters. Psychologists who study the benefits of playing with dolls for kids often cite the opportunity to develop imagination, learn social skills, and cultivate empathy. These scholars have clearly never been to a party or playdate where American Girl stans must decide who gets to be what doll. If you're imagining you and your friends will travel across the prairie (your parents' basement), you must assess which American Girl you will be and what strengths she'll bring to the adventure. This can be fraught. Sure, Molly has natural leadership skills and what some might call a lax appreciation for the rules that we call "outside-the-box thinking." Felicity has a horse. Samantha has cash. Addy has the knowledge of a person who reads books. Kirsten has . . . a stronger immune system than her friend? (RIP Marta.)

These were intense play sessions, as our listeners can relate. "We'd also have American Girl marathons where we went down to our basement and played dolls until we had to emerge for fear of starvation or dehydration," listener Margot remembered. Our American Girl dolls offered us a proxy for traits we wanted to try out with friends. We could be brave like . . . well, really any of the American Girl characters. We could get together and put on a play using the scripts published by American Girl or invent our own on topics that the brand (wisely) did not touch. American Girl didn't put out any content directing girls on how to use their dolls to process the Nancy Kerrigan / Tonya Harding assault via play, for example, but we did. We are still waiting on American Girl to create dolls that will let us tell the Michelle Kwan story.

Other studies of play remind us that it's a way to learn life skills. In 2020, scientists at Cardiff University monitored over thirty children ages four to eight as they played with Barbies and found that such play activated a region of the brain associated with social information processing such as empathy, even when the children played alone. This study, which showed comparable results for both boys and girls playing with dolls, replicates a longer historical pattern of using dolls to teach care and compassion.

Historically, dolls were part of a range of toys that allowed young girls to practice their future roles as wives and mothers through play. Playing for girls like Felicity or Kirsten, who, like the other girls, received a doll as a gift in their series, would be a rehearsal for their lives as adults. This is one of many stark differences between our generation and the girls we pretended to emulate through play. Today, boys might also play with dolls to learn compassion, and kids can enjoy them for the fun of it, not with the expectation of preparing for roles in life they may not choose for themselves, like parenting.

Playing with American Girl dolls isn't necessarily designed to prepare us for our lives as parents or spouses. However, it has led some to explore Munchausen by proxy through play, emulating real parents in true crime documentaries. We've heard from several listeners who put their dolls in harm's way or imagined illnesses for them on an epic scale to gain access to the most mysterious medical facility in the Western world, the American Girl doll hospital. These aspiring Shonda Rhimeses have created plotlines with more casualties than a season of *Grey's Anatomy*.

One listener who preferred to remain anonymous (we get it) told us her sister heard American Girl had a hospital where you could send your broken doll to be fixed. Once she recovered, you would receive not only your healed doll but hospital-related accessories. We all know the siren song of the promise of free accessories. Her sister had just broken her arm in real life, so this was likely on her mind, this listener imagined, putting together a theory of the crime after the fact. Her sister decided to purposely break her Josefina doll's leg and convince their parents to send it to the doll hospital. As an added layer to this story, her sister worried her parents would suspect her scheme if she claimed the leg had been broken accidentally, so she persuaded this listener to claim she'd done it. Bringing the story to a shocking, but not unexpected, conclusion, this listener explained, "There was no way they would actually send a doll to the doll hospital. Josefina was her favorite American Girl[,] and I'm fairly certain it's still broken to this day." While we'll never know why the parents couldn't send the doll to the hospital (the expense? Empowering further reckless doll-related behavior?), we can only assume the broken leg was as painful a reminder of bad choices as the musical episode of *Grey's Anatomy*.

Dolls not subjected to what some insurance companies would deem "medically unnecessary procedures" got to go on adventures, and we love hearing about moments listeners treasure because they shared them with much-loved dolls. A woman named Sarah told us her Josefina doll traveled on all her family vacations, and even to a family wedding, where she wore a flower girl dress made for the occasion. Others brought their Felicity dolls to Colonial Williamsburg, proving that you *can* bring a friend on a family vacation and not have it go sideways.

Our dolls also took part in some surprisingly productive conversations. In the past, for example, explaining something to a doll helped us process it ourselves. For some, this meant talking through the arrival of a new sibling with Kirsten. "Well, Kirsten, they're saying it's a new brother and it's a permanent change. We've asked about the return policy and you're not going to like the answer." For Allison, Molly could be a sounding board when she felt the urge to touch something at a museum. "Molly, they are telling us we can't take artifacts from this museum. As a member of the Greatest Generation, you are probably used to having your way, but this isn't Burger King, it's the Smithsonian."

Walking through childhood with our dolls felt like being in the company of a well-dressed, extremely cultured friend who happened to be a great listener. It was kind of like a children's version of reenacting *Weekend at Bernie's*. They never spoke back, except through our imaginations. What we've learned is that other people imagined a very different line between themselves and their dolls.

At this point, if you have never owned a doll, you may be wondering how you, too, can feel connected to American Girl without dropping hundreds of dollars or forcing friends to give to a private birthday fund. Before we leave the world of playing with dolls, we thought it important to tell you about another avenue for getting a doll into your life: the library.

In Which We Get a Clue: A Doll, in the Library, with Allison

A lot of questions keep us up at night. Some of these questions, such as why we didn't see right through the not-subtle subtexts of Britney Spears's

"Lucky," may never be fully answered. One we did think we could take on in a reasonable time frame was this: What happens to the American Girl dolls who live at libraries?

Many American Girl dolls live in stores or private homes. There is a third path that does not get talked about nearly enough. In addition to "libraries of things," some institutions offer kits with American Girl dolls that can be borrowed and circulated. We had heard of this kind of thing years ago but had never had the time (read as: the courage) to actually do this for ourselves.

After reviewing catalogues, magazines, archival documents, and our own childhood trunks, we just knew it was time. Finally, throwing caution to the wind, we decided to believe our own favorite mantra and remember that having fun is never hard when you've got a library card. Before Allison could slam down her patron ID like a heavy, fancy credit card in a movie made to romanticize wealth, she had to find a library willing to lend her a doll. This proved harder than she thought.

During the pandemic, a lot of libraries needed to restrict access to some materials for the safety of their staff and patrons. There's something profoundly humbling about having to call a slew of lending institutions in your area to ask if you can borrow a doll. Even more humbling? Getting voice mails telling you kindly that no, you, or the child in your life, simply cannot borrow a doll at this time. Yes, this was definitely *just* for an age-appropriate child. Voice mail (kindly) deleted, next lead. Then our luck changed. A Julie Kit was available, at last, and just over an hour's drive away. Allison set the date in her calendar and made plans for a pickup.

When you hear that an adult is checking someone out, you probably don't picture that person somewhat sheepishly reaching for a canvas tote with a doll in it at a public lending library. Going forward, perhaps you should. Truth be told, we didn't really know what this checkout would entail. Unlike a book, which you could grab yourself, this was a far more involved process. Would we need to show medical records? Proof of a good home? Okay, neither of those was required, but we did have to show a valid library card.

The online description for our Julie Kit promised only that we would get "1 American Girl Doll with accessories; in a zippered bag 54 x 24 x 16 cm." This kit was rated "Not for children under three years." That would not be a problem for us. Walking into the library, Allison saw that Julie's kit was just *out there*. She was ready to be taken by any intrepid patron, but she was only destined for one. Was the excitement mutual? We can guess that it was not, but we do know that going somewhere had to be better than just sitting on a shelf in the middle of winter.

Of course, it was a Molly who not only oversaw the checkout, but was kind enough to talk a bit about the lending program overall. We mean Molly in both senses: Her name was literally Molly, and she had Molly McIntire energies. During the time of this Julie transfer, the program had been ongoing for about a year. Molly explained that it came about in response to a "very popular" program running at a "neighboring library"—her team saw how well it was doing and "decided to give it a try!" Of their dozen or so kits, there were two boys, ten girls, and two Bitty Babies. All did well, but the Girl of the Year, the kind of it girl of the calendar year, as you may recall, usually led the pack. As Molly noted, that one "is always exciting for people to check out."

Julie did not seem to be the hottest item at the library, nor among the highest-ranked checkout. But she was special to us and this was a chance to experiment with a doll neither of us owned (without continually hitting the aftermarket and dipping into our life savings). Still ensconced in that bright pink case, Julie would travel home with Allison. Thankfully, she could see outside of it through a small plastic window. After Allison strapped her into the front seat, weight limits temporarily forgotten, Julie was settled in for a decently long drive against evening commuting traffic. Julie seemed to have a lot of internal monologue happening about the ongoing gas crisis, but that was muffled under the sound of a true crime podcast.

Upon Julie's arrival at her new, albeit temporary, home, Allison was stunned to see just how . . . cool Julie's kit actually was. Julie came in her *Meet* outfit, and a New Year's ensemble was also packed inside. She'd come wearing sandals, but since it was winter, those had to go. Julie spent much of her week as other short-term visitors might: cautiously in the mix, not getting too involved in the household (she did zero chores, in case you're wondering) but also adding a little bit of out-of-town flavor. It was nice to see some hippie energy around the house, and to have someone else for Molly to sit beside for a week.

Logistically, returning Julie was easy. It was just a matter of packing all of her wonderful things back into the case, which now seemed smaller than it had before. Emotionally? That's another story. It's as if she was never really part of Allison's household, which hurt a little. It's tempting to believe she has a great life in the library, but we cannot entirely say for sure. We do know that the people who helped us made this as fun as possible and kept the weirdness to a minimum.

At the library, Molly was not just Julie's part-time caretaker, though that would be enough for many of us to take on. Molly also oversaw a good-size collection of other dolls, who were always on display. Some were positioned to permanently have a good time (boating day, anyone?), whereas others were just on stands. Molly assured us that the dolls-in-waiting never waited for very long. "The dolls are almost constantly checked out," she told us. But when they were at home, at the library, "they stay in their soft cases behind the circulation desk in the Children's Room." There were certainly far worse gilded cages.

When we asked Molly about her work with doll checkouts, she recalled a parent asking whether it would be okay for her son, who was about six at the time, to get a doll. He'd already taken quite a few out, but for some reason, this visit prompted his mother to ask Molly, "Is it okay for him to play with dolls?" With her colleagues, Molly "enthusiastically said YES!" Her reasoning in that moment was that perhaps "someday he will be a caring dad, or a pediatrician, or a teacher—it is okay for boys to play with dolls!" The patron's "mother was relieved" and went on to get multiple dolls for her son to play with.

Outside of this library, Molly thought that this patron likely wouldn't "have been exposed to the experience of playing with dolls," even though it was something he seemed to really like. Here's the thing: It's not just that the dolls were there, or ready to be taken out. Molly's words added the bolster of support the patron needed in that moment. We hear from people all the time who remember a staff member at a historic site or a school who said just the right encouraging thing, possibly without even realizing it. You can say that dolls are for everyone, but if they're exorbitantly expensive, never available, or marked as for "girls only," they are not.

Age has also been a perceived barrier for some people—despite the fact that there are not actually any limits in the system. Molly watched as a group of middle-school-aged students considered whether they were too old *to play with dolls*. Did they dare check out a doll, knowing someone might see them? As people who have been twelve, we know that nearly everything can seem embarrassing at that age. At last, these girls went for it. Molly recalled, "They had such a good time and I heard one of them say to the other: 'I feel like a kid again!'" This statement makes us feel slightly old, but mostly happy.

As with most of our informal investigations, we started with questions about a doll and ended up learning a lot more about people who, insofar as we know, do not spend any time zipped into pink bags in library storage areas. From the time that someone thinks of an idea for a doll to the time that she, he, or they enter your life, there are so many people whose labor is made invisible. For some, that's part of the magic of the toy: It seems to simply materialize and emerge from a perfectly wrapped box. But lots of people take the time to make dolls, and lots of human energy is expended in making that magic appear to be seamless.

Talking about library dolls was also a reminder that accessibility to certain toys is not an abstract concept. Molly the librarian (not the doll) puts expensive objects that many people may not otherwise have access to within arm's reach. At the circulation desk where she works, the idea of a doll really being for anyone just might be truer than most other places in the American Girl universe.

The instinct to wonder what happens to unattended dolls, living alone in storage or in family attics, is one that hasn't left us. In the end, we can only hope that Julie is happy and healthy wherever she lands, to paraphrase Olivia Rodrigo and her "good 4 u" energy. We have moved on and enjoy strawberry ice cream with other dolls (we're looking at you, Samantha) and sincerely wish her the best, even if that means a life that doesn't include us anymore. What we really learned from this Julie was that temporary toys can still leave a lasting impression . . . and just one more thing: No matter how old you are, feeling pure, unadulterated joy while playing with dolls has no due date.

True Life: I'm an American Girl Doll

For some, the only thing better than playing with dolls was trying to dress like them. We heard from one Kit fan who recalled, "I always got my hair cut identical to Kit's classic bob and I *begged* my parents, to no avail, to let me live and sleep in the attic of our house because that's what Kit did." She also wore a homemade "feedbag" dress for Halloween and to her Kit-themed tenth birthday party. Clothes can tell a story, and for some (us included), that story was "we're in too deep" and "can't stop, won't stop." While our bangs grew back (as we've learned ourselves), those memories never fade.

We are both on the record as Mollys and wanted to be just like her, glasses and all. Knowing Molly had glasses, too, was the only consolation Mary had when she learned she'd need them in fourth grade. That year, her teacher had asked if she was glaring at the board because she couldn't see it from that distance or because she just hated math that much. Honestly, both. Allison of course dreamed of glasses but was cursed with perfect vision throughout her childhood. Both of us associated glasses with some ineffable part of Molly's personality, which both softened the blow for Mary when she started wearing them and created a desire in Allison that she now gets to fulfill as an adult glasses wearer.

For many of us, the clothes and ephemera of our favorite dolls offered a path to be more like them. For example, we've heard from multiple listeners who practiced writing their "Fs" with a cursive flourish, believing it brought them one step closer to being Felicity. Shoutout to the readers of this book who learned cursive in school not knowing they were the recipients of a dying art. At least our children will never be able to read our handwritten diaries.

Another listener told us she read Samantha's books and was immediately drawn to her. She gleaned from her books that Samantha never wore pants, preferring Victorian dresses and sailor suits. To be like Samantha, she adopted an aversion to pants that has carried on into adulthood. It's interesting to think about the likes and dislikes we adopted as kids, hoping to be like a fictional fave. What else are we doing as full-grown adults that stems from a desire to be like an American Girl doll?

The catalogue of course offered not just dolls and accessories for their use. It also offered clothes inviting us to dress like our fave girls. Angela on *The Office* once claimed to buy her clothes at the American Girl store, and for many that's a dream of both childhood and adulthood. Many fans also collaborated with parents and grandparents to make their own costumes. As Mariah Carey once said of her fans, "They make their own merch!" We've heard from women whose grandparents and parents helped sew matching outfits for them and their dolls to wear trick-or-treating or for everyday wear. Now they've grown up to make clothes for their own daughters and their dolls, fulfilling the kind of generational American Girl love fest Pleasant dreamed of. While we know homemade clothes are truly the best, we continue to dream of Samantha's cape and matching muff, which we still covet to this day.

Some of our favorite stories come from listeners who dressed up as American Girl characters for Halloween, birthday parties, or to celebrate days that end in "y." In perhaps the most epic and dramatic story we heard, one fan named Margot convinced her parents to help her dress as her childhood idol, Molly McIntire, for Halloween. For her previous birthday, she'd received a Molly costume and had worn the glasses so often she'd snapped them in half. We get it. Her sister had also received a Samantha costume for her birthday, and we truly can't fathom such concentrated Molly and Samantha energy in the same space. We would have needed U.N. peacekeepers on site if a Samantha stepped up to us in our own homes and tried to convince us she was superior to Ms. Model Citizens / zero discipline Molly "probably voted for Reagan but we try not to think about it" McIntire.

Armed with her Molly outfit, Margot conceived of a brilliant Halloween costume that allowed her to bring everything she loved about Molly together in one outfit. She described heading out to trick-or-treat "wearing my Molly costume—skirt, sweater, knee socks, nice Mary Janes that I normally only wore to my first day of school or synagogue, of course all topped with signature beret—underneath an enormous foamcore shell, handcrafted by my father, that transformed me into the book *Meet Molly*."

Picture Margot hobbling down the street, literally a cover girl. The architecture of her genius costume added some drama to the proceedings. "The only downside is that the rigidity of the foamcore meant I couldn't put my arms down through the whole night of trick-or-treating," Margot noted. After a long night of her arms sitting at an awkward angle on the foamcore, Margot explained, "I felt like I was being slowly crucified." What an image! What a sacrifice to embody your fave American Girl doll. Thankfully the story has a happy ending, as she was liberated from her costume to finish out the night trick-or-treating dressed as Molly, sans book cover.

In all these cases, the choice to dress like a particular doll tells us something about the child themselves. Pretending to be an American Girl doll let us try out different traits and behaviors, which we could alter with the speed of a costume change. In Mary's case, it was the choice to *not* dress like her friend's favorite American Girl doll that taught her something about herself. She'd been invited to an American Girl party thrown by a friend we'll call "Samantha," whose grandmother was organizing a fancy tea in true Grandmary style. Her grandmother called Mary to invite her and asked her to wear a "fancy dress" in the style of Samantha Parkington. This is 1,000 percent not what Mary wants to wear to any occasion and is what she now refers to as a "dare to be straight" situation. Instead, Mary wanted to wear jeans, an aesthetic she believed she shared with Molly. On the day of the party, Mary arrived in pants (though not jeans), which she viewed as a compromise. In hindsight, this was an early moment of self-realization. At the time, her parents described it as "tomboy behavior," but she can see now that it reflected an emerging queerness that she now treasures. Dressing like Molly helped her get there.

Some fans found it useful to define themselves as the opposite of a doll they hated. One listener born with a vision disability hated Molly because she wore glasses, which reminded her of the thick glasses she wore after eye surgery as a child. Instead, she loved her Kirsten doll. "Kirsten was a confident blonde who fit right in with the whole rugged, pick-yourself-up-by-the-bootstraps ethos," she recalled as an adult. "I wanted to live up to that[,] and the glasses were just a sign of weakness to me."

Similarly, another American Girl fan, who identified with Samantha, auditioned to be an American Girl model at a local show, only to question her choice to appear as her fave doll, not perhaps as the one she most resembled. In particular, she needed glasses to see distance, the length of a catwalk to be exact. Taking off her glasses to walk the runway as Samantha, she had to inch her way down a path she couldn't quite make out. She did not get the job, but we have to imagine Tyra Banks and company would be proud of this top-model behavior.

Listener KM loved Felicity for reasons that proved complicated. "I wanted to look as feminine and pretty as they did," they explained. They remembered seeing Felicity for the first time in a catalogue. "I was daydreaming of whiteness, I think, and I remember begging my mom to let me go to cotillion lessons." Raise your hand if you, too, wanted to pursue cotillion without fully knowing what you were signing on for. "I wanted to have tea parties, eat interesting desserts, and go outside without ever looking dirty really," they explained. Honestly, same. Their mom didn't really see the appeal, however.

"My mom never really valued dolls as interesting or worth the cost, particularly with American Girl dolls; she literally used to bury her dolls as a kid because she thought they were so creepy." We have heard similar takes on dolls many times. Who hasn't had a sibling bury their Barbie (or other doll) in the backyard? Also, how is that *less* creepy than dolls themselves?

However, unlike us two white girls from New England, KM had conflicted feelings about what doll they were "supposed" to like given their Tejano heritage and identity. "I never really connected with Josefina, despite knowing that she was the one I was *supposed* to identify with, but I think for me, whiteness always seemed rebellious," KM reflected. "I now understand it isn't, but when I felt like something was really being forced upon me and was maybe disingenuous, I felt so driven to do the opposite, which felt like Felicity at the time," they recall. Felicity's and Samantha's cookbooks became common ground for KM and their mom. Experimenting with Felicity's gingerbread recipe became a shared activity they both enjoyed.

It's only as an adult listening to our discussion of Josefina's books that they could see the ways her stories resonated with their own. "The service-based exchanges that happen, the emphasis on sadness and mourning, guilt, all do feel really accurate as someone who also comes out of similar contexts of the world Josefina comes from," they offered. "My ancestors were Indigenous peoples, European colonizers, and enslaved African peoples. I likely had ancestors that occupied the same places as Josefina's family, as rancho owners, and people forced to work the rancho and an ever-present blurring of these lines through intermarriage and other less palatable ways. Point being, intergenerational trauma and silence around these traumas. Service, rituals, and gestures are used to ameliorate the trauma[.]"

Still, they think about Felicity and her accessories from time to time. "I remember really feeling like I needed her coral necklace. I still kind of feel like I need a coral necklace like that!!" Thank you, KM, for forcing us to ask if a desire for statement necklaces is perhaps the connecting tie between American Girl culture and adulthood.

Another AG fan explained how playing with Felicity as a child helped make space for his adult life as a trans man. He wrote, "When you're trans, you have this sort of tendency to look back on your experiences and see what 'matches up' to your current identity. Looking back, there were other more 'tomboy'-esque girls I could have projected myself onto (I never really cared for the dolls that looked like you)." A Felicity stan through and through, he explained, "despite how stubborn Felicity may have been, her wanting to break out of the 'housewife' role while still enjoying things like dresses and dolls resonated with me . . . I can see how that duality carried over to me, even if I didn't realize it at the time."

Perhaps the most vocal community of fans who identify with an American Girl doll are Kirstens. We're afraid to even write about them for fear of lawsuits or that they, like their namesake, will make us take shelter with them in a cave with a dead body, let a raccoon into the house who will ultimately burn it down, or force us to participate in a barn raising (yes, all of these things happen in the books). Here are just a few of the reasons listeners have told us they identified with Kirsten as kids:

- They hail from the Midwest.
- They were immigrants, too.
- They were blond.
- They wished they had a pet raccoon.
- They were of Swedish heritage.
- They felt a connection to the music of ABBA.
- They had a parent who worked at Ikea.

We didn't follow up and ask if they all identify as Kirsten Dunsts, too, because there's already enough going on here. Actor Brie Larson so loved Kirsten she adopted her surname as her stage name. As she recalled to Jimmy Fallon in 2015, she was tired of people mispronouncing her last name, Desaulniers, when she was a child actor. Enamored of Kirsten Larson at the time (and knowing

Larson was also a family name), she announced she'd be taking that as her last name, telling her mom, "Kirsten can be in our family!"

While not claiming Kirsten as a family member, listener Aviva Rosenberg still feels connected to Kirsten. To explain her love for Kirsten to us, she first defended Kirsten's reputation. This is peak Kirsten behavior. "Kirsten has always been overshadowed by the Samantha glamor and the Felicity pushiness and the Molly relatability," she explained. This is a classic opening that reveals how drawn we are to reduce these girls to "types." Seeing Samantha as glamorous? That's a pretty universal opinion. Felicity as pushy? Maybe. She gives off the energy of a girl who is, to paraphrase Kelly Clarkson again, a "Miss Independence" horse girl type. She prefers horses to people and is willing to put herself at risk to protect them. Seeing Molly as relatable? That doesn't feel as common a take, but we won't complain. What exactly defined Kirsten? What was she a caricature of? Striving? Surviving? Assimilating?

Aviva tried to help us understand.

Aviva explained what she liked about Kirsten while not so subtly using Felicity as a lesser example. "I appreciated her low-key clothing and wilderness setting, her independent adventures in the woods and on the farm. Kirsten manages the competing facets of her life and personality with more grace and aplomb than Felicity." To all the Felicitys reading this, we hear you, but please stay with us. For this listener, she could identify with what she retroactively saw as a similar approach to what it meant to be a girl in the '90s. "As a kid, I envied how she synthesized the blend of 'masculine' and 'feminine' interests that I shared with her," she explained. "I was reading her books while trying to navigate that awkward line both among my peers and within myself," Aviva noted, "so Kirsten's stories really resonated."

This confusion at navigating what counted as "girl culture" is probably a universal American Girl feeling among girls in the '90s. In that decade, kids were offered two genders and little explanation of what they meant or how gender could be presented as both so obvious *and* so mysterious. Toy stores seemed divided by the aisle with offerings specific to girls and boys with no explanation of what made something so obviously for boys versus girls. Like, how is a G.I. Joe different from a Barbie? Aren't they both dolls? Are dolls only safe for boys if they're linked to the military-industrial complex?

Rec league sports proved equally puzzling. Those not traumatized by gym class could sign up to play T-ball on a team with boys, but by age eight or nine, they were ushered off into softball land to meet other "Molly-types" while boys got to play baseball. Was this the intended message of *A League of Their Own*?

For Aviva, and many other girls, the stories of the historical girls offered that kind of liberating imaginary space where girls *could* do things that seemed to be both masculine and feminine without apology, punishment, or a need to define themselves. Remember when Felicity wore britches to secretly ride a horse at night? We still don't know what made that horse girl tick, but we get how liberating that must read for girls who don't want to live within the confined lines of what it meant to be a girl in 1774 *or* 1994.

Boys appeared in American Girl books, but not as meaningful rivals or as someone to please or alter your behavior to impress. There is no scene in an American Girl book where a girl feels like she shouldn't raise her hand in school because she's intimidated by the presence of boys (or other girls). In Samantha's books, for example, her neighbor is an annoyance who puts salt in her ice cream because he wasn't invited to her birthday party (demonstrating the kind of behavior that would make him a horrible party guest). In response, she takes his coin collection and empties it into the collection plate at church. Shame by philanthropy is the ultimate Edwardian rich people's revenge.

Kirsten could do real work to support the family, go to school, and explore nature without feeling hemmed in by any idea of what was appropriate "for girls." Just like the "wilderness" she explored, ideas about what girls should be and do are not natural but curated. Kirsten's fictional embrace of things Aviva thought of as both feminine and masculine helped her feel seen. It's almost like reading these books, you'd think men and women weren't so different, which must have come as a shock to grown-up girls who now may buy pink razors at twice the price.

The biggest draw of Kirsten for Aviva (and many other girls) was her immigration story. Now, the embrace of Kirsten as a symbol of being different likely comes as a shock to some reading this who may only remember Kirsten as a blond white girl to whom not much happens. (We are talking about us before we reread these books. We truly only remembered that she perhaps saw a bear and thought that was the extent of drama in her life. How we forgot that she tragically lost her best friend to cholera while immigrating *and* saw a dead guy in a cave from whom she *did* steal pelts to sell for the family we will never know.)

"For most of the '90s, Kirsten was there for every American girl whose Americanness was bound up with other identities," Aviva explained. "I'm Orthodox Jewish . . . The immigrant experience, that dual identity, is still very much a part of who I am even a couple of generations later," she noted. "I connected with Kirsten as a new, hyphenated American, even though I was born and raised in upstate New York, because my culture and daily life still aren't the mainstream American life."

Aviva offered a compelling comparison between the challenges facing Kirsten as an outsider to American culture and her own similar feelings of difference. "Kirsten had to work to find her place among people who didn't speak her language or know where she was coming from. She had to work around using one language at home and one at school or among non-Swedish friends: the English I speak at home is punctuated with Hebrew and Yiddish and I code-switch at work and in other situations." Conjuring images of Kirsten in her iconic St. Lucia's Day dress, Aviva noted, "Kirsten approached the holiday season with expectations based on Swedish traditions: my holidays are also unlike the American standard."

For Aviva, Kirsten served as an imaginary role model and friend who made her feel seen. She talked about her as we would describe what we have in common with a friend, saying, "Kirsten and I clicked because we both know what it's like to be balancing multiple identities and values as well as traits that transcend them." Describing them as having "clicked" suggests not only our response to our favorite doll, but that we imagine they like us, too. That imagined intimacy is what allowed us to think of dolls as true friends and for the play we shared with them to resonate over such a long period of time. Even now, as an adult who has lived to see the launch of Rebecca, an American Girl of Jewish heritage, Aviva says, "When it comes down to it, I'm still a Kirsten."

It's critical to note that for all the importance some girls invested in comparing their identities to their favorite American Girl dolls, for many their choice of a favorite nine-year-old playmate reflected nine-year-old concerns. Some girls gravitated to Samantha because they liked her style, or Kirsten because they liked her braids, or Molly because they liked her glasses, or other very important surface details. A major influence on girls' favorite dolls was the imagined connections they felt to a doll's time period, geographic region, or heritage, and its relationship to their own ancestry.

This was true for Courtney Price, famous to us as the first American Girl magazine paper doll. When Addy was introduced, she could appreciate the shared heritage and links to her own family's history, but she really just saw her as "this girl who has her own duties and chores just like I do." She didn't feel the need to adopt her as her fave because of a shared background, instead proudly stanning Molly in the AG book club she had with her friends at school because Molly acted as a bridge to her own grandmother.

No matter our preferred American Girl, we all worked out some ideas about who we thought we were through play. Part of the joy of American Girl was the ways it created a means to invite friends, family, and loved ones in on that process, too.

Playing with the Past

Among its many historically based treasures, Pleasant Company produced historical plays girls could act out at home with their dolls, friends, and perhaps coerced relatives. Interestingly, we never needed a historical play to act out at any age. The plays usually allow one girl to be *the* American Girl and her slightly disappointed friends/siblings to be minor characters weathering a conflict with historically appropriate dialogue. We remember performing these plays at friends' houses. We also remember how salty we felt when our host presumed they could play the lead role. Do we seem like "supporting cast" to you?

We performed one of these plays on our podcast. Inviting *New York Times* TV critic Margaret Lyons and NPR reporter Cassandra Basler to be part of our performance, some of us performed at a level that would make Meryl Streep proud. Could we bring the chops of a Shailene Woodley, Abigail Breslin, or any of the actors who depicted an American Girl character on screen? Likely not. It didn't stop us. Margaret was, no surprise, a natural as one of Kirsten's siblings. Cassandra shone as the narrator. Allison took on the role of Kirsten *and* several ancillary characters, attempting several voices for every part. Mary basically lost control at every turn and should have been cut from the final performance.

Whatever the varying degrees of talent we brought to the piece, it took us back to the sheer joy of embodying these characters and imagining yourself in some historic scene in a moment of sheer fantasy. Acting in a scripted American Girl play, whether at a friend's birthday party or in the privacy of your parents' basement reimagined as Colonial Williamsburg, you could take yourself back in time. Hitting those moments of peak imagination, we wonder if it ever occurred to us to ask, "Are you having a breakdown or a breakthrough?"

Maybe that question suits the situation of two adult women hosting a podcast about American Girl, but we digress. What matters to us here is thinking about what it meant that so many girls believed they could reenact the past through physical play and literal plays. We aren't going to revisit the lyrics to the Spice Girls' "Wannabe," mostly because of copyright, but we're pretty sure it was written about the attempt to dress up as a historical girl from the distance of the 1990s. So much of the fun of playing with American Girl was the weird imaginary space we created in our heads that maybe re-created the worlds of the books, or maybe invented something entirely new. As Aqua said of a different, too-sexy doll and her world, "life in plastic, it's fantastic."

When we wanted to imagine the past as our playscape, grandparents could be a vital resource. First, they used their time, talents, and in some cases cash to hook us up with dolls and books in the first place. Many also generously took their grandkids to historic places relevant to the dolls' stories. Fans have written to us of the cherished memories they have of visiting Colonial Williamsburg with their grandparents and Felicity in tow, for example. Grandparents also made matching dresses for their granddaughters and dolls, items now cherished especially if their grandparents are no longer with us. For many, the dolls and their stories acted as a bridge to talk to their grandparents about their own histories, and to create opportunities for play based on those experiences.

Listener Katie Ward shared a really touching story of the way her grandfather encouraged her love for Kit. "Kit's story helped me build a strong relationship with my pawpaw," she explained. "Kit wrote her little daily newspapers on her typewriter, so at some point, my pawpaw gave me my nana's typewriter. Modeling Kit, I too wrote daily newspapers and have found a couple of them." What began as an effort to encourage her by providing a family item to channel Kit's Depression-era journalistic ambitions created a greater connection between them. "I was also inspired to interview my pawpaw about growing up during the Great Depression," she recalled. "I also followed up with other grandparents about their experiences growing up in a different time than me." This is a frequent refrain we hear from our generation of American Girl fans, and know to be true from our own experiences. Becoming fans of a particular doll and her story positioned your grandparents as consultants who could help you determine if your interpretation staged in your parents' basement was accurate. It also helped us to see them as real people with stories that predate our existence, which is honestly hard for most fire signs to fathom.

Using family history to feel connected to broader history can be fraught. When Mary went on a family car trip to Gettysburg at age eight, she remembers being led around a cemetery until her dad pointed at a headstone that bore their last name, "Mahoney." Pointing at it with pride, her dad asked Mary and her brothers what they thought of someone with their last name fighting and dying at Gettysburg. Taking a beat, her younger brother Patrick, then five, asked with total seriousness, "Dad, did you know him?"

Sometimes the past seems very far away, but to kids it can feel very immediate when they're presented with tactile reminders and relatives who share stories that bring it to life. No, Mary's dad was not at Gettysburg, but he could share stories passed down to him through generations of relatives who did fight in the Civil War. Grandparents especially played this role for a lot of our listeners (and us), shaping our understanding of these stories according to what did and did not seem real to them.

For one listener's grandmother, Kit's story of life during the Depression was not relatable content. "Her family was not affected by the Great Depression," this listener explained, "which is a weird message she made sure to always remind us of growing up. She would, however, often talk about how hard the Depression was on her because 'we had to go down to only one maid' and 'only had one turkey at Thanksgiving.'" Her grandmother was a real Samantha, and in fact bought this listener and her cousins their first American Girl doll (a Samantha, of course). As much as this listener loved Kit and told us how important playing with her and reading her stories was in her childhood, what emerged was how much she loved learning about her grandmother through American Girl.

Her grandmother's life sounds like something American Girl themselves would not print because it sounds too unreal. She grew up privileged, had a portrait painted of herself at eleven that still hangs above her fireplace because, to paraphrase the legend herself, it's the best piece of art she's ever seen. She attended Mount Holyoke and falsely inflated the tuition to her parents, keeping the balance to pay for adventures with her friends. Her own education and interest in seemingly everything made her intent on raising daughters and granddaughters who also saw their lives as full of possibility.

This didn't necessarily extend to all her grandchildren. "Iconically," this listener noted, "when one of my male cousins said he wanted to be an author, she said[,] 'Oh boy, another book by a man no one wants to read.'" Harsh but fair, Grandma. Learning about our grandmothers' stories gives us a sense of the possibilities for our own. It reminds us, too, that family history is a space that has always valued women's stories even if popular histories haven't.

Other grandparents were here to offer a reality check on some of the privileges of our play in the past. Specifically, sometimes we needed to hear from our grandparents who grew up in the Great Depression that, "No, you're actually not reenacting the Great Depression by buying a doll for $100, dressing in perfectly good clothes shred to 'rags,' and pretending you know hobos" (to paraphrase one listener's grandparent).

Grandparents are great for spoiling us, caring about us, and, in some cases, loving us enough to tell us the truth. Play is about fantasy, and it developed our imaginations in all sorts of directions. One defining characteristic of our love for American Girl is how easily we could collapse the distance between ourselves and the girls we so loved who lived in the past. Part of the reason we could so easily make that leap was because we were nine, and, as Courtney Price noted, at that age you're more inclined to see characters your age as girls who share your interests and inclinations. Addy was not a character fraught with myriad meanings and implications, for example, but a girl with chores like Courtney who loved her grandma, too.

Part of the reason we could so easily imagine ourselves like them, perhaps missing some key differences, is from sleight of hand by the brand itself. We could play dolls at birthday parties, perform plays after school with historically accurate props, and make colonial gingerbread from the cookbooks because we were presented with toys that implied that they were approximate to things the American Girl dolls would have had or done. In many cases, this was based on intense research and fair to say. However, the insistence on the girls all having birthdays and birthday parties is a tell. If American Girl wanted us to see ourselves in history and as a part of it, they did it most by insisting on birthdays for historical girls, many of whom would not have recognized their own celebrations. Birthdays were not always an important celebratory occasion in the past, but they were for a lot of girls growing up in the '90s.

This is an interesting bit of the tail wagging the dog, as the plentiful birthday-related content and merch made it possible for us to have American Girl birthday parties and to receive on-theme gifts that the American Girl dolls themselves perhaps would not have understood. Honestly, could anyone understand the chaos of '90s birthday party culture? In an attempt to revisit the magic of growing up in the '90s, we want to take you on a tour of our American Girl birthday parties and speculate about what a birthday would mean for *the* American Girls.

Happy Birthday, Girls of the '90s

In our next life, we may become party planners. We have a flare for it. In the past few years alone, we've thrown a JonBenét-themed birthday party, a "Hail to the Bale" Christian Bale film festival birthday party (mainly to watch Winona Ryder in *Little Women*), and a Free Britney / Miss Victory birthday party for our show that we held virtually with our listeners. No one ever asked us to link the plight of Britney Spears with that of women on the home front during World War II, but then again, no one had to. We love a chance to celebrate and revel in some niche interests along the way. It creates an occasion to have fun, hang out with people, and force them to discuss things we care about. (Which March sister are *you*?) We are not alone in that instinct. Since our show debuted, we've received lots of mail and messages from women who grew up partying like it was 1774 and with an assortment of other non–American Girl themed birthday parties. Even when their parties didn't revolve around American Girl, listeners still reach out with stories in part because they know their extremely niche theme will impress us (it does), and it will reveal something about what they were like as kids.

One listener told us about a "Spice on Ice" themed party she had when she was ten—notably, the American Girl birthday of note in all the books. At this party, this girl and all her friends dressed up as the Spice Girls of their choice and then went ice skating. (Quick aside, is it too late for us to RSVP yes to this? Who gets to be Chilly Spice, or Nancy Kerrigan Spice?) Another hosted a joint party with a friend with an *American Idol* theme, which they used to judge their friends. We can imagine that the *American Idol* catchphrases slipped into other parts of the party, with reluctant children declaring, "It's a no for me," when faced with an undesirable hot dog. These two party planners are terrifying geniuses whom we assume now run the Who Wore It Better? section of *US Weekly* or are actual judges (PS: Was there a Ryan Seacrest impersonator at the party? Asking for Allison). Many other listeners poured hours into special slumber parties and made favors that took hours to craft to be just right.

We are all shaped by and saturated in the cultures we live in. Listeners who have shared stories with us clearly recall the superlevel creativity they had as kids to make special moments their own. This is true for people who loved American Girl, and those who felt attached to other aspects of culture (seriously, can you imagine the possibilities of a Baby Spice skating outfit? Limitless).

Mary can relate to this. She thinks her 1996 Olympic-themed birthday party was perfectly on brand with who she was then as now: a tomboy who loved the games themselves as much as pop culture's camp obsession with the iconic Kerri Strug. Mary still loves a contender and can always get down for a very well-coordinated party. We also still stan the U.S. Gymnastics Team, if not the shadiness of their organization.

If you asked Mary's parents what birthday party was the most telling of her personality, they would describe her brother's pirate party held in the same era. The pirate party consisted of ten eight-year-old boys running around Mary's childhood backyard. Beforehand, they'd worried she'd be overwhelmed by all the "boy energy." During the party, they watched from the window as the boys all ran in one direction like a school of fish to escape Mary in hot pursuit wielding a bow and arrow. Disclaimer—no partygoers were harmed in the course of that event or in the writing of this chapter.

Allison's parties, to the surprise of no one, contained a lot less athleticism. Before going further, she would like to formally apologize to the friend who hosted a gymnastics party when she was seven. This was Allison's personal nightmare, and she can't remember if she took that out on anyone, but she does know it wasn't any fun for her. Maybe everyone else was into it, but it was hard to focus when the overwhelming fear of breaking her neck clouded everything in sight. If you're going to serve bright red punch and have a balance beam, you should honestly give people a heads-up.

Now, we will be the first to tell you that neither of us ever had an American Girl birthday party ourselves (yet). However, Mary's eight-year-old kid party was doll themed. That said, there was no American Girl required dress code, no games pulled from a historical era of her choice, and no desserts reminiscent of the past (sorry, but the wonders of a '90s Carvel ice-cream cake can never be improved upon). The only memory she has of the party is a craft that involved decorating doll-size straw hats for teddy bears. Before you ask why they decorated hats for teddy bears and not dolls, just know Mary's grandma Fluffy worried not every guest might have a doll to bring, and she found a good deal on teddy bears and doll-size hats at Christmas Tree Shops (a New England chain that sells everything and nothing you need).

What exactly does it mean to have an "American Girl birthday"? Is an American Girl birthday one in which you receive a doll as a gift, or one where your friends all bring their dolls and you vibe out on a shared fave character? Or do you subject your guests to an American Girl play of your choice? For answers, we turned to some fellow millennial / Gen Z fans for their experiences.

One listener's story stands apart because all of her birthdays are American Girl themed. Before she was born, her parents went on yearly vacations to Colonial Williamsburg and bought her sister a Felicity doll. After buying one thing from American Girl, they were now on the company mailing list for life and got in the habit of flipping through the catalogue. There, they saw and loved the name "Kirsten," inspiring this listener's name, Kirsten Dahl.

According to Kirsten, she only recently got this admission from her parents. They also seemed puzzled when she asked if they thought it was strange "to name their daughter after a doll and have her last name *be* Dahl?" Because we thrive on drama, we truly wish these parents had been brave enough to name her American (Girl) Dahl and try to scam free products for life. Perhaps the biggest surprise of all is that even though Kirsten received a Kirsten doll for a birthday gift, her favorite has always been Samantha.

For listener Holly, her American Girl birthday was the year her grandfather gifted her Kit. She has a fond memory of spending her birthday at a Pizza Hut with her family, along with its newest member. Kit got her own seat at the table, and Holly celebrated with a BOOK IT! free pizza. Was there any better philanthropic endeavor to reach kids than BOOK IT!?

Angela educated us on the fact that a girl could have multiple American Girl birthdays if you counted the year you received a doll and the year you made her the centerpiece of a one-woman show / birthday party. When she was nine, her mom let her choose from the then original three dolls as a birthday gift, and she chose Samantha. The following year, she had a Samantha-themed party with petit fours and ice cream. She invited her friends to act out one of Samantha's plays from American Girl's theater kit and had her parents videotape it. We wonder if she had half of her friends eat dessert in the kitchen as a form of method acting preparation to play staff? Kids are known to respond well to upstairs/downstairs party dynamics. We love that her parents made this party happen for her.

As children's parties became another signifier of class and comfortability in American culture, parents often felt a pressure to do more. They might have grown up with some pretty good family parties or other gatherings, but the 1990s presented whole new party worlds to navigate. Why just re-create your own traditions when you have hundreds of years of history to pull from? Listen, if parents could make up entire stories based on the Samantha bedroom set, we know that this level of extra was not only possible but happening.

Especially for parents who wanted to provide their children with *meaning-ful* or *educational* toys, an American Girl party was the best of both worlds. No, it wasn't a little bit country and a little bit rock and roll, but it was a way to introduce some learning into the world of partying (which is what we all want when partying, right?). Often, parents or other caregivers went to great lengths to create or purchase matching outfits and to really set a mood. Pleasant Rowland and others encouraged this kind of studied approach to birthdays. Looking back, we can see this as part of a larger caretaking trend Anne Helen Petersen summarizes in her work on "concerted cultivation." It's not just about raising smart or talented kids, but also the endless curation of curiosity and a studied approach to life. Even a birthday party for nine-year-olds needs to *mean* something.

With so much riding on this, how would parents (and kids) plan an American Girl party? The historical characters' books themselves are pur-posefully vague on planning details. With the exception of Addy, most of these characters don't interrogate how their birthday magic is happening. Friends, parents, caretakers, servants, and enslaved people in all of these books somehow just *know* what to do for these special days. In some ways, this reinforces the kind of "innocence" that Rowland and others wanted to be built into the early historical narratives. The fact that Molly can worry about her English-tea-party-themed birthday during a period of sustained bombing in London is part of the complexity of these stories, which are both very much of a moment and outside the messiness that makes them worth writing about.

Fortunately, American Girl came through with a guide on how to plan the perfect American Girl party. *The American Girls Party Book* opens: "Since the earliest days of America, American girls have found lots of ways to celebrate . . . these tips will help you plan a party that's fun for everyone." Planning a party that's "fun for everyone" is literally an impossible dream, but we love this intention. The book is divided by historic characters and their eras. Flipping through the book, parents and kids could explore games, crafts, and desserts their favorite characters may have enjoyed on *their* birthdays that they can co-opt for their own. Cultivating a love of crafting and baking explains in part our big-time love for *The Great British Bake Off* (Felicity may object), crafting blogs, and she sheds.

Some of the suggestions in this book are extremely niche, like the game of quoits (or ring toss) from Felicity's time. By the time you flip through to every kind of party, the note that colonial gatherings could have "lasted for days!" feels as much like a threat as anything. The strong focus in the party book on emulating imagined historical birthday traditions strikes us now as singular to that moment.

While we don't have kids, here is a sample of themes we've seen at kid parties we've attended: "*PAW Patrol*," "baseball," and, let's not forget, "princess." We feel sad for kids today, who will never know the pandemonium of a birthday party where you genuinely try to convince your guests they should pretend to have "whatever Marta had" to lean into the "frontier theme" of a compulsory Kirsten birthday play performance. Or a party where you're told you can't have cake until you "finish your quilt square craft" and "win the revolution," as Mary was once told at a Felicity-themed bash.

Whatever kind of American Girl party you were planning, the brand's guides stressed decorum, procedure, and manners. Even dogs needed to get in on the act. A Fall 2003 American Girl catalogue offers a Coconut (the official American Girl dog of the early 2000s) birthday party favor kit for ten girls ($65) or a fuller package with cards, cupcake wrappers, confetti, and other fixings for $70. Literature is also recommended: *Birthday! Pages and Pockets* "features pages for recording party plans and memories, flaps where friends can write predictions for the future, and envelopes for holding secrets and souvenirs." That one cost you $12.95, but the price of losing a book riddled with possible land mines and friend secrets may be incalculable.

As you have likely deduced, none of these elaborate parties came cheap. Along with these party kits, for $70, girls could also get a dress and cardigan set and matching doll's birthday outfit. These ensembles came in what can only be described as dELiA*s purple. The promise of a perfectly accessorized doll birthday is pretty alluring. The catalogue reminds hesitant readers: "Your American Girl doll will feel like a queen . . ."

As this line from the catalogue suggests, birthday stories can reveal inequities even as they appear universal. What these catalogues offer is an ideal, not a reality. Birthdays are yet another moment where class matters—a lot—in the way people experience their childhoods. In the song "Juicy," the Notorious B.I.G. remembers, "Birthdays was the worst days / Now we sip Champagne when we thirsty." While growing up surrounded by the birthday-industrial complex, B.I.G. experienced birthdays as another day that he went without; as an adult, he was able to bring a birthday mood to his daily life.

Would an American Girl Doll Understand an American Girl Birthday Party?

The American Girl birthday section of the catalogue features a variety of accessories and outfits perfectly designed for an AG birthday celebration. This, along with the books themselves, which always center a birthday party (and gift), made us think birthdays were natural and always a thing for these ladies. They would likely have a lot of questions if invited to some of our AG birthday parties growing up. As we know now, for many of the American Girls, birthdays themselves were a privilege denied or part of the self-emancipation process.

Addy was born into bondage and, like many enslaved people, did not know her date of birth. Famously, Frederick Douglass claimed a day to celebrate his birth after freeing himself. He chose February 14. The fictional

Addy Walker chose April 9 as her day. In both instances, the act of choosing a birthday is also part of a larger process of claiming a life as a free person. Within the Addy series, the struggle to reunite with a younger sister, who was an infant when Addy and her mother ran away, is one of the central crises driving the family to seek reunification. Although Addy's sister is physically absent, she is on Addy's and Momma's minds all the time. Author Connie Porter ensures that she is a reminder of the acute dangers faced by enslaved mothers and their children.

Much of what Addy faces day-to-day revolves around serious personal crises and the painful loss of family, but the bigger picture is also always in view. Addy's choice of April 9 also brings the national context of the Civil War. Addy opts not just to be an Aries (she may not have been as invested in her star chart as we are) but to honor herself and her life on the day the Civil War ends. Just weeks later, she and her father would have seen the body of a dead president coming into their chosen city. But for that day, April 9, Addy gets to revel in the moment, which she memorializes with a banner that says "my ◄ is glad my country is free." We just know Addy would have an amazing Etsy shop today fighting white supremacy with explicit cross-stitch patterns.

Historic sites interpreting the histories of history and freedom of which Addy is a part have taken inspiration from her story. One of the best examples of interpretation of not only Addy's story, but of her birthday, is in Historic Stagville in North Carolina.

Addy's story is a work of fiction (and really, art), but it is also a tribute to a specific woman and family from history. Her story is based in part on the life of Mary Walker, a woman enslaved by the Cameron family, owners of a plantation in Stagville, North Carolina. A portion of this former plantation, now called Historic Stagville State Site, interprets the history of the Bennehan-Cameron families, where, their site explains, "from 1771 to 1865," the families "profited from the forced labor of enslaved Africans and African Americans" and controlled "over 30,000 acres of land and enslaved over 1,000 people."

Vera Cecelski, assistant site manager of Historic Stagville, appeared on our show and shared some of this history. Mary Walker was enslaved by the Cameron family, with whom she traveled as a servant to Philadelphia in 1848. There, drawing on a local abolitionist network, she escaped and claimed freedom. "While she was technically living as a free person for much of this time," Vera explained, "she did not really feel free." This was in part because, unlike in Addy's stories, she'd had to leave her children behind, including a daughter named Agnes, often called Aggie.

Historic Stagville interprets and shares this history today, and does so in part using the Addy story, including a birthday party they host in her honor. While some of the features of the Addy party, such as ice cream, are pretty standard for modern children, there's another layer of meaning to what goes into these parties at Stagville. Historic Stagville issued a press release for an Addy birthday party in 2018 that explained party guests would get to make "cloth dolls and cowrie shell necklaces" as part of the event. These "accessories" from Addy's line link to key elements in her stories. What is perhaps less known, the site explained, is that "many of Addy's personal items . . . are based on archaeological artifacts discovered at Stagville, such as her family heirloom cowrie shell necklace."

The event honoring Addy doesn't shy away from discussing the harsher realities of her life on the plantation. At this party, children might "learn more about tobacco and the hornworms from Addy's story." Unlike other parties, they are not asked to reenact these aspects of Addy's world, but to appreciate them. This is not an Addy experience, per se, so much as a window into her world. For this reason, partiers are also likely to be asked to spend the time learning about Mary Walker, the self-liberated woman who inspired Addy.

Re-creating Addy's own birthday experiences is not the goal at Stagville. The idea is to garner appreciation for her story, and for Walker's family. Addy is the draw, but the backstory is really the main event. But there are other, strategic elements of these get-togethers that show how to build a bridge between past and present at historic sites in a way that is still respectful of the true history. One of the moments of joy in the Addy books is when her father is able to provide ice cream. It is not a treat that she takes for granted. After living without her father for so long, she finds the ice cream extra sweet, for Addy knows how hard her father had to work to make it happen for her.

As with far too many aspects of U.S. history, ice cream is a Black invention that is almost never credited as such. Brilliant public historians working in the intersection of food history and material culture have made this story better known in recent years. One of our favorite food historians, KJ Kearney, a Black food historian and founder of the James Beard Award–nominated social media advocacy initiative Black Food Fridays, collaborated with Harlem-based and Black-owned Mikey Likes It Ice Cream to share the history of Augustus Jackson, called "the Father of Ice Cream." Their TikTok explains that Jackson served as a chef in the White House in the 1820s and later relocated to Philadelphia, where he innovated the mass production and sale of ice cream. It's fun to imagine if Addy would have enjoyed mint or strawberry ice cream, flavors attributed to Jackson, when she arrived in Philadelphia.

By enjoying ice cream on a warm spring day at Stagville, visitors aren't expected to know exactly what her parties were like, but they are able to step outside of their own experience. Without flattening the space between modern partiers and Addy, making a necklace or eating a fresh cone of ice cream can reveal how the past is both present and very far away.

When it comes to birthdays, Addy isn't always the star of her own show, and in that regard, she has something in common with Josefina. Her "special day" is also not entirely about her birth, but a celebration of her family and the faith that guides their lives. Born on March 19, St. Joseph's (San José) Day, Josefina is proud that she gets to celebrate along with a saint who is important to her Catholic faith. Josefina's birthday aligning with a feast day allows an opening for a grander occasion in the book than would likely happen in reality. A girl from a devout family who was born on an important saint's day would be far more likely to enjoy sweets and time with her community. For the sake of consistency across the series, all the girls *need* to have a moment on their date of birth, but a "real" Josefina may not have known her birthday.

This is true of all the characters to varying degrees. Looking broadly at eighteenth-century history, there is not *actually* much evidence that Felicity would have been so spoiled on her day (in spite of her wealth). Kirsten's family would have also been more concerned about survival and colonization, but we can't rule out the fact that her kind of party might have happened. Yet these differences aren't really the point.

Reading our listeners' stories and reflecting on our own has taught us a few things. Buying apparel matching their worlds, or attending a party in their honor, girls are not just looking to live inside a character's experience or history. They are making a new, hybrid experience that allows them to connect with the parts of these girls' stories that feel important to them. All of these examples, in various ways, are the epitome of what Pleasant Rowland dreamed of decades before.

Still Playing

Since we started the show, we've heard from fans our age who have been inspired to dust off their childhood dolls and accessories from their parents' attics and have them around again. Some handed them to their own children. Others are trying out new hobbies and making modern outfits for dolls in a return to the joy of playing with them as children themselves. Some of you are making some quick cash by selling your dolls and accessories to the likes of us. Will we ever be able to retire someday if we keep chasing discontinued accessories on eBay? Asking for us, currently bidding on a stuffed Sombrita.

One such listener, named Kristi, wrote to us that she recently sold her childhood Kirsten and made some quick cash (congrats). She still loved Kirsten and reflected on their shared immigrant stories. What resonated with her was the fun she had listening to her mom tell her improvised stories about what her Kirsten would get up to with her brother's toys and pet beta fish every night before bed. In these stories, Kirsten was a "a two-faced b****; on the surface, she was sweet and kind, and when you turned your back[,] she was narcissistic, manipulative, and evil" (her words).

When she let her mom know she'd sold Kirsten at a nice profit and would need help shipping her from her childhood home to her new life, her mom sent her one last story with photos imagining Kirsten's eviction from their house. Iconically, Kirsten didn't understand the change in her station and was simply informed "business is business." Kristi may have been ready to let Kirsten go in part because she knew the source of her joy and the fun she had playing with Kirsten, her mom's truly engrossing stories, could continue without the doll itself.

There's a quote that pops up on message boards and memes from time to time with hazy attribution that says "At some point in your childhood, you and your friends went outside to play together for the last time and nobody knew it." Taken sincerely, this could make us sad. We know we can never return to our early years with American Girl, when we, like the American Girl characters themselves, had no idea what was before us or what we would be when we grew up. However, the magic of American Girl is that there is no cutoff date to fun. This is not like going outside to play (which adults also still do). For all we know, Kristi mailed her Kirsten to another adult looking to revive her childhood fandom. We are living in a culture of burnout, and play is arguably important for adults now more than ever.

In 2022, the *New York Times* reported on a new pop culture phenomenon that seemed to embody the sense of play so many adults (like us) desperately need. People our age (and slightly younger—hey, Gen Z!) were celebrating their birthdays (and just normal days) at American Girl Café. Taking their dolls along for the party, they would invite friends to join them to sip mimosas at the café among parties of nine-year-old girls and their families also celebrating *their* big days. Often recording the experience for history and TikTok, these influencers wanted to play on the juxtaposition of adults in a place designed theoretically for kids, having fun without them. Gleefully posing their dolls for photoshoots, seating them in high chairs designed for that purpose at the end of their tables, these people were living their best lives. We could only ask how our invite somehow got lost in the mail.

We've heard from listeners who couldn't wait to pass down their treasured dolls to their own children, only to learn that their kids didn't understand the appeal. In a bleak moment, we've tried to imagine a child reacting with disgust—or worse, indifference—to receiving a treasured Molly doll from a parent. Did Molly win a war for *this*? While Pleasant may have wanted to share her dolls and books through generations, sometimes kids just aren't interested in helping her make that happen.

This only increases our love for these videos and pics of people our age having fun with their American Girl dolls. They are throwing caution to the wind, credit cards to the waitstaff, and any potential judgment out the window. We live for the storylines these influencers create starring their childhood dolls in scenarios Valerie Tripp definitely could not have dreamed up. (That said, we would love to see what she would do with a TikTok.)

Considering how slowly Pleasant's magazine and brand were to adapt to the internet, her head would spin at the prevalence of American Girl travel blogs, influencer accounts, and other forms of storytelling by generations older than the imagined target of the brand.

The influence of millennials may in fact be something that is now increasingly on the brand's radar. Courtney, the historic doll from 1986 (excuse us as Mary screams into a pillow at the thought of her birth year being "history"), in many ways feels like an attempt to lure back grown-up fans. We could now buy in miniature form the accessories of our own childhoods. A mini cassette Walkman that costs more than an actual Walkman we likely owned? Was this designed to bankrupt us?

Like *Ms. Pac-Man*, whose arcade game was also for sale as part of Courtney's line, we gobbled up every bit of nostalgia they threw at us. Actual youths would never know the stress of trying to tape songs off the radio on cassette, and yet seeing a cassette tape in miniature took us right back to those memories. The accessories would represent fantasy for kids today and nostalgia for us.

In ways we could not have predicted, both for us and for other fans who grew up on the brand, American Girl is the gift that keeps on giving. This is not to say that its legacy isn't complicated. If our childhood love for it was defined by play, adulthood allows us play with perspective. How *do* we make sense of some of the stories we grew up on from the perspective of adulthood? What can the experiences of girls offer the lives of adults? To find out, we had to look for some heroes.

Tips for Throwing a Birthday Party for Your Doll When You Are Past Childhood Age:

- First, abandon all preconceived notions about who dolls are for. If you want to throw your doll a party, do it.
- Consider your friends for whom dolls may not exactly spark joy. Evaluate the guest list a few times.
- Know your doll's sign!!! We can't emphasize this enough. (Do you think you should have a small gathering for your Leo companion? No, you should not.) Addy's birthday choice is a sign to make yourself the main character in your story. Also, a lesson that being an Aries can be by birth or by destiny.
- Don't overlook the small things. Make Felicity feel at home with guitar music. Comfort Josefina with "Las Mañanitas" and remember that kind words never go out of style.
- Do not give anyone involved a puppy thinking they are one-day gifts! Maybe Molly's dog could disappear with impunity, but most are long-term commitments.
- Try to avoid greasy foods that may leave lasting stains on expensive merch. This is especially true for the hard-to-replace items.

- Remember Samantha's ice-cream disaster (salt instead of sugar, courtesy of a jealous neighbor) and keep it close as a lesson in maintaining boundaries.
- Cake, cake, and more cake. If it were easy to make a cake or other historic confections for an eighteen-inch plastic being, everyone would do it. Don't be just anyone. Go for the gold (this reminds us that an Olympics party is always in style).

CHAPTER 5

Heroes Come Along

In which we hit the books and look for life lessons about saving the day. While the stories may be formulaic, we meet adult fans who have been inspired to make American Girl stories a useful and important part of their lives in truly original ways.

Never underestimate the power of a ribbon.

When we were kids, few things made us feel more dignified than a ribbon bookmark. If we were going to live in a material world, we were going to read with style. Who knew that such a small investment in a ribbon could not only hold someone's place in a book, but also have a vise grip on someone's heart? Looking back, the people behind American Girl and Dear America knew exactly what they were doing when they filled our Scholastic Book Fairs with volumes that looked like they had been pulled off Samantha Parkington's shelves.

We grew up in an era of really great historical fiction specifically marketed toward girls. The Little House books had gotten an earlier generation of readers hooked on history. For us, historical fiction came in the form of diaries and series like American Girl. Did we have anything in common with kids who struggled through a journey on the *Mayflower* or a winter at Valley Forge? Not really, but that did not stop us from pining over those beautifully bound books with illustrations of girls right on the cover.

For years, we begged our parents to take us out and buy books that would drag us through countless historical tragedies. We were also not above solving mysteries with kids living in a boxcar or spending time with the little sisters who got a spinoff from the Baby-Sitters Club. We were just also desperate to know whether girls living through winters hundreds of years ago also had ChapStick.

As you well know from coming on this journey with us, American Girl became a huge, multifaceted brand with seemingly endless product lines during the 1990s and 2000s. Over the years, American Girl products have made their way into our birthday celebrations, our closets, our magazine racks, our attics, and, of course, our hearts. The toys were built to last, but there's another huge piece of this empire that endured beyond the shelf life of any pair of Felicity's shoes. Long before we found ourselves scouring the web for vintage American Girl letter jackets to match Just Like You dolls we don't even have, we were adoring readers of American Girl books. We were not professional historians, but kids who loved stories bound in beautiful little volumes.

Like all American Girl products, the books had more than one purpose. Though they made for a pleasing picture when all lined up on a shelf, small silhouettes facing out, that wasn't their only role in our overstuffed childhood bedrooms. These books were supposed to entertain us *and* teach us things—what, we were not always sure. Revisiting those stories has been a strange process. Sure, the books are the same, or just a little bit worse for the wear, but we're different in so many ways. Looking through that old bookshelf or box of books can feel like going to a high school reunion. Even if you're looking forward to it, you know some weird feelings might come up.

We started hearing from people who, like us, had loved these books. They'd casually mention that their choice to work in a certain profession had been inspired by Samantha's fearlessness. Or they'd cite their choice to stand up for a divisive position could be tied back to Addy's courage. Erin Reilly, who wrote to us about her decision to change career paths, knows that these books sparked more than a childhood "love of history." While reminiscing about her favorite story, *Kit Saves the Day*, Erin expressed that this process was about more than nostalgia. It was really a way of thinking about what she was doing with her life and the career she "fell into." Making a pivot from marketing to public history, Erin explained, had to do with her love of American Girl and finding her own way "to tell my favorite kind of stories."

We became really curious about how these historical books set us on the messy paths to becoming our grown selves. Clearly, Kit was offering Erin and others more than a template for how to serve looks in overalls or ways to survive a major economic downturn. While there were many connections we weren't expecting, one thing became consistent: the depth of feeling people had for the stories that empowered them. American Girl can be so motivational it makes its adult fans feel like the embodiment of the "We need an American Girl doll who can . . ." meme. Fans who replayed and remixed the stories online clearly weren't just nostalgic for their own childhood toys, but actively vibing on stories that continue to do work for them as adults. We became curious about the stories within these stories in our inbox and online, and the ways that narratives from childhood *could* change and become something else in the process of their retelling.

The *Saves the Day* books are a strange element of the original six-book formula. The only requirement for the plot is that at some point in the book, our central character will become a hero. Through conversations with other adult fans and our own reflections, we want to explore how American Girl empowered us through these stories of heroism as kids. For example, why was it on girls to save, if not run, the world? What else might they have taught us, and did anything really prepare us for living through this many recessions and global meltdowns, not to mention climate change?

We know these books *did* empower us, but what does that look like? We set out to find some adult sheroes to guide us in discovering the real value of revisiting treasured stories from childhood. Through cool video and photo work, costume and historical interpretation, and lol-worthy social media posts, they demonstrate how we can revise and remix something we loved as children to make it even more meaningful as adults.

But we are getting ahead of ourselves. If we're being honest, the clarity to focus on one particular kind of story came not just from patterns in fans' testimonials, but another kind of storytelling. Like with all great twenty-first-century cultural analyses, it was actually a reel on Instagram that inspired us to hit the *Saves the Day* books once again.

The Real Reel

A lot of people put American Girl content out onto the web every single day. From the American Girl Wiki to Tumblr and Twitter, there's a pretty much endless stream of fan content out there to explore. When scrolling through feeds of American Girl doll photographers, there are a few creators who stand out. Sydney Rose Paulsen is one of those creators. Simply put, she is really good at what she does *and* she can rock a Kirsten bonnet.

As she notes in her Instagram bio, Sydney spends much of her time "telling stories through dolls." We have followed Sydney's work for years and admire her ability to photograph her dolls in elaborate scenarios, re-creating famous scenes in movies, TV, and, of course, American Girl books. Sydney's unassuming social media handle is also her inventory of pets—@5hensandacockatiel—and she is known for her uncanny ability to make dolls, and their worlds, come to life. While looking at her videos and photography, you can't help but really think that her Kirsten doll is about to be swarmed by bees, or that her *Ferris Bueller* tableaux is somehow just as compelling as anything out of the movie.

Dolls are Sydney's main focus, but she appears in some of the shots, too. In the summer of 2021, Sydney got into her 2006 Samantha sailor dress (a birthday gift from her parents) and took a Samantha doll out on a small boat. She wrote: "The sleeves don't button and the skirt is probably a bit scandalous in length for 1904, but I still felt like Samantha for a magical evening." During her photo shoot, Sydney and her small team found "about 4 feet of beach" and launched Samantha on her own, sturdy craft. In one shot, from the longer reel from the shoot, Sydney hugs her Samantha close. In another, she peels away her high, thick socks so that she can run and then splash in the water. Both seem to make her unspeakably happy, or maybe that's just how we felt watching it.

The video is short but powerful. During this beautifully lit sunset photoshoot, Sydney radiates pure, seemingly unfiltered excitement. To her thousands of followers, Sydney explained in voiceover, "The things that have been bringing me the most joy lately are the moments I wish I had created as a kiddo." This resonated with us, and we felt such a happy energy coming from her work when we first saw it.

Of course, we don't know what Sydney's doll made of all this, but she may have been relieved (if sentient) that it wasn't direct book-to-boat cosplay. Samantha's actual boat story, which comes from her *Saves the Day* book, is a pretty traumatic one. In addition to dealing with ongoing family issues (and trying to connect with the memory of her lost parents), Samantha watches as a person who is close to her nearly drowns. She is almost forced to witness a moment that resembles the circumstances of her parents' tragic deaths. This could be a villain origin story, but it's not. It's an American Girl book, and the ten-year-old saves everyone instead.

We kept thinking about Sydney's Samantha scene, particularly in trying to process the power of these books and dolls for adults who love them (including us). What felt so amazing about her scene was the way she made space both for Samantha's story and her own experience of it.

In this process of refashioning something from her own closet, Sydney used this shoot to create a profoundly different take on Samantha's nautical experience *and* something from her own childhood. Her bold choice to wear a vintage Samantha outfit (and her ability to make it look like her doll was rowing a boat!) caught our attention. But we wondered about the deeper meaning of this play long after the reel was over.

Not to make this about us, but we're very aware we're just two people among many fans who have chosen to reimagine the dolls (their aesthetic, books, contexts) to tell new stories as adults. On our show, we love to speculate about what we wish had happened in some of the books, or what some characters would be like as adults, for example (no one is ready for our fan fic on Molly's golden years). This desire to revisit, reimagine, and re-create moments in the characters' stories (and our own) for the benefit of our adult selves is not a desire unique to us, which is perhaps why Sydney's work resonates so much. She reminds us we're not alone in still finding meaning in these stories even as adults.

A review of social media posts by what we'll call "AG Adult Influencers" demonstrates the range of reasons fans stage, reenact, or speculate about the characters today. Sometimes it's to improve on story choices that wouldn't play now (like the very concept of expecting nine-year-olds to be responsible for saving anything), or to create room for other identities the brand ignored in the '80s and '90s. Others have revisited the stories to consider the impact that nine-year-old sheroes expected to "save the day" had on their own choices, career or otherwise.

Pressuring kids to save the day may feel odd now (like watching Julia Stiles audition for Julliard in *Save the Last Dance*. We could also not save any dance with our skill set, but we need a town hall meeting on what exactly she was being asked to do in that routine). However, these books still loom large in our memories, and we wanted to survey the experiences of other fans who have found meaning in interpreting, remixing, or holding on to American Girl as adults.

But first, what did these books *think* they were doing?

Hero, Shero

For most people, American Girl books would have no place near stories about "real" heroes. However, we are not most people, and we seem to have walked away with more from *Meet Molly* than most would from a cursory read of *The Iliad*. That said, we did wonder how these books stacked up against other books about heroism, aside from being (much, much) shorter.

Well before there were superhero movies, or conventions, people needed stories about brave people, to paraphrase Barbra Streisand. From stone tablets to modern tablets, humans have pored over stories of heroes on difficult journeys of discovery, some of which may take a lifetime to complete. There's Gilgamesh, one of the oldest heroes on record, and "classics," like Achilles, with his well-known podiatric issues. Mariah Carey proved herself everyone's hero with her 1993 ballad about heroism achieved through self-possession. Enrique Iglesias put out a single called "Hero" in 2001, which led people listening to the lyrics to think it was about romantic love and other casual listeners to think it was about 9/11.

If you are unacquainted with these songs or books (or like us, half remember them before a reread), here is what you can expect from picking up any of the *Saves the Day* books in the historic girl series. In *Saves the Day* world, we are asked to focus on one crisis to get the blood pumping. Each time, the hero's arc hinges on whether a girl can make a crucial decision in time. As with all hero stories, it would be easy to focus on the formulaic bits in these books, but they have also thrown us for quite a few loops. One of the thrills of the *Saves the Day* books is wondering how each girl will actually pull it off.

Notably, these books are often tightly focused on a small window of time and might only cover a few days. Bucking lots of conventions, like a young girl on top of a stolen horse, these books are *not* like *The Lord of the Rings*, where friends must embark on an epic journey. In many ways, these books sometimes even seem like they are outside of the character development that is usually well underway. Bigger problems and most of the crises that give the girls a historical context may even fade or go away entirely for sixty pages. These girls have already been through a lot by the time we reach this book, but the hero moment is a kind of exclamation point, preparing us for the next big event, which is the highly anticipated Change.

Before we can get into how people have reimagined these books or revisited their meanings, we want to give you the 411 on *Saves the Day* books of the American Girls we grew up with.

A Quick 411 on 911-Worthy Situations

Going chronologically, we just have to start with the redhead who could have changed the course of the American Revolution as we know it, if only she had been real. Felicity has already flirted with treason quite a bit by book five. Then, during a family trip out of town, Felicity has to read a man's (Ben's) sloppy handwriting and risk multiple relationships to save a life. There is also a major, long-lasting war coming, but that's not her biggest issue, at least not yet.

For her part, Josefina also gets caught up in a wayward man's drama and makes a trade she's afraid will hurt the people she loves. In this case, Josefina has to assess the trustworthiness of a single guy and what being so close to folks in the United States will mean for her. The larger issues surrounding U.S. imperialism are not exactly on her docket, but we know they're there.

Kirsten, on the other hand, launches straight into a full-on wildlife scenario that honestly few could see coming. As she's living in the age before the teddy bear, we can kind of understand her point of view, but if you remember nothing else, just know that no honey is worth the risks this girl takes in book five.

Moving ahead just a few decades, a major war has ended, but other struggles are only getting more pressing for Addy. At a fundraising fair, Addy has to use her quick assessment of a new person to figure out how to save a much-needed cash box. While she's working so hard to establish a free life with her mother, new friends, and community, this feels like yet another potentially huge setback. Thankfully, Addy gets the money back and understands why the person trying to take it acts the way she does.

Cut to the Samantha and Molly books, which have surprising tension given that the girls are on summer break during their stories. They are also living comparatively much easier lives. Thankfully, both have their minds sharp even if school is out of session. Samantha saves a close family friend during a sudden storm, and she succeeds in part because she chooses to act (and fast). Likewise, Molly finds herself in an aquatic nightmare, though she is in an actual camp-sponsored color war game. An ongoing war, in Molly's case, and the pain of not having a parent (or parents) around continue to simmer in these stories, but for at least a few chapters, other concerns bubble up. And these girls? They rise to the occasion.

Save the Day, but Make It Camp

Something that always struck us as odd about these books in the series is that they felt like a one-off. They often take place without any reference to bigger stories playing across the six-book arc, and seem like a retreat or pause from the rest of the books. Take Molly's *Saves the Day*, which takes place at a summer camp, as a telling example. The book's events have nothing to do with the rest of the series and don't impact anything outside book five. We'd love to say the plot feels truly "from nowhere," but we knew it had to come from somewhere.

Thanks to a listener/informant, we learned that the plot of the Molly book may have been inspired by the life of the original shero, Pleasant Rowland. Pleasant is an alumna of the Red Pine Camp, a Wisconsin girls' retreat first created by Richard and Helen Wittenkamp (with a last name like that, how do you *not* start a summer retreat?). We do not know what Rowland and her pals' experiences were like at the camp during their own stay, but we hope they were truly Molly-ish.

What many fans of American Girl may not be aware of is the fact that Rowland also saved her own camp. According to Red Pine's own brief history of their site, "after 70 successful years of family ownership and operation, a group of alumnae expressed interest in owning the camp. With their encouragement, Red Pine was purchased by the Pleasant T. Rowland Foundation of Madison, WI." Within two years, Rowland "gifted the property to Red Pine Camp Foundation, Inc." She had been moved to save the camp because of what it meant to her own life, but also because of the promise it offered girls in the early 2000s.

In an open letter, Rowland explained, "Red Pine Camp is an oasis from the incessant media message to grow up too fast. It is a place blessedly free of cell phones, YouTube, instant messaging and consumer pressure. It is a place with deeper values and higher aspirations. I give you my word that it will remain so." We can almost imagine Aunt Cornelia nodding along, or Grandmary thinking of her own multigenerational camp featured in *Samantha Saves the Day*. Notably, the camp could be "blessedly free" in this way because Rowland was secure in her millions and therefore did not need campers to also be consumers at all times.

Armed with this knowledge, we had to reassess a story that had never really been at the top of our lists. Yes, we are admitting that even as Molly-types, we had not connected with this book as much as we'd have liked. Molly's win at Camp Gowonagin is cool and all, but that moment does not really have super serious consequences for the rest of her life. Ultimately, she helps her team win a game during a rough year of their adolescence. If you went to camp and loved color war games and are screaming at us right now that we are just NOT GETTING IT, that's totally okay. We know that we just do not know the thrill, nor can we go back in time and understand the stakes. Molly's exploits aside, that story has taken on such greater meaning with the knowledge that it allowed Rowland to actually keep a girls' camp afloat.

Rowland went full circle with loving camp as a girl, having her friend Valerie Tripp write about camp and girlhood, then finally saving a girls' camp with her fortune. Still, to really get to the heart of how American Girl shaped ideas about modern heroism for girls, we'd need more than just Pleasant's example. Maybe no one else had been inspired by a *Saves* book to become a millionaire who could support girls' retreats. We did not want to rule that out, but we had to stay curious about what else continued to resonate with readers.

"What Does It Mean?": Miley Cyrus, Philosophers Across Time, and Us

In spite of their somewhat forgettable, occasionally outlandish heroes' arcs, we knew there was something here if people still felt an attachment to these girls and their bravery. It would be easy to simply exclude these girls from an American heroes' pantheon and move on, but we knew better than to do that. Samantha did not give up on an all-white outfit even though she was in the woods, so we will not just give up on these books. Like pretty much all aspects of American Girl, the *Saves* stories have taught their millions of readers a very wide array of lessons, and we'd just scratched the surface.

Taking this extended "peek into the past," we also realized just how much these formulaic books can sometimes jump out of or seem to deviate from their longer historical timeline. In her story, Molly goes all out (and actually becomes ill!) to win a camp game with very low stakes during her *Saves the Day*. While we hadn't easily recalled all the details at first, something seemed a bit off, upon reread, about her out-of-time hijinks at camp. As adults, we were looking for a little bit more intelligence related to her historical context. Molly was at camp during a period of national crisis and global suffering, so what gives? We're not alone in thinking this, as it turns out.

Other readers admitted they did not learn much of anything about the war in this book, and what they did take away somewhat baffles them. The Holocaust is completely absent, and Molly's camp experience seems to happen in a total vacuum within the United States. Except, Molly is aware of the war, or at least knows enough to copy a famous *amphibious landing*. According to one of our sources, Molly's *Saves the Day* accessories included "a 'sit upon' similar to what Molly used in the book that was stuffed with newspaper." This toy included a "faithful, tiny-print re-creation of a *Chicago Tribune* front page on D-Day that you could actually read . . ." Writing to us, this fellow Molly lover was curious, as an adult, what this was all about. What did it really mean to make Molly a hero for girls, some of whom may have lost relatives during the war, a generation or two back? Knowing what we do now about June and July of 1944, we are left scratching our heads that a major moment in World War II could become an almost throwaway plot point.

Even briefly revisiting these *Saves* plots might leave you reconsidering what *you* were supposed to take away from the *Saves the Day* titles. Where is the line between bravery and foolishness, and how does it move as you go past age ten? Can you love a book that seems to totally miss major traumatic events that are important to understanding history? At the risk of sounding like "these books about girl heroes aren't like *other* books about girl heroes," indulge us in finding some of the more inspirational silver linings of these stories. In the logic of this universe, all leading girls get a chance to be heroic, at least once in a sixty-to-seventy-page story. What does that do for a reader who may not see herself elsewhere in heroic stories?

Looking back, and with the benefit of time and a daily face cream routine, we see different things and look over or around some of the plot points. When left to their own devices, these girls do not rely on divine or adult intervention—they *alone* save the day, for better or for worse. Each girl in the historical series seems to be giving off some Amanda Lovelace energy (*The Princess Saves Herself in This One*) combined with the stubbornness of a repeat reality-TV contestant.

All of these girls have to summon something from within themselves to save the day. There are no ghosts giving them morality lessons. Nearby, fully living adults seem to be either clueless or unhelpful. None of these girls even seems to have a talisman that would be of use. Instead, across the centuries, no matter how serious the situation, these girls wait for no one, even when, honestly, they probably should. All of them feel empowered to trust their own instincts to be brave. Right on time, these girls buck the idea of the damsel in distress to become their own heroes.

Given the persistent infantilization of women and, frankly, the dismissiveness with which children are often treated, it is both amazing and scary that all the girls become active agents in their own life-altering situations. A few even take a stand in moments that have much larger echoes for U.S. history, giving their one day of heroism even greater significance. Addy was not just getting some money back, after all. She was continuing to fight for her family's place in an unfree "free" society in Pennsylvania. That kind of courage is just amazing.

When we think about the lessons we take away from these stories, this might be one of the more intriguing. According to American Girl, none of us, no matter how young, need to wait for heroes. Nor do we need to be afraid about meeting them up close. Instead, we can just look in a mirror. We think it was Spider-Man, writing about American Girl, who taught us "with great power comes great responsibility." After reading book after book with heroic girls, it just might be easier to imagine yourself *becoming* one, too, at least for one day. Does it matter that these characters are only ten, and perhaps should not be *asked* to save the day, at all? In book five of the American Girl series, it absolutely does not.

Now we need to pause here and ask why girls needed to save the day. Where are the adults during Samantha's near drowning, or Felicity stealing/liberating a horse, or Kirsten's raccoon play? Yes, the placement of girls in the past carries the expectation that girls would have held far more responsibility in their family life than perhaps girls in the '90s or today. That said, can we please speak back to the need for kids to be *the* heroes in their worlds? Where are the adults?

American Girl builds on a trope we've talked about on our show of the expectation that it's women's jobs to make everything okay for everyone in their world, putting their own needs last. The girls are not the most selfless people in their worlds (cough, Molly), but they are presented in family units where their mother *is* often very self-sacrificing (if she's still alive; RIP Samantha's and Josefina's moms). The suggestion in asking them to save the day as girls is that it's in some ways preparing them to not only be brave, but also be the hero, or savior, of their families as adult wives and mothers.

We can see this in Felicity's books very clearly. Her mother (along with enslaved labor) is in charge of making everything work in the family. In the lead-up to the holidays, she works herself to the point of illness. This creates a crisis in the family that Felicity steps in to help solve by taking on as much of her mother's work as possible. Allison noted on our show that that same instinct for mothers to make holidays and special family times perfect for everyone else still persists today and has contributed to the kind of culture of adult burnout that Anne Helen Petersen and others have written so much about.

There's a chance you are finding it difficult to place Felicity or any of her peers within your preexisting pantheon of "real" heroes. If that's the case, we understand. In addition to the cultural biases that make these girls unusual candidates for the category (young, female, long dead, and fictional), there's the simple fact that some of their brave moments may seem a bit strange or even uncanny, in retrospect.

In returning to the *Saves the Day* plots, we can agree that the heroics are all relative, and some are a little extra. We do not want to name names, but some of the situations also seem avoidable (Kirsten). Again, if we *were* to focus on one character, and if we picked Kirsten at random, we could concede that it's not as if she cures cholera. However, she does still save the day, and she remains a hero in the world of American Girl. Thinking about other shows and books we loved as kids, we believe it's still something special (and daunting) that she did it all on her own.

Following Threads

We noticed an interesting element of feedback from fellow AG fans about the *Saves the Day* books. For a lot of adult fans who grew up with the brand, the outfits from these books live longer in our memories than some of the plot lines. This makes sense as clothing can be an important way of imagining a character or world. After all, nothing says rich girl of the Edwardian era like a nautical vacation look.

An entire industry of people in cosplay could have told us that what you wear matters, and they are onto something about assuming the role of a hero. Perhaps without realizing it, so many people took to Samantha's look because it gave them confidence in her abilities to actually take command of a nautical nightmare. A great outfit can empower us all. For proof of this, look no further than AG expert and influencer Harry Hill, who wore Samantha's classic *Meet* look out and about in NYC. (Please look this up on Instagram; it's incredible.) A city has not been so rocked by an outfit choice since Carrie Bradshaw's tutu.

Kirsten also had a remarkable *Saves the Day* look. During her misadventure, she can be found in a beautiful blue printed dress. For Jessica Quirk, a seamstress and designer who shares her creations online, Kirsten's outfits are definitely much more than just great summer looks. In fact, they inspired her to create *The Kirsten Project*, a series of re-creations of Kirsten's signature looks that she modeled herself on her blog and Instagram accounts.

Growing up in Indiana, Jessica felt a kinship with Kirsten, which she described to us when she appeared on our show. For her, this was a very active love. After exploring the catalogues and devouring the Kirsten books in the school library, she wanted to live in Kirsten's world. "Both my mom and dad were super supportive of the Kirsten world that I wanted to live in," she explained. Her mom taught her how to sew and even made some of her clothing. She wore Kirsten-style dresses to school and "dyed fabric with berries in my backyard and made a quilt."

Having lived in a "Kirsten world" as a child, Jessica returned to it in adulthood through her skills as a seamstress by way of Jane Austen. Some months before beginning her *Kirsten Project*, Jessica attended a Jane Austen festival, though not in costume. She described the event as a "magnificent display of beauty," as she marveled at the range of looks, from hand-stitched period clothing to "cosplay." Inspired by the festival, she set out to explore different historical eras by researching and making fashions from the past.

This led her to re-create Kirsten's world by researching and making all her signature looks. "It's really fun as an adult to go back and look at something that you loved so much as a kid with a new lens," she explained on our show. Part of that "new lens" includes an understanding of the work that would have gone into making one of Kirsten's outfits.

To re-create Kirsten's summer style from *Kirsten Saves the Day*, for example, Jessica had to make or refashion a Kirsten-style dress, pair of boots, and hat for herself. Her process builds on her costume history coursework and experience in fashion design, and begins with scrolling through Pinterest and Instagram to get references for costume silhouettes and style. For *The Kirsten Project*, she also had to balance what she knew of costume history and what defined different eras' fashions with the expectation of fans following her project online who wanted exact reproductions of Kirsten's looks.

To understand what inspired the Pleasant Company illustrations of Kirsten's clothing, Jessica spoke to Renée Graef, iconic illustrator of the Kirsten books, who told her that in the early days, Pleasant Company drew on the works of Swedish painter Carl Larsson. He was known for creating beautiful portraits, using his children as some of his most frequent models. Did we mention he had a daughter named Kersti? Jessica recalled seeing a portrait he'd created of a child wearing a striped dress and striped hat. Working in the early twentieth century, he reproduced images of children's fashion that more closely resembled Samantha's era. A straw hat / stripe energy screamed Samantha to us.

Historic fashions collected in museums could also assist Jessica in her work, but most museum collections draw on clothing that's been saved and passed down by elites. Fabric in Kirsten's family might have been reused and eventually stripped to rags, making examples of this kind of clothing from the 1850s scarce, she explained. This emphasis on practicality in Kirsten's clothing also suggested to Quirk that Kirsten would not have worn short-sleeves, as she does in her *Saves the Day* cover look. As Quirk explained to us, most women in Kirsten's era wore long sleeves to shield themselves from the sun as they worked outdoors.

We spoke with Jessica Quirk in January 2020, when she was still in the midst of creating looks for the project. At that time, she spoke about the challenges of balancing historical accuracy, fan expectations, and her own inclinations. The work that has resulted since is incredibly beautiful. In her updated *Saves the Day* look, she included sleeves in her dress to be historically appropriate. The smile she offers her audience while modeling this dress is, like the disease that killed Marta, truly contagious. Perhaps the most significant (and aspirational) piece of this for us is the reflection Jessica offered about how wearing costumes makes her feel. On our show, she recalled a time when her husband asked if she feels like another person when she's dressed up. "No," she told him. "I actually feel like my most true self when I'm all dressed up."

Our conversation with Jessica Quirk reminded us that part of the joy of reconnecting with American Girl or the things we loved from childhood is not the return it presents to childish ways, but the opportunity to take part in things that make us feel like our truest selves. We may not be costumers of Jessica's caliber, but we can certainly relate to the ways that revisiting the books, dolls, and accessories has similarly reminded us of things that make us feel like ourselves, whether it's talking about history, pop culture, friendship, or more.

La China Poblana

The world of costuming has taught us a lot about history and American Girl. In addition to learning we can make adult-size copies of the brand's looks (still dreaming of Samantha's cape), costumers doing important work in living history communities modeled how to create and model historic fashions without taking on the biases of the past. One of our favorite projects that demonstrated this was called *La Vida Josefina*, a costuming project by historic costuming expert Katie. On her Instagram, YouTube channel, and blog, all entitled *Latina Living History*, we loved following her journey of re-creating Josefina's signature looks beginning in early 2020.

In an Instagram post introducing the project, Katie explained her personal connection to the brand and what inspired her work. She began by acknowledging that she was inspired by Jessica Quirk's *Kirsten Project* and the costumer @historic_heroine, who had made life-size versions of Felicity's costumes. Like Jessica Quirk, who was inspired to explore her own heritage through research and re-creation of historic clothing, Katie also wanted to explore her ancestry. "I didn't have many opportunities to delve into my Mexican heritage growing up," she explained. "AG released Josefina just a little too late for her to be 'my' girl." She went on to explain she had Kirsten, who spoke to her "Minnesotan roots and Nordic ancestry on the other side of my family." In a thoughtful intention, Katie begins the project by reflecting "part of me does wonder what it would have been like if I'd been invited to learn more about the Mexican part of my family at a young age—so, I'm finding out now!"

In a video called *La China Poblana*, Katie recalled that years earlier, her mother had chosen to buy a Josefina for the family. "She looked like us . . . and had these fabulous clothes and stories," Katie shared, adding that her mom "bought the family a Josefina doll because it meant so much to us to have that representation." Katie's project models what can be so powerful about re-engaging an interest from childhood like American Girl. Making Josefina's clothing for herself invited Katie to reflect about her own connections to the heritage and history Josefina represents.

Katie started her project with the clothes of Josefina's lifetime, circa 1824. Using her extensive experience in costuming, Katie chose to "explore what life might have been like for Josefina . . . through explorations of fashion and reconstructing garments from Josefina's collection." Doing this research led Katie to quite a few "uncomfortable" moments, which she wanted to share with her audience through vlogs.

Starting with Josefina's *Meet* dress, Katie explains that the outfit includes a *camisa* (shirt) typical of the "China poblana" dress. The origins of this term made Katie curious. While unraveling the Asian influences on Mexican fashion around Josefina's time, Katie traced the outfit back to a story about human trafficking and slavery. In her clear, authoritative tone in her posts and videos, Katie reminded us that history is not simply about making a bonnet just so, nor is it merely a world to play in. History is also about looking at the parts of our own genealogies that are uncomfortable or even disturbing. Katie cares a lot about the *things* of the past, and getting them right, but she also cares about how people use those objects to tell the truth.

Katie is not just a fan of Josefina, or a multilayered costumer. She is also a leading voice in the "costube" world, and serves as "the main wrangler of all the daily posters and designers" on Costume Entertainment Network, CEN. According to its code of conduct, the CEN "is a collective community-run free service to help promote YouTube Channels with a focus on costuming." During #CostubeSymposium2021, Katie interviewed fellow BIPOC creators who had dealt with racism in the costuming community. In a YouTube video

"What Your Indigenous & POC Costumer Friends Want You to Know," a panel of experts talked about how whiteness and white comfort were often privileged at meetups and other events. They all had years' worth of experiences to share, but a particular event was really the impetus for this discussion.

Prior to this symposium, a Jane Austen meetup was planned and set to take place at a plantation. Historic Locust Grove, a Louisville historic site, was the home of an elite family "built by enslaved workers" in the 1790s. Posting later about the event, Katie asked, "Why would you visit a plantation wearing the finery and fashion of a human trafficker?" Notably, she did not tell other BIPOC creators, or anyone, to boycott the event. Instead, she offered suggestions for how to participate in costume events without glorifying traumatic historic sites. "Consider going to learn, rather than to dress up," Katie recommended. "Take your costume photos in nature or photo backdrop settings, rather than sites of historical trauma." On her Instagram account, she also offered a primer for white costumers who caused harm on how to craft and present a genuine apology online entitled "So, You Done F*cked up on the Internet." Her instructions on how to own the mistake, acknowledge wrong doing, present a plan for changed behavior, and ask forgiveness are useful for anyone working in history genuinely interested in de-centering white comfort and dismantling white supremacy.

Josefina's books are filled with struggles over mourning, conflicts with family, and fear of change on the horizon. At a time when people are speaking out about problems in the reenacting and living history worlds, Katie uses her rich knowledge and expertise to amplify other creators' voices and to continue claiming space for her own. What Katie does is unbelievably hard. She has taken a new accounting of something that a lot of people have loved or cherished and gone out of her way to teach others to do the same. We really admire the way she has reckoned with history and moved beyond the stories her peers might have admired long ago.

Decades ago, American Girl once thought it was okay to release "Plantation Play" kits, for girls who liked the Felicity stories. Now, there are more and more experts speaking out about problems in the reenacting and living history worlds and about things that might evoke problematic history. These critical consumers (like Katie) are offering another vision of how living temporarily in the past is possible. American Girl told us to take a "Peek into the Past" at the end of each book. Often, this meant learning some history and trivia about a year or two in American history. These creators ask you to look with your eyes wide open.

Lesbian Kirsten

In another corner of the internet, a content creator named Sarah caught our attention with a simple tagline for her specialty Instagram account: "Kirsten was a lesbian, change my mind."

Sarah's first post under the @lesbian_kirsten account features "a throwback of me and of course, lesbian Kirsten. Made this account to get back into my childhood love of American Girl and how I headcanoned all of them as gay ▀ Excited to be here!" Although a quiz online informed her, and us, she is actually only 35 percent Kirsten, that hasn't stopped Sarah from pursuing her leading Kirsten thesis or her excellent doll photography.

In a highly relatable Instagram post, Sarah shared that she also grew up spritzing herself with Bath and Body Works scents (Apple Blossom, to be specific) and poring over American Girl magazines. Receiving American Girl mail, she explained, was "an absolute highlight of my childhood." More than just a hobby, however, Sarah saw American Girl as the thing that ignited an "interest in history and women's rights. I attribute my love of learning and strong sense of justice to these wonderful characters." Sarah shows this appreciation often in her posts. When American Girl turned thirty-five, Sarah gathered three original dolls, a Kirsten, a Molly, and a Samantha, and put them in impeccable birthday outfits. With arms outstretched, they are standing in front of a massive piece of rainbow cake.

Sarah had started her Instagram account over a year earlier, back in January 2021. At that time, fans were discussing a new doll named Kira, and a particular plot point about her aunts Lynette and Mamie. Though most of Kira's story was about her work with animal rescue, a passing reference to Lynette and Mamie's marriage was enough to make homophobic buyers enraged. Julie Parks, who does public relations for American Girl, responded in a statement to *Yahoo Life*: "We know for girls who can directly relate to Kira's circumstances (i.e. a father who has passed away or a couple in a same-sex marriage), we're glad to show them that the make-up of one's family doesn't matter—it's still a family and that's all the counts."

Along with other collectors, Sarah found that among some people in the American Girl community, homophobic comments would be put forward under the guise of "appropriateness," with people questioning "how 'appropriate' it is for girls to read a story with lesbian characters." There was a lot that she loved about Kirsten and other characters, but a lot that was lacking, too. As she explained in an Instagram post, "Having positive lesbian representation in children's media when I was a kid would have been life-changing. Kids deserve to have this and more."

Mary can attest to how powerful this would have been for her, too. She grew up gay in a Catholic household where anything gay was never discussed, making for a world where being gay seemed simply impossible. In hindsight, it's easy to see how she gravitated toward characters like Kristy in Baby-Sitters Club, or Molly McIntire, or *Daria* (which she convinced a babysitter to let her watch on MTV when her parents were out). While not signaling queerness overtly, there was . . . *something* going on there (if you know, you know). Was it normal to secretly tape *South of Nowhere* on the family DVR, watch it, and then delete it before anyone might ask why you were drawn to the lesbian content? Asking for Mary.

Mary often wonders what it would have been like to have openly queer characters in the things she read and watched at a younger age. Maybe she would have come to certain realizations sooner, had the kind of teen years she saw on *South of Nowhere*. She is not the only person who feels that way. There's been a lot of great writing by queer writers at Autostraddle and other sites about the delayed adolescence queer people have when they are deprived the experimentation of teen years due to repressed sexualities. This may be in part why adult fans of American Girl so delight in reading queerness into the characters now. We're having the fun we couldn't have with it as kids and delighting in creating the representations we still want to see for ourselves, and for kids growing up now.

Sarah created an iconic Instagram persona in the form of Lesbian Kirsten. Her Kirsten is not a flat, one-dimensional character, but a lesbian who has something to say about current events and representation within the brand that created her. In addition to Ariana Grande tributes and a mini-me shoot, Sarah poses her Kirsten doll with a trans rights flag. Her Julie and Ivy dolls are photographed embracing cheek to cheek, more than just friends. A Samantha and Rebecca set from her collection are holding hands with a valentine and glowing heart hovering over them. In another post, "Miss AG Bear is getting ready for her Galentine's date." It's no surprise that some fans have called her the greatest Kirsten stan on Instagram.

On the cover of *Kirsten Saves the Day*, the "hero" of the book is startled by a bear. It is one of the better-known stories from the Kirsten series. Of note is the fact that this frightened-half-to-death girl has perfect braids, and her hand is over her mouth. Like a lot of creators, Sarah could probably re-create this cover and many scenes from memory. Sarah grew up loving Kirsten and uses some of her precious time now to make her a more usable mirror. It's not as if she's forgotten what really went on in these stories. Rather, she's choosing to imagine Kirsten from a fresh perspective, much like Jessica Quirk, who steps inside Kirsten's world in a totally different way.

In a 2021 post showing her "Kirsten posse" of three dolls, Sarah's "Mattel Kirsten" expresses surprise at yet another Kirsten joining the group. When they're standing side by side, it's easy to see how a doll from 1987 differs from one made years later and one made in 2021. Sarah's post imagines a conversation between the three, and Sarah herself asks: "Which version of Kirsten is your favorite?" Unless you're a true doll expert, it can be hard to formulate a good answer to this question, but honestly, we don't really need to. Our favorite is the Kirsten who inspired a girl, who became a woman, who made the exact kind of doll she never had. That's the story that's going to stay with us.

Saving the Day with Trauma and Play:
Addy and Complicated Stories

Addy's *Saves the Day* book and overall story offer clear points of difference from other early characters' books and stories. The *Saves the Day* books for Molly or Felicity hinge on conflicts that are mostly self-made, for example, and blunted by a white privilege that will mostly keep them out of harm's way. This put the Addy books and the trauma she confronts in much starker relief. We wanted to know in particular what Black fans made of her arrival in their lives as children and what meaning they make of her story now as adults. This is history we can acknowledge but certainly not claim.

Addy Walker's stories asked readers to confront histories of slavery and the Civil War through the eyes of the first Black character offered by the brand. In telling her story, author Connie Porter, brand researchers, and the advisory board of external experts created to support Addy's development had to both offer a historically accurate depiction of what life would have been like for Addy and her family while also not defining her life by the trauma she would have experienced. Author Brit Bennett, who would go on to write the Claudie series for American Girl beginning in 2022, wrote about the complexity of consuming her stories as a child. "She is a toy steeped in tragedy," Bennett wrote in "Addy Walker, American Girl" appearing in the *Paris Review* in 2015, "and who is offered tragedy during play? Who gets the pink stores and tea parties, and who gets the worms?" Her writing on Addy identified the expectations placed on Black girls who received Addy as a gift. "When I received an Addy doll for Christmas," she reflected, "I was innocent enough to believe that Santa had brought it to me, but mature enough to experience the horrors of slavery."

As Polly Athan, the in-house research coordinator at Pleasant Company during Addy's development, told Aisha Harris for a 2016 history of Addy's production, "The Making of an American Girl" appearing in *Slate*, the advisory board compiled to create the first Black character "wanted Addy's Civil War–era story to show the struggle and survival of African-Americans as a major human accomplishment." As Harris reported, Connie Porter and the advisory board involved in creating Addy's story "agreed it had to be a story of a self-authorized flight to freedom," quoting one board member as saying, "We were all very concerned that the experience of slavery not be white-washed." Black characters would self-emancipate and appear as powerful, joyful, and thoughtful actors in their world without relying on whites to "save" them.

Connie Porter had a monumental task before her. She had to research the histories of lives approximate to Addy's and her family's experiences in order to present accurate representations *and* humanize these experiences to make them understandable for children (see worm trauma). She also had to produce something of value for Black kids who had never been offered a Black doll in American Girl history. And, we imagine, Connie Porter had to somehow do all of this *and* work in plenty of opportunities to highlight available merch and accessories. Aisha Harris accurately described the scale of this challenge in her *Slate* article. "In 1991," she wrote, "the doll company set out to introduce its first black character. All she had to do was represent the entire history of black America."

Part of Connie Porter's skill in creating Addy's world and stories lie in her ability to distill complex and cruel histories in the experiences of one character. As Porter herself explained, "I wanted children to see African American people as part of strong, loving families, caught up in slavery, doing what they had to do to survive." Recalling her own performance as Addy in a public library play, Brit Bennett reflected on the power of identification through Addy's stories. "This is the particular joy of an American Girl doll," she explained, "she is a doll your age who arrives with her story told; she allows you to leap into history and imagine yourself alongside her." This sense of identification is possible for all the American Girl dolls and their stories. As Brit Bennett argued, the stories' capacity to humanize history carries special significance in Addy's books. "Addy humanizes slavery for children," she wrote, "which is crucial since slavery, by definition, strips humanity away."

As Brit Bennett, Aisha Harris, and other writers have explored, it is complicated to ask Black children to take on trauma with their play. When we covered the Addy books on our show, we heard from several Black listeners who were unfamiliar with the story because their parents did not want them to have the doll or books. By comparison, we also had Black listeners who grew up with Addy and are navigating the meaning of that childhood play today as adults.

One such listener, Kayla Chenault, an author and historian, wrote to us to share her own reflections on how she felt about Addy as a child and now from the distance of adulthood. Kayla grew up with a Molly, Addy, and Kaya. She can remember her first chapter book in first grade being *Meet Samantha* and being "obsessed" with *Meet Molly* (same). As an African American, "it was so rare to find a doll that looked like me, and my parents basically thrust Addy into my life," Kayla wrote, "much to my own objections."

To understand her objection to Addy, Kayla told us she was then living in a predominantly white town and "I felt a sort of shame associated with the Addy doll that I could never quite understand." Having considered this shame as an adult, Kayla explained, "What I experienced when I got her was a reminder to me of my own otherness through a material object," adding, "She had dark skin and very coarse hair that was difficult to play with, the latter of which I was often teased for in my very small, very white school."

Still, Kayla noted, she was appreciative of the opportunity to read the Addy books. "Much of the historical and racial trauma that black children were taught centers on real people, especially young people," she explained, citing Emmett Till and the Children's Marches. "To a 7-year-old, like I was when I read *Meet Addy*, that is overwhelming. But with Addy, I could engage with those stories of black trauma and understand the reality of racism, while still maintaining the safe distance of fiction."

We so appreciated Kayla's childhood memories of reading Addy and her suggestion for the ways the books can still offer a safe space to communicate history to young readers. Specifically, she shared that a family friend was reading the Addy books to their young granddaughter to help explain the incarceration of a parent. "Even though the child is still very young, even younger than I was when I read Addy's books, she is still able to connect the fact that Addy's father and brother are removed from the family to the fact that her parent is removed from her life in a very similar way," Kayla explained. "I now see Addy as emblematic of the ways we can use fiction to tell the realities of racism." While we more than respect the choice not to engage Addy because of its traumatic connotations for particularly readers of color, we can also appreciate the connection Kayla makes between the histories of slavery and the realities of racism still very much alive in our world.

Kayla's framing of her own Addy story and her understanding of its continued uses with young readers reveals her own instincts as both a museum educator *and* a storyteller. In 2021, Kayla published her first novel, *These Bones*, and continues to create exhibits that offer challenging but true narratives to the public. She is not alone in pursuing storytelling in adulthood that draws on her complicated Addy feelings. Knowing Brit Bennett's connection to Addy's stories, it's exciting to know she wrote the Claudie Wells's books focusing on a Black girl growing up during the Harlem Renaissance of the 1920s.

Settlement and the City

In another museum, and in an entirely different city, two women are hard at work. One was told, decades ago, that as a child from a German family, "You don't need American Girl dolls!" She did, however, have access to the books. Her name is Danielle. Another spent hours playing with Felicity and Samantha dolls. She's a self-identified "Horse Girl, capital H and G." Her name is Grace. As adults, they met while working at the Tenement Museum, on the Lower East Side in Manhattan.

During her interview for the job, Grace McGookey casually mentioned that "as a kid, I would be dressed up like Laura Ingalls Wilder, you know, and that was my playtime." She did not think this was unusual. Her future boss seems to have thought it made her a great fit to work with people presenting history in costume, speaking as interpreters of the past.

Danielle Wetmore pursued public history and fell in love with the Tenement Museum's work on a tour. She works with people in costumes to "facilitate conversations." In layperson's, or laydoll's, terms, she explains that some of the programs she's part of are similar to "if you got to meet an American Girl doll. It has the same magical quality that the books do, where you're pulled into this moment, and you get inside the mind of another individual."

When asked about heroes, both Danielle and Grace noted that they didn't have just one. Both had learned how to appreciate the stories of ordinary people, like the ones they've researched at the museum. Visitors are drawn to the museum from a similar instinct. The museum, which explores histories of immigration from the late nineteenth century into the twentieth century, allows many to see how ordinary people lived after arriving in America. For many, this can inspire a curiosity about relatives who immigrated. Other visitors are motivated by a desire to learn more about two extraordinary girls, Samantha Parkington and Rebecca Rubin, an American Girl released in 2009. Rebecca, the first Jewish American Girl, lives in New York and is the child of Russian immigrants. Her books follow her journey to deal with the challenge of assimilation and self-discovery.

Though they only deal with "real stories," Grace and Danielle have seen quite a few Samantha and Rebecca dolls come through the door. Dolls have brought girls and families into the museum, and informed questions people ask of Victoria, the most popular costumed program figure. Grace noted that she dates from the same era as settlement houses and speculated Samantha may have grown up to work at one. Though intrigued by Samantha's story and exploits, neither Grace nor Danielle is asked to perform a boat rescue at work. They *are* asked to talk about the lives of people like Nellie O'Malley, Samantha's friend who of course doesn't get an invite on this (dangerous) summer trip. Thinking more about heroes, Grace revealed, "The process of having a single hero is something I rejected a long time ago." Yet both have deep admiration for the figures who made changes within the tenements. Talking about the laundry yards that would have served as meeting points between buildings, Danielle added, "Real change happens when a lot of people" are "brave together."

There's not a straight line, really, from American Girl dolls or books to working at any single place, except maybe American Girl. But these stories made Grace really wonder about the world around her. She once asked her first-grade teacher, "Is this real?" upon completing one of the books. Her teacher replied, "Yes, it's real . . . it's a real book." But that wasn't what she was asking. Today, Grace and Danielle play with what is real on the programs they run in a very historic place that requires a bit of acting and storytelling to make the past come alive.

Telling the stories of "people who are totally regular," in Danielle's words, is an important thing to do when so much of history is still focused on elites (ahem, Samantha). In thinking about all the ways Samantha could have made a difference right in New York City, it's striking that she goes "off set" to save the day. Maybe Samantha would have gone on to work in a tenement or become a social worker. Or she might have ditched her friend Nellie altogether in a few years. Still, lots of people have found Samantha's *Saves* book and her overall energy inspiring.

We once received an anonymous message from one such woman working in politics who felt particularly inspired by Samantha. "The American Girls series had a profound effect in my life," she wrote, "especially the Samantha series. I loved Aunt Cornelia and thought being a suffragist and someone who fought for equality was awesome. I believe that's where my love for elections started." For over a decade, this woman has "worked and studied campaigns and election administration," work she directly relates back to Cornelia and Samantha. Yet it wasn't just the politics but a note that made her a firm Samantha stan. "Valerie Tripp hand wrote a response to me when

I sent her a letter when I was 7 years old." In that moment, a woman who wrote about children as heroes also became one.

Molly's War: The Greatest Generation and Historical Erasures

In true revolutionary style, we find ourselves on this journey to discover heroes right back where we started. When Rowland thought it might be handy to have a story that reflected her own time at a camp (a place she has since come to save from financial ruin), she never could have imagined the lives these stories would take on. Bizarrely, no one has written to tell us that Molly's camp rescue changed their own amphibious tactics. We have met a woman who learned to fall in love with history, not just through American Girl, but by connecting with voices from the past.

The artist known as J.Mix came into our lives in the most fateful of ways. After we talked about the WWII Museum in New Orleans on our show, listeners reached out to tell us we just had to get in touch with one of the former performers there who was involved in community efforts to dismantle the museum. J.Mix is a singer, skater, and activist who also performed World War II–era songs for veterans as part of her day job. While J.Mix could not remember what American Girl doll she had, she *could* speak to the erasures in typical World War II narratives that are important to correct. She inspired us by sharing her own experiences being marginalized within the museum and through her descriptions of the feeling she gets when making memories for people who served during World War II, and particularly veterans of color, whose contributions are still too often sidelined.

For years, J.Mix has been involved with local politics in New Orleans and national conversations about memory and race; she is a leader in a movement to change representations of World War II. J.Mix does not idolize any single doll or story, but she appreciates that we all come to history in our own way and time.

Talking with J.Mix helped us to understand how complicated myths about heroism and patriotism can be to untangle. If it were easy to break away from some of the nostalgia about World War II that gave us books such as Molly's, we wouldn't have massive tomes about single war events still lining many of the shelves at popular bookstores.

J.Mix was somewhat on the edge of American Girl fandom, but others who remember being deep in it are also having to spend time rethinking the work some of these books do for us today. Part of what makes the Molly books challenging upon reread, and especially her *Saves* story, is the fact that the struggles have very little to do with the context she lives in. The war is a kind of backdrop, but it is not a character. This is at least partially a reflection of her privilege and her upbringing.

As a girl, American Girl devotee (and Taylor Swift superfan) Chana was just plain confused by *Molly Saves the Day*. In an email, she explained that this and other Molly books didn't really even make sense to her "because here was a girl who was living in the time of the war but seemed further removed from the Holocaust than I was in the 21st century." In her childhood, "it seemed [odd] when I was younger reading the Molly books and having there be no mention of the Holocaust." Chana was also fortunate enough to know "Great Grandparents who were Holocaust survivors (they both managed to escape from Europe)." She explained, "I love American Girl, but I'm here to listen because my great-grandparents survived."

When we started talking about Molly's camp experience, we received more emails, messages, and letters like this than we could have imagined. Talking about this kind of camp, when others were suffering in concentration camps in the United States and in Europe at the same time, only served to highlight the many gaps between what can be taught and what is still often taught about World War II. Thankfully, other brilliant historians stepped up, including Leah Sauter, a Holocaust historian and educator, to teach us what Americans would have known about the Holocaust in 1944, and what they would learn only later. Appearing on our show, Leah also introduced us to some real-life heroes from this period, girls who had no choice but to be daring. Their bravery floors us still. The people who have given these stories entirely new meanings through their own research, family conversations, and efforts to share will never cease to amaze us.

Back to the Present

Some of the people we have met along the way have owned thousands of dollars' worth of merchandise. They can easily pluck any book off the shelf and remember their American Girl moments fondly while looking through a large and preserved collection of toys. That is not the case for American Girl fan Sravya Tadepalli. Sravya remembers longing for a doll in first grade, but knowing they were out of her budget. It was at the library that she was able to get "a bag full of American Girl books" and to find a story that resonated. Sravya admits, "The American Girls were nothing like me, an Indian-American girl living in a small town in Oregon in the 2000s, [but] I wanted to be just like them, courageously fighting the powers that be."

In her case, this meant going full Kit Kittredge and opting "to write a letter to the editor to my local newspaper condemning the Iraq War. Though not exactly Mearsheimer, it was published a few days later in the opinion section." Sravya does not put Kit up on a hero's pedestal in her email; after all, it's hard to type and write from way up there. What she's far more interested in—and us, too—is what Kit has meant in her life.

Sravya's note to us got at something deeply important, which is that all of these "books made me fall in love with history and politics, participate in speech and debate in high school, and eventually led me to pursue a political science and journalism degree and enter a career in public service." An award-winning scholar, Sravya explains, "I don't talk about this often because it's a little weird to say that my democratic-socialist anti-imperialist beliefs came from Mattel, but this series I started reading in the first grade truly set off the trajectory for my life."

A wise woman once asked whether these girls were the heroes America needs or the heroes America *deserves*. Actually, the wise woman was really just us, stacked in a trench coat. These books are a reminder that in life, there is plenty we just cannot plan for—the opportunities to intervene and to make a difference. When we looked past and through the plots of these books, we were left with the voices of people who really have been changed by these stories.

We have also discovered that these books may have been so meaningful to people (even when there were major issues they had to confront) precisely because other girl-heroes were so hard to come by. Long before Tripp and others took to writing these characters into being, plenty of other authors (most of whom did not care for what children read) had tried to set the record straight on heroism in the United States. As early as 1805, American historian Mercy Otis Warren was annoyed that too many people, "amidst the rage of accumulation," were not paying the necessary "respect on the fortitude and virtue of their ancestors [.]"

The American Revolution was barely in the rearview mirror, but Warren already felt as though *kids these days* were forgetting how difficult it had been. One of the reasons historians took up their pens so early to write histories of the United States is they wanted to be sure the *right* people and lessons got into the books. They would need to show people meeting challenges, overcoming adversity, and, of course, becoming heroes.

The country's first hype people got to work early. They formed historical societies and wrote really long books, undaunted by even the longest run-on sentence. Keen on showcasing what they perceived to be their nation's high points, many chose to narrow the frame. This meant extolling the virtues of the rich, white, and male people who had been in charge. Sometimes women would get a shout-out (yes, we mean Martha Washington), but these early books were like modern-day money. Presidents and elite colonists were in, almost everyone else out. Warren was afraid people might forget the legendary people and sacrifices of her lifetime. If anything, the same lessons have been taught and retaught, almost too well. The small number of people we now think of as extensions of these *Saves the Day* plotlines show that we can find kernels of heroism in all sorts of places.

In the summer of 2020, as people were physically changing history by taking down statues of folks whom they no longer wanted to be seen as heroes, it became all the more obvious what had *not* changed in more than a century. Pressing down hard on a fast-forward button, it's amazing that in over two hundred years, the ranks of national heroes and heroines remained limited and, mostly, white and rich. Children no longer sit down to read moralizing stories about Washington cutting down trees. Instead, you can now put a bobblehead of Superman or Spider-Man right next to the Founding Fathers on your desk while you type on a machine unimaginable to people who lived even a few generations ago. You can also use that machine to buy a Frederick Douglass magnet or an Eleanor Roosevelt finger puppet that will complement your phone case.

But when it comes to the mass marketing of heroism, what's really changed? American Girl does not offer the most diverse cast of characters when it comes to heroes. The brand is part of a larger, if still very slowly evolving, change in imagining more heroes and younger heroes in fiction. After all, Felicity Merriman was not made in a vacuum. It took a team of people thinking just outside the box to reexamine moments such as the revolution, and to ask what would happen if a plucky girl were in fact plotting with an apprentice behind the scenes in Williamsburg. She would still be wealthy, non-disabled, and interested in boys. But she was not cast in the same mold as other heroes, namely, young men ready to fight for the revolution. Felicity's story presented a different kind of hero: one that is still imperfect, and possibly not the hero one would want to promote uncritically for the next twenty years given her own cultural biases.

A few years later, another team would move into the next century, and imagine a girl brave enough to free herself from slavery. One of the lessons from this turn toward social history was that brave people could be found doing all sorts of things, in all walks of life. In writing *Saves the Day* stories featuring girls, they insisted that kids could be heroes of their own lives, pushing through one of the strongest implicit assumptions about who gets to be a hero. In a country where children of the past had operated danger-ous machinery, worked in coal mines, witnessed war, and suffered through bondage, it was not a stretch to imagine an ordinary, extraordinary kid sav-ing the day. But these kinds of stories were not really used as fodder for instilling values like bravery or integrity. Few children really rose to the ranks to be called *heroes*, even temporarily. Kids were supposed to read about adults doing great things and build up to the hero stuff.

Reading or rereading American Girl books as adults, we are reminded how often we are asked to look up to elders, or peers, in comparison to kids. It is also far too easy to publish a think piece on how uncomplicated it is to be a kid today. Yet we also know that many children today still face incredible challenges. These heroes often go unremarked upon simply because of their youth. Adults are rarely asked to emulate children, or to look into the inner worlds of brave children. Next to the piles of G.I. Joe figures, Barbie dolls, spy stories, and trinkets dedicated to presidents, American Girl entered the picture with kids who rose to the occasion and acted in surprising ways.

We can acknowledge that their central conflicts are often pretty contrived or against the backdrop of some outlandish situations. Still, every American Girl had a kind of confidence that we *do* find really admirable.

Decades later, some readers are also still wondering when American Girl will better reflect their own ideas about heroes and role models. Writing to us, one American Girl fan wondered why the Asian American representation was still so limited, and why "AG has flummoxed many of its attempts." Whereas feedback groups were carefully curated to include consultants and community members during the development of characters like Kaya and Addy, this fan confessed that when it came to Asian American and Pacific Islander dolls and content, "I can't help but feel a little underwhelmed. After thirty odd years, is this all I can really offer to my baby cousins and nieces?" With the introduction of Nanea, who lives in Hawaii, and Corinne (an Asian American Girl of the Year), some fans have hope for an even wider range of stories. Understandably, for many others, such changes have come too slowly.

Make Our Day, the American Girl Way

These *Saves the Day* books continue to resonate with readers (including us) even if we're a little skeptical of the need for nine-year-olds to save anything or anyone. While we may have read these books as kids and thought it would be dazzling if we, too, could win a color war at summer camp / steal a horse, etc., we're choosing not to see these stories as aspirational for ourselves now as adults. Frankly, it's just too much pressure, and Mariah Carey said we can be heroes just by practicing introspection, so we'll go with that.

What's both aspirational and inspirational is the example of all the adult fans who have made truly original contributions to the world of American Girl through their interpretation and creative work inspired by the brand and its stories. Some mark silences in the brand's stories, and others create those needed representations themselves through their own work.

Some fans use their various platforms to model the fun we had with our dolls and books as kids. As they've shown us, loving American Girl can be a lifelong commitment. It's also a relationship that can change to reflect our lives and tastes today. While it still resonates with us to follow along as American Girls save the day, we have real respect for all the adult fans out here making our day and reminding us we're never too old for American Girl.

Can We Phone a Friend?: A List of Situations When We'd Ask the American Girls to Save Us

1. If we were in a cave with a dead body and had no clue what to do next, we'd know exactly who to call. When Keith from *Dateline* didn't answer the phone, we'd call Kirsten and hear the words everyone in a crisis longs for: "You may not feel safe with that body right now, but you can steal their possessions for resale to save your families!"

2. If we somehow made it into the Bachelor mansion, only to realize

we were not in fact there for "the right reasons," we'd call Molly to get us out. Not only does she have the World War II–inspired leadership skills of someone who maybe read about D-Day in the paper one time, we know she wouldn't get distracted on her way out, because something tells us *The Bachelor* is *not* her brand.

3. We don't really see ourselves getting lost in nature (Thoreau left Walden for ice cream, and that's the only kind of camping we can support at this time). However, like Kirsten, we would risk a bear encounter if it meant getting honey. To paraphrase white people on the frontier everywhere, "If we can't extract resources from nature, why does it exist?"

4. If we're at a party with a person who tells us they don't "see color," we will draw them a vague map to an afterparty and then never have to "see" them again. Thanks, Felicity (and Ben)!

5. The next time someone we're no longer in contact with texts us to ask "if we're still using their Netflix password," we will respond simply and with conviction, "I shall take no tea." According to Felicity, that is a protest that, though completely unrelated, is both polite and dramatic.

6. When we download an app and are prompted to agree to its endless terms of service in fine print, we will ask Addy to stop us from mindlessly clicking "I accept" without reading. We would trust her to spell out key details in letters made from cookies, which is truly the best way to consume knowledge.

7. We'd call Samantha if we ever found ourselves in a financial emergency, like when we don't have cash and the Girl Scouts are selling cookies door-to-door, etc. Sometimes someone's presence is their present, and other times their greatest assets are their assets.

CHAPTER 6

Changes for American Girls

In which we take stock of what we've learned and how we've changed, contemplate creating a utopian town, and leave you with a call to community.

Is there anything more challenging than a reflective exercise? We're thinking of class conversations after a field trip where you're forced to recap something significant you took away from, say, walking through a museum or seeing a play. Once, Mary went on a lackluster field trip to a local newspaper's office with her Brownie troop. Sitting in a booth at Friendly's and waiting on post–field trip ice cream, her troop leader asked the group to share what they'd learned. Mary considered sharing a secret a fellow troop member whispered in the car ride over, that she believed she was "part cat," but that felt off-topic. Unable to pull any important lessons from what she'd learned, Mary pivoted instead to summary and said, "That happened." Reflection is hard.

Perhaps Mary's troop leader was pushing for meaning because so much of culture in the '90s aimed at kids insisted on some kind of moral as an essential ingredient. An emphasis on a concluding lesson may also be recognizable to anyone else who grew up in the '90s and watched the TGIF lineup of *Family Matters* (the title itself a lesson), *Boy Meets World, Step by Step, Full House, Hangin' with Mr. Cooper*, and please don't forget *Sabrina the Teenage Witch*. Most episodes of these classics ended with a "hugging and learning" moment with earnest-sounding music playing through a scene in which an adult helps a kid face a challenge or reconcile a tough life lesson. Sometimes they learned something, sometimes they didn't, but a hug was usually part of the process.

The emphasis on growth or change is no different in the final book of the American Girl traditional six-book arc. Molly's dad comes back from war. Samantha's (maybe straight) Uncle Gard and Aunt Cornelia announce they plan to adopt her orphaned friend Nellie and her sisters. Kirsten burns down her house after inviting a raccoon in (not much we can say about the growth in that act), but also starts to feel more American than immigrant. Felicity learns to appreciate multiple viewpoints as she prepares for an oncoming revolution, and, most significantly of all, Addy's family is reunited after separation forced by slavery. When we look at the scale of their change over time and compare it to our own over the course of writing this book and making our show, we feel . . . pressure.

We are not prepared to weather a revolution, adopt children, or engage in raccoon house performance art as a result of this experience. However, we can appreciate how much we've grown over the course of this process. And after all, the *Changes* books aren't really so much about change as they are about growth.

A few years ago, we could scarcely tell you what was in an American Girl catalogue except for a few hazy memories. We had a loose handle on the plots of these books and only rough leads on the whereabouts of our childhood dolls.

If playing with toys in childhood can predict a professional interest or reveal an emerging personality, what did our adult revisiting of our childhood faves do for us? There are many ways to track change and growth beyond the fading colors of doll eyes. Allison owns more dolls now than when we started. Mary still doesn't know where her childhood dolls are, but also hasn't tried to find them. In some ways, that is on brand for us both. However, reading the stories and talking about it with each other and with listeners has made us think about the thing we loved with only some memory of its contents. We found more things to laugh about together, to question, and to reflect on.

At the end of this experience, we can't stand back from our stories, the stories shared with us by a generation of fans and the story of the brand itself, and say only that "it happened." We're channeling our best '90s selves, so brace yourself for some hugging and learning as we attempt to reflect on what we make of this journey. Are we still Mollys? What can we do with our love for American Girl now as adults?

Changes for Allison

What you just read is right: I, Allison, have a lot more dolls than I had just a few years ago. This is one of the scary perks of reengaging a childhood hobby. Has this been a cheap process? No. Has it made me feel so rich, beyond anything I would have thought as an eight-year-old? Yes.

If you've made it this far, you've been to a lot of places with Mary and me. You may have also revisited some important spaces in your own life and rediscovered some friends who've been gathering cobwebs over the years. At some point, you may have felt an urge to pull out an old photograph of you in a bonnet, ready to go to elementary school and/or a barn-raising birthday party.

With this whole journey nearly behind us, let's indulge for a second and go on one more little trip, this time to a doll museum. Some might say there can never be enough museums, even if there are over 35,000 in the United States alone. Among these thousands, there are dozens of doll museums, which still seems like an undercount. We'd know: We've visited as many as we can in our time on this planet. Many doll museum curators and owners have taken to writing their own superlatives, so it can be hard to know where the biggest, best, or oldest is actually located in the fifty states. What we can say is that we have made an effort to peer beyond the plexiglass and to really see what makes some dolls museum-worthy.

The philosophical among us know that Rihanna befriends the monsters under her bed. Nietzsche, another single-name great thinker, had something else to say about monsters. He cautions us against becoming one when fighting the monstrous. Nietzsche also cheerfully warns, "If you gaze long enough into an abyss, the abyss will gaze back into you." This may be true, but here's the thing: Neither Nietzsche nor Rihanna told us what happens when we stare into the eyes of a doll, who may or may not be under our bed, for just a little too long. Or what happens when we can imagine them staring right back at us.

This thought materialized in my mind during a visit to a small but densely packed dollhouse-and-toy museum located in small-town Vermont. Like a Gilded Age lady, minus the money part, I'd gone out West (by this, I mean western Massachusetts and vicinity) for some refined air and to see some art. I found myself arranging a private viewing at a bright purple house, at a place proudly called THE Doll and Toy Museum of Vermont. If this all sounds very refined, add one more visual to this: my bright red Honda Civic is usually filled with random debris from my life, including a truly chaotic combination of doll stuff and work attire. I was able to park a few blocks away from the doll museum, which could not have been situated in a more charming home. Upon entry, I saw a somewhat alarming number of elves, but I was quickly pulled away from that scene and had a fantastic guide to show me around some of the exhibits.

Mostly, though, I was on my own, and I got to stare at lovely dollhouses for a couple of hours. I learned the story of Madame (Beatrice) Alexander, a largely self-made woman from an immigrant family who imagined a whole powerful role for dolls and small bits of fabric. I will admit that this is also the kind of place that some people might call "creepy," though not to my face. There're plenty of horror stories, after all, where the girl who is gazing lovingly at her doll is frightened when, suddenly, that doll blinks or looks back. I happen to find large cabinets of marionettes and porcelain dolls calming, but I can see this is not for everyone. What always charms me the most, though, is being around other people who love dolls.

Part of me understands the fear of toys coming alive, and part of me knows it's something I used to want to happen so badly. Long before I was a thirty-something road tripping to doll museums, this was actually something I dreamed of. If you are of the *Toy Story* generation, or were traumatized by

Chucky, you have experienced something that has long been part of being human. In the act of playing and making the world around us make sense, sometimes we desperately want things to be more than passive. We want them to be part of our story, and we want them to be real. What's changed, for me, is knowing just how much power *I* have to actually make that happen.

In a younger season of my life, I'd beg to go to the dollhouse store near my hometown. To be fair, I never really had to drive a hard bargain, and usually, I got a yes out of my parents or my sister. As often as I could, I wanted to look at all the precious small things I could collect. I'd also admire the beautiful dolls put out on display and the sometimes-baffling number of expensive teddy bears this store also carried. I unabashedly loved all of these things, and this was not questioned, merely supported and encouraged in various ways beyond providing transportation. No one around me mocked these interests, nor did they question me spending hours imagining my dolls were on Rumspringa. I see how special that is now. I just *liked* these things and had fun with them. With the distance of time, I am so grateful for that.

Looking back, it's clear to me that when I made a lot of my early connections to history, it was alone or with my family. Mostly, I enjoyed being with my dolls and other special things alone, or apart from people my age. If you'd told me that I would eventually have a community of friends who also love American Girl, I would have been really surprised. A younger me, who loved playing with a tape recorder, may have also been happily curious about the idea of a podcast. There was also that small thing about me wanting to be a doctor (which, to me, meant medical doctor), and also having no idea that being a historian was an actual job.

Now I continue to make memories with my dolls and get to work in a job I never even dreamed of having. When I'm lucky, I get to spend time at historic sites with friends and to talk about dolls with family. If you think my nephews and niece did not receive endless historical books and dolls from me truly as soon as possible, you are kidding yourself. What's changed is that I also get to share all of this with people from around the world. These are people who never met the girl who loved to adjust her dollhouse swing set or make playthings for her Felicity dolls. I like to think that we have a kind of friendship, and special connection, too.

Revisiting American Girl, and making some kind of yardstick about how I have changed, and how this whole world has changed, has meant pulling some stuff out of the attic, figuratively and literally. Many of the things we've loved throughout our lives can end up discarded, hidden away, or even on the aftermarket. If we're lucky, though, we have people who've kept memories of that time close all along, and at least some of those memories are good. People who love me and know me well find delight in continuing to buy me American Girl products; they know I am not playing with them as I would have years ago, but the expression of love is what stays the same.

Some people found it shocking that American Girl would release a doll with scrunchies and a Walkman. I found it thrilling because this new doll, Courtney, reminded me of my sister growing up. As a historian, collector, and American woman, it's gratifying to see what has changed and evolved in my lifetime. I'm also glad that at least for a while, I grew up and out of American Girl. It was something I could return to, with great pleasure, after accumulating other life experiences. Looking back, I sought out American Girl during another season of figuring out who I am, and my own place in history.

When all of this started, I would have said that I was interested in what American Girl represented in another time. I was curious, after all, about investigating this thing that had a hold on an early chapter of my life. Arguably, that is a chapter that has been long closed and, lacking access to a time machine, one I won't be returning to even if I wanted to. The reality, though, is that I don't want to. I much prefer American Girl as I understand it now: through the experience of adulthood, with the knowledge of a historian, and as part of a community of global friendship.

In the past few years, I have been asked, "So, are you still a Molly?" I have also been asked, in not always the most generous way, "So, you're an adult who thinks she's a doll?" Most of all, though, people want me to help them figure out what American Girl doll they are. In these moments I can only say, I wish I could help you, but please know I'm still navigating how taxes work, what the blockchain is, and if Bitcoin is a new form of commodity or the Bitty Baby of currency. Mainly, I can't help others answer this question because I'm still navigating an answer to it for myself, too.

Compared to my eight-year-old self, I don't even need to fake fail an eye exam anymore; I can do that just as well all on my own. But returning to Molly, with new lenses, in both the figurative and literal sense, has been an absolute blast and a challenge. The decision to see American Girl through a twenty-first-century lens has made me ask what I love and why. It's made me think hard about my values and the problems with a story I've come to call my own for decades. The short answer is that I was always both fully a Molly and also becoming myself. There's very little left of my eight- or nine-year-old self; true crime aficionados know that my skin cells have long turned over since the day I opened Molly. What hasn't changed—for me, at least—is the enduring desire to curl up and spend an afternoon in another place and time.

My love for that story, and for the people who have continued to make American Girl special, has brought a lot of joy into my life. At the end of the day, it's kind of fun to joke about which American Girl would invest in cryptocurrency, or to speculate as to who might try to sell an image of their pet as an NFT. It's also fun to imagine what kind of apartment they might have if, by some chance, they all ended up living on the same timeline. Humor can be one of the great glues that hold us together, especially in hard times.

But reading these books again, it's clear to me that there's also something serious at stake. We use these characters as a means of better understanding our place in the world. Americans, of course, are not the only ones to do this (hello, Canadian Girl and Australian Girl doll fans, we see and appreciate you). More recently, American Girl has tried to speak directly to the newest generation of activists and, well, American girls by creating a new line called World By Us in 2021. This line is made up of characters who live in the here and now. They are young people who are looking to actively make a change and to combat serious social issues, including climate change. There are real girls doing just that, on TikTok, on television, in their local meeting halls, and at school.

Maybe these World By Us characters provide an opportunity for kids to see themselves within history. But if we've learned anything, they are just the starting point. We should listen to the girls who are out there making change here and now, too.

While I can love much of what these books and toys represent, I can—and should—also see them as embedded within a marketplace. I see more clearly now how these books center a certain kind of girlhood, and almost always, whiteness. I know that they were partially about elevating a certain kind of womanhood, and usually, girls who looked, moved, and worshipped like me, at the expense of others. American Girl is many, many things, but it is ultimately a brand. What do brands do, other than leave a mark? The question I've tried to think of, in terms of personal and social change, is how we shape that mark. If you still care about American Girl, is it because these stories help you to understand yourself? Or are they stories that make you question the world as it was, is, and could be in the future?

In the beginning, every girl got six stories. Then, they got many more. Soon, there were mysteries, crafts, puzzles, and of course games. There were a variety of places to seek out pleasure and even some guides for how to deal with pain. As in life, none of us can be distilled to just a few character arcs or plot twists. We all contain these multitudes, and more. Maybe playing a Victorian parlor game empowered you to learn something about yourself, and candidly, maybe it did not. However these pieces fit into your story, I feel confident in saying that American Girl changed lives and pushed the boundaries of play in our childhoods.

In the end, what's really changed in the past thirty-plus years of American Girl? Even as more and more products flooded the pages of the glossy catalogues, it was clear that there was still a lot of work to be done. Right up to the present, there are still many experiences missing from the picture. American Girl is also a product of a country obsessed with stories and myths about itself, and with nationalism. Exclusion will likely always be part of that equation, as much as boosterism and inclusion. What gives me hope is that my favorite American Girl characters are no longer the ones who can be bought and sold or featured in a magazine. The most important characters are all of you. They're not Molly, Samantha, or Josefina, nor are they catalogued in my mind just as Mollys, Samanthas, or Josefinas. They're the people who've grown up and decided to become themselves: through lessons, birthdays, nautical disasters, changes, and all.

Changes for Mary

When I think about how my relationship to the brand has changed, it's hard to separate it from the life of the show. We began by identifying as Mollys and now hear from people who identify as an "Allison" or a "Mary." I am still not entirely sure what that means, and I *am* Mary. I think if American Girl offered me a connection to a thing I loved (studying history) and to people I loved (my grandmother), our podcast has offered a means of bridging the things I was born to with the things I've become. This is a life that looks a lot like the dreams I had as a child—to go on adventures, to have great friends, to have meaningful time with family—and it's different.

Rereading the books for the show has been a wild ride. It's strange to think that when we started, I didn't remember the stories at all, but never questioned what they meant to me. I have always been certain that reading the books set me on a path to be interested in history *and* to be confident in the things that made me feel like myself. Having glasses became cool to me the instant I knew Molly also wore them, for example. If reading the books had made me a curious and confident child, rereading them as an adult made me reflect on all that had changed for me in the interim. The books had not changed, but I sure had.

The differences became apparent to me not in rereading books I'd loved as a kid, but when we reached a character whose books I'd never read before. Josefina is a Catholic girl living in Mexico in the early nineteenth century in territory that will later become New Mexico. Reading her books was some of the most fun I've had making the show. We imagined at various points that author Valerie Tripp drew on the plot of the movie *The Piano* when writing these books and created an aunt character who was secretly a serial killer. The hashtag #TiaDoloresdidit became something our listeners used frequently on social media and in writing to us. One even created a Twitter bot that tweeted out various ways Tía Dolores may have committed crimes. This brought some needed levity to what were actually very sad books.

Josefina loses her mother before we meet her in book one, and much of the books is about her grieving process and attempts to find meaning and joy in life as her family moves forward. I could not help but imagine how I would have read these books as a child. Growing up in a devout Catholic family, Josefina relied on her faith as a coping mechanism, which would have likely been something I could relate to in a world that was otherwise very foreign to my experience. I, too, grew up organizing time around religious holidays and holy days. When someone died, we prayed for them and understood this sadness through shared beliefs. Reading this as an adult, and as someone who has left Catholicism, I really struggled with the pieces of the story that would have made me feel at home as a child.

The way I talk about the dolls and their stories now reflects the changes I've made to my life as an adult. For example, Josefina at one point breaks a ceramic belonging to an aunt and runs away yelling "Shame! Shame! Shame!" As a kid, I might have read that moment and felt sorry for her, but thought nothing of it. As an adult, it's a painful reminder of what Catholic guilt feels like, this ineffable desire to blame yourself for things that are not inherently bad. As Bruce Springsteen once said in what I'm reclaiming as a statement on queer desire, "It ain't no sin to be glad you're alive." That makes more sense to me now and is a more positive message than that moment in Josefina's story.

The show also changed the ways I think about Molly, my favorite doll. What if she was my favorite not only because she offered a connection to my grandmother, but because I sensed something in her that I now understand as queerness? Are saddle shoes a gateway to an "alternative lifestyle"? Would Molly be the older lady I saw at a resurrected Lilith Fair who was truly only there for the Indigo Girls? Hard to say.

I often wonder what my grandmother would make of the show and its success, and the ways I talk about my life and the American Girl books on it. She died in 2015, and I still grieve for her in ways that made Josefina's books feel very real to me, even as an adult. My grandmother was the ultimate phone-a-friend, and I often wish I could call and tell her about the books I'm rereading and the response we've had to the show. She would have loved it. I can just imagine calling her up and hearing her say "Hey, pal," which is how we always greeted each other. She'd tell me what she'd been up to, give me a rundown of crimes she'd heard reported on the local news, ask if I still have the rape whistle she bought me (yes), tell me about local fires she'd heard about, and then ask if my mom knew I used the stove in my apartment by myself (also yes). I'd love to tell her that on the show I feel free to talk about not just history or American Girl but the people in my life who make the books' themes of friendship and family resonate for me, like my wife, Anna.

I met Anna on my twenty-ninth birthday (July 31, shoutout to every Leo reading this). Being with her turned my life upside down in the best possible way, as I never saw myself as a person who would be partnered or married. I'd spent most of my teens and early twenties in and out of hospitals dealing with chronic illnesses, and that experience had made me someone who believed it was my fate to be alone. I didn't think anyone would want to take on my ongoing health issues that I have to think about daily, or the scars from these experiences, both visible and not.

My grandmother tried to combat this notion at every turn. She was known for making pronouncements as if she had psychic powers. One of her most famous was her attempt to predict the death of my ailing great-aunt. Routinely, she'd call me up and say, "It's happening on Christmas!" Days later, and with my great-aunt still very much alive, she'd revise her prediction and say, "She's going out with the new year!" Months into this process, I was going to see my great-aunt and my grandmother called to warn, "Don't buy her green bananas! She's not long for this world!" Perhaps to spite my grandmother, my great-aunt outlived her expectations by months. It's hard to know if my grandmother was sad at my great-aunt's eventual passing because of the loss or the temerity of my great-aunt dying on a day she didn't predict.

When I was growing up, she'd tell me, "I will dance at your wedding!" as a kind of similar prediction she hoped to manifest. On the day that I got married in 2020 in my parents' backyard (we love a pandemic wedding!), I thought about her and her wish to be with me. I'd known that wouldn't be possible since her passing years before. In a ceremony before a crowd of ten people, I carried a handkerchief on which I'd printed a note she'd written me, so that some part of her could be there.

I wish I could have spoken to her about parts of my life with the candor I use on the show. She never knew I was gay or that Catholicism didn't offer me the comfort it provided her. I wish I'd felt that kind of bravery growing up, like an American Girl character about to steal a horse / burn their cabin down / liberate some orphans, but I just didn't. It's strange to think that the show has helped me normalize speaking about the parts of my adulthood that my childhood taught me to feel ashamed of, Josefina-style.

Podcasts are a surprisingly intimate medium in both directions. For listeners, we travel with them on their commute, as they feed their babies in the middle of the night, or as they do chores. We are speaking to them through headphones, and, but for their inability to speak back directly, it could feel like a phone call to a friend. For me, the ability to speak to Allison—and by extension our listeners—honestly and openly about my life has been a gift. I treat Allison and the listeners like my phone-a-friends and, in doing so, have found community. It still shocks me when people write to me and mention something I said that resonated with them. I was floored by how many absolute strangers were so thrilled for me when I got engaged. A few listeners even wrote in offering to plan my wedding.

The intimacy of audio would not have surprised my grandmother. She fell asleep every night to the sound of talk radio. This was where she got her news (for better or worse), and she truly thought of the hosts as her friends. I think she would have loved that this is the way I've chosen to share stories about history. The value of this medium would not have surprised her at all, even though the role it's played in my life was certainly something I didn't predict.

When I was a child, American Girl created a deep curiosity in me to learn about the past. It also led me to believe that being a historian and getting to research and write the "Peek into the Past" section at the end of each book would be the greatest job in the world. At various points in my childhood, I imagined I might be an archaeologist, Egyptologist (every child has an ancient Egypt or *Titanic* phase that I can't explain right now), or historian. I thought about attempting these simultaneously in adulthood, but only Barbie seems to pull off that kind of multihyphenate career path. These and other experiences led me to think it would be great to teach history at a college and write books on my research. The show presented the culmination of the realization that the life I had long dreamed for myself did not actually fit me in practice (we won't get into the job shortage and great adjunctification of higher ed that makes this not ideal or realistic for many).

We started the show just as I finished grad school and had my PhD. I never quite felt like the conversation in grad school was the one I wanted to have. This may in part explain why I learned how to record and edit audio in those years, as a kind of gesture toward storytelling that better suited me. In grad school, I had the chance to read deeply in different areas and debate various interpretations of the past with experts. I learned how to do research, and those skills all continue to serve me now. I think I always knew, however, that the conversations I wanted to have were not solely in the more insulated spaces of a college or university but with the broader public. What got me interested in history were popular books, shows, and experiences that welcomed me without condescension. Revisiting American Girl as an adult has reified the importance of that for me and for what I feel most inspired doing.

When *New York Times* television critic Margaret Lyons wrote about our show in 2019, she identified a vital element of American Girl and its value to those for whom it mattered: "If you play making apple butter, or goat-herding, or sturdy perseverance in the face of unforgiving winters; if you play with loss before you have to encounter it; if you play survival, or freedom or girlhood—who knows what you'll be prepared for." Explaining that her play with her American Girl dolls prepared her for a life in the arts as our play with the same dolls prepared us for an adult interest in history, she understands the meaning of play in our childhood as something that can suggest or direct us. This is a real value to play. What I have been reflecting on in the course of our show and researching and writing this book is the value of revisiting the source of childhood play for adulthood. What can we get from returning to American Girl now?

The plotlines are definitely repetitive as we read through each series one after the next, but what has been inspirational for me is the theme of change and possibility. Rather than seeing change as something to stave off, or imagining growth as something that's the province of nine-year-olds wondering what they might be when they grow up, rereading these children's books has reminded me of the importance of seeing myself as being in progress. We are all perpetually in a process of becoming, and that doesn't end in adulthood. Margaret Lyons is right in noting the importance of play in providing a safe space for kids to try out new emotions or imagined professions or interests. What returning to these sites of play might remind us as adults is the value in allowing ourselves that freedom to imagine what we might become. As Miley Cyrus reminds us, "It's the climb."

This is something I've noticed in myself as we've done the show and reread all the books I grew up on. Rather than be sad that our time with each character is coming to an end, I think about the possibilities for them. I love to speculate about what Molly would be doing today. Would she take her tap-dancing routine to Hollywood? Be part of a generation of emerging television stars in the '50s? Question the moon landing in the '60s? Score a guest-starring role on *Columbo* in the '70s and vote for Reagan in the '80s? I am terrified to know.

But that same speculation seeps into my thinking about my own life.

How might I grow and change? Specifically, how might I grow and improve on what I now see as limitations of some of the early books? Should I let a raccoon into my house Kirsten-style? (Likely not: I have seen TikTok videos where grown adults do this and not as American Girl cosplay, and I'm scared of the results.) I want to see myself as a partner in my community's pursuit of freedom and not as a white girl savior offering charity (the Samantha fanfic we really need). I may call myself Miss Victory and dance for a cause in a revue tentatively called *This Is a Huge Mistake.* Who knows! The point is, it's never too late to be who you are, or as Pleasant Rowland might say, to be a girl who not only loves history, but makes history.

This brings me to an important question: What did Pleasant think we would do with our adulthoods?

Her own life offered a pivot from the wife/mother expectation her more traditional values might suggest. Instead, she was an educator, early female TV journalist, and entrepreneur. In her retirement, she's funded countless philanthropic causes and has been slowly rebuilding a town in her own image of the past. Sound familiar? The town, Aurora, New York, is the home of Wells College, from which Rowland graduated in 1962. In a speech reopening the town's inn in 2003, she described her affection for the town as a place that reminded her "of the values and traditions of another, more tender time." Hard to say what that time was. For many residents, some of whom sport bumper stickers saying "Aurora Was Pleasant Before," there is likely doubt about whether their town needed to be transformed into a dollhouse or Thomas Kinkade painting. Rowland's retirement has inexplicably taken the shape of the Rockefellers, whose own utopian project at Williamsburg first inspired American Girl.

Let's assume we're not all on a teacher-to-utopian-leader trajectory. I simply don't have the millions or the time (yet). While I admire Pleasant Rowland's adaptability to different professions and willingness to take a chance by changing careers and starting new businesses, her desire to remake a place in her own image is not necessarily the vibe I want to define my adulthood. I have zero desire to be a "girl boss" or even as Taylor Swift might say "The Man."

This is the difference (to me) between American Girl and our podcast about American Girl.

The brand I grew up on empowered girls as individuals whose thoughts and dreams mattered. That had real value to me then as now. It also had a kind of one-size-fits-all approach to girlhood. However, as we all know by now, girlhood and womanhood are not like the jeans in *The Sisterhood of the Traveling Pants*. One pair cannot fit all (my apologies to Blake Lively and all cast members). Pleasant's presumption to present girlhood in a more limited scale or one that presumed differences could be presented equally like a multicultural fair is—I hope—a relic of the '90s.

It reminds me of the melting pot metaphor. In 1914, Henry Ford created a school for his immigrant employees as they prepared to become citizens where they could learn civics and English. At graduation, students would ascend a stage designed to resemble a "melting pot" in clothing from their home country. They'd then go down into the "pot" under the stage and emerge dressed in suits and waving American flags. Thank God Vitamin C didn't live in these times, because truly no one could put this graduation experience to song. The point is, in many facets of American life, we know that not all groups experience the same kinds of acceptance. Race, gender, sexuality, and class are just some of the lenses that create need for real equity that embraces difference without eliding it.

To me, that has been the benefit of rediscovering American Girl through our show. The title of our show suggests it will just be about us. However, it reflects entire generations of people for whom this brand mattered from the time of its inception in 1986. While the brand may have spoken to us individually, revisiting it in adulthood has made us aware of the community of which we're a part. Hopefully, by exploring the facets of the history it presented and continues to explore in its dolls, books, and swag, we can continue to think with our shared past for the benefit of our lives now.

Does this mean that owning American Girl things is essential to being in this community? Not at all. Capitalism is a scam and there is no ethical consumption within it. That is not to diminish the disappointment not having access to these things created for people without my privilege growing up. However, our experience both revisiting the brand and writing this book has reaffirmed for me that it's the stories we've read, shared, and heard from listeners that have given this experience so much meaning. Not only did our memories of the brand inspire us to share our stories, but we've been able to hear stories from many others who did not reflect the brand's overwhelming emphasis on privilege and whiteness. Centering these kinds of stories is just one way we can prevent a new generation of girls from growing up thinking girlhood is defined solely by similarly limited ideas.

Community is vital to our lives, and I think the memory of the connections we shared with others is a key part of the memories we associate with American Girl; the time with grandparents making doll clothes, reading with parents, playing with friends. Especially now in a digital world where we can feel so easily isolated from others, the world of the books and of our show has reminded me how much my life is immeasurably improved by connection to the care and concerns of other people. To me, this is the greatest part of being a fan of American Girl; it has put me in conversation with so many interesting people whose lives are not like mine.

Our show has never been about Allison and me, but about the memories it surfaces for all of us and the language that gives us to connect with family and friends, new and old. That is the thing I will treasure about both American Girl and our show.

Millennial Possibilities and a Call to Community

It would be very easy to focus on American Girl and keep our attention on individuals, whether specific dolls or Pleasant Rowland herself. When we reflect on what this has all meant to a generation of people, and not just us, the thing that seems most significant is the relationships American Girl created, between caregivers (grandparents, parents, etc.) and children, children and dolls, and among kids themselves.

For us, it reaffirmed the value of friendship. As bell hooks wrote of friendship and its power, "Friendship is the place in which a great majority of us have our first glimpse of redemptive love and caring community. Learning to love in friendships empowers us in ways that enable us to bring this love to other interactions with family or with romantic bonds." Dolls also have a place in this story, and in learning how to be a good friend. For many kids, dolls were their first (if not overly talkative) friends. These friends were the first playmates they can recall sharing secrets with and playing with for hours. From there, it was possible to learn how to play and pretend we were our favorite characters with friends at school or at friends' houses. We could read about what friendship looked like between girls our age, and then try to play that out ourselves.

We started our show because American Girl was something that drew us together as friends. It was an early common language and source of some early and fierce debates (who had the best wardrobe? best friends? We mostly picked Molly, but loved at least considering the others). With the show, we've been able to connect with so many others. We've seen the hunger for meaningful connection as adults, and in particular, the hunger to develop meaningful friendship in adulthood. Friendship gets surprisingly little play in pop culture, and yet it's clear it's something that is vital to so many. Our most treasured messages from listeners are ones in which they tell us they feel like they're our friends.

We wanted to end the book with some ideas to inspire a similar journey into your own American Girl past. Think of this as a combination *Care and Keeping of You* journal / pen pal program / activity book that will help you remember your own hot takes on American Girl and the fun it inspired with friends. We may not have a Comic-Con for American Girl fans (yet), but if this trek through history, fandom, and the world imagined by Pleasant has taught us anything, it's not to wait for anyone or any brand to make the thing you can't wait to see in the world. Look for it within yourself, your friends, your community, and just maybe, within the recesses of those closets where you've saved the things that gave you joy years ago.

It's never too late to meet new friends, learn some lessons, celebrate, and change. We have some ideas to get you started.

Original-Generation American Girls (OGAG) Call to Community:

- Think about who loved American Girl with you all those years ago. Connect or reconnect with these friends and see what they remember. What are they up to now? Social media sleuthing may stand in for actual connection depending on how brave you are in your DMs, but this could also be a plausible reason to drop in on an old friend.

- Connect with some friends you've made in adulthood and talk about American Girl or something else you once loved, but have maybe lost touch with over the years. Who did you identify with as a kid and why? Who are you now? Ask your friends to guess answers to both questions and do the same for them. Discuss. Also, feel free to play this game with your parents or childhood caregivers.

- Pull out your old photographs and scrapbooks, or look in other places where you keep your memories. Can you remember the most epic escapade you took an American Girl doll on? Can you revisit the scene of said crime with someone in your life now you'd like to share that story with?

- Explore a museum or historic site to learn more about a favorite American Girl's era. Take it from us, you will never regret a historical vacation (just work in a hot tub and seltzer breaks).

- A lot of archives have made historic books, recipes, and even video games available for free online. Invite some friends to get together and try out some things that American Girl characters may recognize from their own time periods. You can make meals from different eras and regions using recipes posted by museums and archives, read books in the public domain the characters may have read, and even play the computer game *Oregon Trail* to reenact your own childhood tribute to Kirsten.

- Every American Girl learns a lesson. What do you want to learn more about? Find a friend and explore learning a language, craft, new skill, or new ideas together.

- Do your own Samantha cosplay in your community. WE DO NOT MEAN YOU SHOULD HELP ORPHANS ESCAPE AND KEEP THEM IN YOUR ATTIC. You *could* explore the social justice work already being done in your community, and invite a friend to join you in supporting it. White girls (and women): This means decentering yourselves in questions of race and doing your own work to educate yourself without putting further strain on communities of color to educate you about racism.

- Flex your creative muscles and consider what a millennial or Gen Z American Girl would be like—and when she would get made. Would her story feature time-period-specific plotlines? Who are her friends and what are they like? What accessories would be part of her line? Throw a PowerPoint party and ask everyone to come prepared to present their vision of their American Girl.

  - Not to make this about us, but what if the eventual American Girl of the Year dreams of being a podcaster? Can you imagine the accessories? A microphone with a girl power sticker? A sample meal prep kit to talk about on an ad? An email about a man complaining of vocal fry? If the catalogue ever attempts to take on podcasting culture, please never tell us. Or alternately: American Girl, if you're reading this, we're available.

Peek into Our Past

The "Peek into the Past" was an iconic element of American Girl literature informed by some combination of thorough historical research and patriotism. This concluding section of each traditional book asked a lot of its brave authors. Specifically, it had to describe key elements of work, play, and family life for girls across historical eras in terms we could understand. The section covered a lot of ground in just a few pages, and we imagine the only template ambitious enough for such a project was Billy Joel's "We Didn't Start the Fire." Like Billy's "this is what it feels like to prep for the AP US History exam" classic, the references were random, mostly accurate, and entirely subjective. So, of course, we couldn't help writing one of our own.

We may have been born in the '80s, but we grew up in the '90s and early '00s. To understand where American Girl fits in the broader scope of our lives, we want to give you a peek into our past and paint you a picture of life in those years. Consider this historical survey an unsolicited answer to Madonna's question from 2000: "Do you know what it feels like in this world for a girl?" We could spend all our time describing national events like Bill Clinton's presidency (1993–2001), the first Gulf War (1990–1991), 9/11, and the Global War on Terror (2001–today)—but this isn't a textbook. We're focusing instead on the places and things that defined our everyday lives as kids. Peeking into the past, American Girl–style, isn't about forgetting the bigger background stories, but putting people (and really, girls) back at the center. Here is our survey of the decades that made us.

At Home and Online

Girls in the '90s got to live through arguably one of the greatest transitions in American history, from living in blissful ignorance of the internet to having the capacity to be extremely online. While the internet has a long history dating back to the Cold War, it became available for unrestricted commercial use in 1993. By 1996, about 36 million people were using the internet, a number that would grow to 248 million worldwide by 1999. According to the International Telecommunication Union (ITU), an estimated 4.9 billion people have used the internet as of 2021, or roughly more than half the world's population. Most are using mobile phones to connect. More on those in a moment.

Perhaps the greatest advent of the internet was access to a lot of new information, like how many Vanilla Ice quotes your friend felt safe using in her away message on the AIM instant messaging app. Yes, before texting on cell phones, kids would use the online messaging app AIM to chat with friends, families, and in some cases, bots (shoutout to SmarterChild, iykyk). If you were fortunate enough to have a computer, you may have shared one desktop with your entire family in a common space that made jockeying for computer time a competitive sport. In perhaps the greatest reversal of all, our parents, socialized to be our teachers, were immediately forced to defer to their children for instruction on how to connect to the internet and use the computer. That power dynamic remains unchanged.

Our parents would also remind us that the computer—a big investment—had a higher purpose. They wanted us to use technology to actually learn things, which was not hard for those with access to Encarta, Microsoft's encyclopedia, or Music Central 96, a music encyclopedia. Imagine if YouTube was highly curated and abridged, limiting you to brief clips of artists ranging from Patsy Cline to Queen Latifah. You haven't lived until you've watched '70s era Aerosmith sing "Eat the Rich" and then immediately rolled into a video of Iggy Pop singing "Now I want to be your dog" followed by Ella Fitzgerald scatting to "How High the Moon." Aside from AIM, Mary spent a lot of time on the family computer scrolling Music Central. After seeing a clip of the Talking Heads performing "Psycho Killer," she requested the cassette at her local library only to be told that "the psycho killer song" is not for ten-year-olds. Little did that librarian know Mary would grow up to be part of a demographic (sometimes problematically) associated with true crime.

We thought we were super tech savvy, living in an age of wonders like computers, the internet, and the Talkboy, made famous in *Home Alone 2*. Some things remained unchanged, however, like our reliance on landline phones. Sure, we had *67 to help us disguise our home numbers when making prank calls, but brick-like cell phones or car phones seemed the province of Zack Morris and other fictional dreamboats on TV. Did some of us dream of owning the iconic '90s clear plastic phone to operationalize an entrepreneurial babysitting club? Sure. Did we think we'd ever look as cool as Claudia doing it? No. Do we still want that phone even though roughly only 30% of Americans use a landline in 2022 according to a CDC poll? Absolutely.

At School

School in the '90s looked a lot like school today, with some notable differences. Our own kids may never know the joys of learning cursive, for example, and the thrill of proving our cursive skills enough to get to write in pen instead of pencil. When cursive was no longer required by the Common Core standards in 2010, it fell out of popularity nationally. What is the equivalent communication style today? Just regular print? Printing in all caps like a textual scream? Coding? That might have "real world application," but it will not let you cosplay as Felicity with greater authenticity.

With the prevalence of email and then texting, kids today are far more proficient with using computers and tablets seemingly from birth. Many schools invite note-taking on tablets instead of paper. This is not a change everyone has welcomed. Since 2010, at least fourteen states have passed legislation to require teaching cursive. In part, this was motivated by a desire to develop fine motor skills and retention. While this debate is ongoing, we can attest that being able to read cursive is a good skill to have if you want to pursue a career as a historian.

Speaking of poor life choices, kids in the '90s were subjected to D.A.R.E. (Drug Abuse Resistance Education), an anti-drug program founded in 1983. Kids in this era may recall D.A.R.E. as a program you'd have in fourth or fifth grade, often taught by a specially trained D.A.R.E. police officer and featuring lots of cautionary tales about doing drugs. Truthfully, this program taught us all just enough about drugs to be dangerous, and as a result, it was already facing scrutiny in the 1990s when we encountered it. We can remember being in D.A.R.E. class and learning all kinds of slang words for drugs that were 100% news to us. We felt like extras on *Law & Order*, a feeling that partially prepared us to act in the mandatory anti-drug skit capstone performance for a captive audience of our parents. D.A.R.E. instructors also really wanted you to spread the word, which meant writing a persuasive, five-paragraph essay that no one would ever want to read again. Allison came in second place in her D.A.R.E.-sponsored essay writing contest, probably because she used an overly complex metaphor about spiders. School drew us into many webs, but the pull to explain anything with a metaphor remains as attractive as anything in the American Girl catalogue.

Acting coaches may have fairly assessed our performance in D.A.R.E. skits as "tone deaf," "unconvincing," and "sad." Interestingly, this is reminiscent of actual criticisms made of the D.A.R.E. program itself by experts. As the *Washington Post* reported in a 2017 history of the program, a 1994 study concluded the program had little to no effect on preventing teen drug use. Iconically, the *Post* quoted the then executive director's response to the study's results saying, "It's like kicking Santa Claus to me. We're as pure as the driven snow." Clearly, this director's word choice demonstrates he either watched some *Law & Order* or was comfortable drawing on the drug lingo he may have learned in D.A.R.E. In recent years, the program eventually relaunched with a new curriculum called "keepin' it REAL," which is too bleak for us to cover any further.

Girl Power?

In 1996, we were immediately under the spell of the Spice Girls when they debuted with "Wannabe." We were taken in by their frequent use of the phrase "girl power" in public and their enviable style, looks which we could hardly keep up with while wearing our slap bracelets, light-up sneaks, butterfly clips, and other fare for which we'd now have to pay top dollar at Urban Outfitters. In that heady time, choosing which Spice Girl you identified with was as fraught as understanding what "girl power" actually meant, though that did not stop us from yelling it often, unsolicited, and likely out of context. The Spice Girls, though representing our former colonial overlords, had clearly liberated something inside us. What exactly was "girl power"? Well, as the Spice Girls explained in numerous interviews when they made their debut, "it's about equality and fun and trying to rule your life." As kids, we likely interpreted that as an invitation to recreate the "Say You'll Be There" video in our backyards.

Now we can look back and wonder just how progressive this period was for women and girls. Newspapers across the country proclaimed 1992 as "the year of women" after the Clarence Thomas hearings the previous year created public conversations around sexual harassment and gender discrimination. A surge of women candidates was elected to Congress that year, benefitting in part from public outrage over the televised testimony of Anita Hill in which senators questioned her with little restraint or respect. The drive for greater representation of women and policy protections for issues affecting women's lives and bodies continues to this day. The Clarence Thomas hearings were so important in part for the threat his appointment could pose to *Roe v. Wade*. In 2022, *Roe v. Wade* was overturned, demonstrating history is not always a story of progress but can be something to grapple with as we process and protest contests over bodily autonomy.

With the passage of Title IX in 1972, girls in the '90s likely had more rights and support in terms of athletics than our own mothers and grandmothers. We also had more coverage of women excelling in sports, thanks to the national obsession with women's figure skating in the 1990s (Hello, Michelle Kwan, if you're reading this), the U.S. Gymnastics Team (maybe you owned the iconic 1996 Olympic Gymnast Barbie), the advent of the WNBA in 1996, and the U.S. Women's World Cup victory in 1999. With more exposure came more respect and equity, right? Well, the U.S. Women's Soccer Team only reached a settlement in their lawsuit over equal pay in 2022. In a poll that same year by the AP-NORC/National Women's History Museum, about half of those polled said things had gotten better for women, but not all women. Specifically, 49% of white women said there had been real progress since Title IX, to which only 36% of women of color polled agreed, along with 33% of LGBTQ women, and 26% of low-income women.

This trumpeting of progress hiding persisting structural inequalities may be what media critic and journalist Jennifer Pozner meant when she noted it's "probably a fair assumption to say that a 'zig-a-zig-ah' is not Spice shorthand for 'subvert the dominant paradigm'." While we still love the Spice Girls and that phrase, it is true that some of the pop culture that helped us celebrate being girls also wanted to sell us things at the same time (pausing to think of another prominent example . . . perhaps not British, but?). That doesn't mean these things weren't genuine in holding up women and their experiences, even if they didn't use their power to call out real structural issues affecting them. It is just a case, then as now, of people or brands promoting valuable ideas for their own gain while likely erasing or eroding the origins of those ideas and their creators. For example, "girl power." The phrase is itself alleged to date to a zine created by riot grrrl band Bikini Kill in 1991. This zine transparently drew on language dating back to earlier histories of Black power movements.

This same desire for "equality and fun and trying to rule your life" that drove the Spice Girls in 1996 still inspires us, even if we use different phrases to pursue it now. Unlike the Spice Girls, we want to remind everyone to look beyond the brands or slogans that sell us catchy phrases about rights and be aware of the structures that may be influencing our rights to our lives and bodies today.

Like American Girl itself, which has made major strides in supporting transgender and queer fans, we want empowerment not just for girls but for all underrepresented and vulnerable groups in our politics, sports, and pop culture.

We Bust a Block and Explain It All (the Pop Culture That Ruled Our Lives)

Clearly, pop culture made a big impact on us growing up. It still does.

American Girl books were not the only ones we read. If ever we were worried about pirating too many songs off LimeWire or Napster, music sites with dubious legality, we could take ourselves to the library. There, taking advantage of free books is entirely the point. At the library, we built on our burgeoning interest in the past by reading the *Little House* books, any of the books in the Eyewitness series, perhaps on a topic of a current obsession (*Titanic*, anyone?), and every single *Dear America* book. Brave readers could take on R.L. Stine's books, which ruled the decade, and even non-fantasy fans were drawn into the Harry Potter series after their debut in 1998. (Our love for Harry Potter is certainly complicated now that J.K. Rowling is firmly in her transphobic villain era.) We'd love to tell you we spent our childhoods reading Shel Silverstein's poetry, dreamily staring into the middle-distance and imagining our future lives as poets laureate, but we also knew we were living in a golden age of TV and movies. Kids in the '90s had a lot of TV offerings to take in, and by TV we mean actual television and not streaming. For those who could figure out how to tape shows on their VCR, they could watch shows and rewatch them whenever they chose; for those without that intel (Mary), you had to guard the family TV at the appointed hour so as not to miss key programming like the prom episode of *Saved by the Bell* (still thinking of Zack and Kelly slow dancing outside the gym).

We grew up in the age of the sitcom, and if our parents allowed it, we could watch episodes of *Friends*, *Living Single*, *Seinfeld*, and every other show that is experiencing a resurgence now. In 1992, *Golden Girls* aired its final episode, offering us an early vision of chosen family and non-traditional family structures that flew in the face of the more traditional world of *7th Heaven* and similar shows from the period.

Though it may have been the age of the sitcom, we benefited from TV that offered a whole new world of options to kids. Beginning in 1992, Nickelodeon offered an entire block of programming for kids called SNICK, aka "Saturday Night Nickelodeon" that felt like appointment television. *Clarissa Explains It All* offered a model of a cool teen who seemed to truly know it all, or at least fake it to get out of self-created drama. *The Ren & Stimpy Show* (along with *Doug*, *Rugrats*, *Hey Arnold!*, and so many others) offered the kind of chaotic animated storytelling that likely launched a thousand dreams of art school (or at least thousands of kids singing "Happy, happy, joy, joy" to the annoyance of their parents). *Are You Afraid of the Dark?* posed a question to which our answer is still yes while offering tame spooky stories for kids.

Shows like *Wishbone* on PBS followed an adorable dog as he interpreted the classics, combining an avowedly educational mission with a desire to make learning fun (never forget his iconic turn as Joan of Arc). Not all TV had to be "edutainment," however. ABC's TGIF lineup, *Family Matters* (the title itself an argument), *Step by Step, Boy Meets World,* and *Full House* all made navigating friendships and family seem like *the* very stuff of life. In its positioning of hetero families and their hijinks at the center, these shows weren't all that different from the sitcoms our parents grew up watching.

However, some shows really did want to speak to the times. Claire Danes in *My So-Called Life* perfectly spoke to the angst of teens (or aspiring teens who watched to learn what teen years might be like, aka us), and featured kids with real family drama and *gasp* a gay character. Okay, maybe the other shows tried to innovate, too. We all remember Jessie Spano's caffeine pill "moment," which really just taught us all a hard and early lesson about the perils of breaking into the music business and the fantasy of multitasking (she was trying to study for midterms *and* prepare for a gig with her girl group). We have to wonder if things would have been different had Jessie had access to the D.A.R.E. program.

Speaking of being way harsh, we have never forgotten the lessons we learned from Cher in *Clueless.* For many, this was *the* foundational high school movie and our introduction to Jane Austen. How many reading comprehension tests for Austen's *Emma* cite Cher's statue of liberty address? If, like us, you felt brave enough to cite Wishbone during a classroom conversation on Frankenstein, why not casually cite Cher's scholarship in everyday life? In a story of a rich, popular, high school girl (not relatable content to us), Cher learns not to be casually cruel, not to presume to know the wishes of other people, and to understand the value of Brittany Murphy (RIP). This movie also left us with a powerful measure for the technological prowess of our times. Unlike some who keep holding out for jetpacks as the height of progress, we're still waiting for someone to replicate Cher's virtual closet.

Movies in this era offered kids some truly heartwarming content, including

Homeward Bound, The Little Rascals, and *The Lion King* (scary but heartening—a fair assessment of most Disney films from this period). Other movies taught us some perhaps unintentional lessons: for example, *The Sandlot* (a film that made us believe talent was tied to a pair of Converse sneakers), *Sister Act* (a film that made us believe musical talent was tied to a nun's habit), and *Selena* (a movie that made us believe J.Lo was Selena). Amazingly, *Empire Records* romanticized the decline of record stores, falsely preparing us for a future when records would be irrelevant. In 2022, Taylor Swift sold more copies of her *Midnights* album on vinyl than CD, a future we never thought possible. (Although, considering how many scratched CDs we're still holding on to, we're open to a new or perhaps better vintage technology.)

Kids could also learn a lot about history from movies. Scholars are always trying to identify gaps in our knowledge and tell underrepresented stories. Nowhere was this more evident than the heroes who produced *Newsies,* starring a young Christian Bale as the leader of the newsboys' strike of 1899. We may not remember the facts of that event, but the interpretive dance Christian Bale offered about his character's dream of escaping to Santa Fe is likely some of the best free advertising that city has seen. We would be remiss to not acknowledge the phenomenon of *Titanic* upon its release in 1997. Kids would see marathon screenings, which is truly impressive at its over-three-hour runtime, and fell in love with the musical stylings of Celine Dion. While we never believed Leo couldn't fit on that door, we recognize that perhaps everything with the Titanic had to end in tragedy.

Many of our movies were rented for either two- or five-day windows from Blockbuster, a business designed to offer movie rentals at a markup. Kids today will never know the joy of renting a movie on video tape and feeling the real frustration of discovering that it had not been rewound by the previous user. Will kids today even understand the true kindness of those who heeded the invitation to "be kind, rewind"?

Imagine being beholden to Blockbuster or an actual movie theater for the latest flicks? For those of us who were law abiding, that was exactly the kind of limitation we had to accept. Unfortunately, because of the power dynamic we've mentioned, our parents had no knowledge of the development of Napster in 1999 or its many competitors. This allowed some of us who won't be named to find movies we weren't allowed to watch (hello, *Romeo + Juliet*) and discover all kinds of music. Kids today will never know the special kind of fear that accompanied waiting for a download on one of these sites and sincerely wishing you would receive what you'd hoped you were downloading, and not, as happened to one of us, a live recording of Debbie Gibson singing the score of *Les Mis* in a nightclub as a fan loudly annotated her performance (to be fair, still an iconic recording to have).

Now That's What We Called Music

Let it never be said our childhood was without some of the most iconic music of all time. Ours was the era that allowed Sugar Ray, LFO, and the Macarena to coexist. Imagine a world where Mariah Carey is a constant in the news cycle (then as now) and claims to be celebrating her twelfth birthday (she says this every year) while singing about emotions and Christmas (a forever icon). Like our hero Molly McIntire in her '40s era childhood, we took all of this in as kids by listening to the radio.

While we were pretty young for the popularity of grunge, and the advent of hip hop in the mainstream (which really began in the '80s), we certainly got to benefit from both. Radio stations focusing on different genres created a means for listeners to distinguish themselves among fellow music fans. Favorite stations became simultaneously a sign of taste (I listen to this college hip hop station, you've probably never heard of it) and identity (I listen to the indie station! You wouldn't get it!). There were lots of musical fads in this period with less staying power and we remember those, too. For a brief window, swing music had a resurgence ("Zoot Suit Riot," anyone?), along with ska (No Doubt, Sublime, Less Than Jake, etc.). Perhaps this would have made Molly feel safe; it's still unclear how it made us feel.

The '90s also began a major era for boy bands, and allegiances to *NYSNC, Backstreet Boys, 98 Degrees, and more could divide entire friend groups. People convened sleepovers to impress upon friends the superior quality of their favorite band, as if they were courting votes at a presidential convention. That rivalry paled in comparison to the ways the music biz pitted women against one another, whether Britney vs. Christina vs. Mandy. We can only say we have always respected all divas.

Never forget the first VH1 Divas Live concert in 1998 featuring Aretha Franklin, Mariah Carey, Celine Dion, Gloria Estefan, Carole King, and Shania Twain. We can still remember the group performance of "Natural Woman" that demonstrated Aretha believed this show was titled Diva Live, and who are we to question that?

The greatest pop focus of music in this period was the advent of *Total Request Live*, or *TRL*, on MTV in 1998. It's hard to overstate the importance of *TRL* as a common show kids could watch to learn what was popular at the moment. Also hard to recall that the arbiter of cool on this show was Carson Daly (moment of silence for his single black-painted fingernail, which was being asked to do a LOT of work).

On weekday afternoons, the show counted down the top 10 music videos for songs that garnered the most votes from viewers, presenting itself as a beacon of democracy in the midst of corporate music culture. A typical countdown would bring together different genres to present a survey of what was popular, or curate a sense of what either kids and/or MTV believed *should* be popular.

TRL also had the improv nature of a live show that felt equal parts strange and exciting. For example, this was the kind of show that would host Snoop Dogg for an interview, then maybe do a segment with Ashley Parker Angel of the boy band O-Town, and then let Eminem perform old Marky Mark lyrics to rebooted actor Mark Wahlberg's face as deeply uncomfortable spoken word. It was the kind of stuff that had to be seen to be believed (and you can find it on YouTube to this day).

Music videos are less relevant now than they were then. We can't recreate the anticipation fans had for the latest Destiny's Child video, or the sight of Times Square being shut down for a visit from the Backstreet Boys. This is also where we learned some early interpretive skills, spitballing the possible artistic "choices" behind the pairing of imagery with sound. Like, why did Britney go so hard in the "Toxic" video as a flight attendant? How did she know that *this* occupation would tell the story of a toxic workplace environment? Had we known the full backstory, we would have argued Britney should have starred as herself, a woman perpetually done wrong by her own family (and the media) in the name of capitalism and casual misogyny.

It may seem silly now that videos drop with little fanfare on YouTube, but sometimes *TRL* would tease the debut of a new video for days in advance. We will never forget where we were when we saw "Independent Women Part 1" by Destiny's Child intercut with clips of the 2000 *Charlie's Angels* reboot starring actor, lifestyle guru, and talk show queen Drew Barrymore, actor and iconic painter Lucy Liu, and wine entrepreneur and actor Cameron Diaz. Talk about synergy.

It would be wrong to paint *TRL* and its impact as purely nostalgic as it did carry some of the burdens of its time. Specifically, it focused on mostly white artists with big corporations behind them, making little space for cool indie artists. This is the benefit of things like YouTube (or podcasting) in our own times that lets anyone share their work widely to find an audience. However, we did like the shared experience of watching the show or having places to turn to (even if just on TV) when life got hard.

True Life: The '90s/'00s Could Be Terrifying

We're living through '90s nostalgia now, which like all memory projects, only chooses to remember unproblematic things. The ubiquity of fashions, TV shows, music, and more from those years may delude us into thinking everything from the period is worth a nostalgic re-embrace (slap bracelets hit different as adults), and that it was universally a good time and a good time equally for all (we are pretty sure that it was not for Monica Lewinsky, for example). The reality is always more complicated, and not as rosy as our pink jelly sandals may have suggested.

Some major national tragedies in the period still feel fresh to us and have shaped much of life today in ways that would be recognizable to kids growing up now. The Columbine school shooting on April 20, 1999, was a shock for everyone, especially kids who grew up assuming school was a safe space. It may have reminded an older generation of the shooting at Kent State University in 1970. In the days after Columbine, the news coverage echoed calls that such tragedies never happen again.

Now kids learn mass shooter drills in school, reflecting the reality that such shootings have continued ever since.

When national tragedies like these (and others) happened, kids had a range of places to learn about the news that were aimed at them. Linda Ellerbee hosted *Nick News* (1992–2015), which was designed to produce stories on issues of the day by kids for kids. The show featured reporting by teens and opinion pieces, including a story on a young Meghan Markle then writing letters to ask a dish soap company to change an ad she viewed as sexist. The show also covered Magic Johnson's announcement of his HIV diagnosis, climate change, presidential elections, and family issues like divorce. It aired on Nickelodeon, though it was also available in schools where it supplemented magazines like the *Weekly Reader*, which also presented current events to kids. Before the advent of social media (Myspace was created in 2003 and Facebook in 2004) when the capacity to share personal opinions no matter your age felt perhaps *too* accessible, these kinds of shows and resources put kids and their concerns at the center and purposefully involved them in conversations about events and ideas shaping their lives.

Kids in the era faced increasing political divides, environmental stress, looming college costs, and a whole host of pressure points (though at least Y2K didn't cause the chaos some feared). Added to this was the enormity of the impact of 9/11 and the resulting war on terror. Videos of *TRL* or blogs and message boards from the period show kids hungry for a place to process the enormity of this event, understand it, and assign some meaning to it. Our own classroom conversations at the time explicitly asked us to link our personal memories of the event to the larger national story, inviting us to see ourselves as historical actors.

Many American Girl books similarly choose traumatic national events as a point of departure that a girl and her family must survive, whether the revolution, the Civil War, or events like Pearl Harbor. Felicity's decision to politely decline tea becomes a symbol of her own burgeoning independence, for example, in mirroring the revolutionary events in the colonies. We wonder what an American Girl book based on these years might be like and imagine it would be shaped in some ways by an awareness of these events. For those who lived through these events like us, consider how such large national stories have impacted the history of your own life or that of your family and friends.

Our Attics Are an Archive

In the Peek into the Past in the *Meet Kirsten* book, readers are reminded Kirsten could take very few things with her from her home in Sweden to her new life in Minnesota. Turning the question on the reader, the book asks "How would you know what to bring with you?" And, perhaps more importantly, "What would you leave behind?" At this point in her book, we should have screamed "bring clean water for Marta!" Alas, it was already too late. But these questions aren't just helpful in thinking about Kirsten's history. They can also be useful in imagining how we can move forward with our own histories. As we get older and accrue more personal history, what do we keep, and what do we leave behind?

For American Girl, each character's accessories suggest things they love so much that they'd survive the transition to adulthood. Courtney Moore, the American Girl character set in 1986, lives in an era closest to our own childhood, and we can easily recognize some of her accessories as things we ourselves owned and treasured: a cassette Walkman, Trapper Keeper, Care Bears sleeping bag, etc. When we want to see the cache of items we insisted on keeping for our adult selves, we need look no further than the free storage facility and time capsule that is our parents' attics. For Mary, her original Polly Pockets present both memories of fun playtimes with neighbors and a modern-day choking hazard.

If you're reading this and are roughly our age, what are the things you've kept from your childhood? (Please say a Skip-It.) What have you left behind? If you kept a Princess Diana Beanie Baby, is that currently the basis of your retirement savings plan? Maybe you, too, grew up with the pop culture of the '90s and have been talking back to this brief history with your own memories. We want to close by inviting you to create your own peek into the past.

History is something to think with, not memorize, and can help us organize our worlds and our place within them. What would your peek into the past look like?

What were the national stories that stayed with you? Consider the local histories or gossip you return to in your mind that seemed to unexpectedly shape your own memory of being in school, in your family, or in your hometown. What were your most important "accessories"?

Our favorite thing about Peek into the Past, besides the historical survey of different time periods, was its attempt to present histories of ordinary people, like us. History does not just belong to presidents or celebrities appearing on genealogy shows. It belongs to you, too. If you enjoy investigating the past and thinking with history, consider volunteering at your local historical society. There you will find the real heroes preserving the histories and culture of your community for generations to come. You can be part of the valuable work that ensures future generations understand what exactly Pogs were (we can't actually recall) and what currency they held in our lives (incalculable).

Acknowledgments

Our Shared Thanks

We'd like to thank our intrepid editor, Kat Brzozowski. Thanks for giving us this opportunity. We so appreciate your guidance through this process and your hot takes on *The Bachelor* and every relevant pop culture matter of the day. Special shoutout and thanks to Kat's sister Sally Brzozowski, who told Kat about our show and helped us get here.

Thank you to our agent, Lauren MacLeod. Your expert advice and pep talks truly made this book possible. We're so happy to have you in our corner.

Thanks to everyone at Feiwel & Friends for all their hard work on our behalf.

Thanks to Pleasant Rowland for creating American Girl. While we may have tough talk for some of your choices, we are still here talking (and now writing) about the brand you made all these years later. Your work made us feel like we could be at the center of our own story, and we so respect that you always took kids and their needs seriously.

Thanks to everyone who has shared their American Girl stories with us through the years. We treasure all the stories and experiences that have so enriched our lives and this book.

Last, but not least, thanks to all our *Dolls of Our Lives* podcast listeners. We can't believe something that started as a conversation between friends led us here. We are gratified to know we weren't just shouting (or laughing) into a void and so value everyone in this community. The two of us owe a unique kind of debt to the people who reached out, shared their stories, and generously allowed us to share them with you. Our community on Discord, Instagram, Twitter, and other internet spaces has been sustaining and lots of fun. Additional thanks to these official and unofficial AG experts: Aubre Andrus, Kayla Chenault, Michelle Cude, Ingrid Hess,

Grace McGookey, J.Mix, Elisabeth Montanaro, Courtney Price, Jessica Quirk, Leah Sauter, Helen Schultz, Sravya Tadepalli, Danielle Wetmore, Mary Wiseman, and Lindsey Wood.

Mary's Acknowledgments

I'd like to thank Allison for, in *Bachelor* terms, going on this journey with me. It's truly been a Tripp.

I have had the benefit of great teachers in my life, inside and out of classrooms. I want to thank all my teachers at Corpus Christi School, East Catholic High, Trinity College, and UConn. Special thanks to Mrs. Hulse, Mr. Nevins, Mrs. Ward, Mr. Duffy, Mrs. Jacobs, Jonathan Elukin, Ron Spencer, and Jack Chatfield.

I want to thank Dr. Alex Flores at Boston Children's Hospital. I would literally not be able to write this book without your care. Thank you for giving me the chance to do this (and so much more).

Thanks to all my friends at Trinity College who have encouraged this project. I am grateful that the list is too numerous for me to name. I want to specifically thank Yoli Bergstrom-Lynch, Joelle Thomas, and Cait Kennedy, who sent me a cheesecake during the writing process, proving once again that I am also reached by the same things that appeal to the Golden Girls: friendship, drama, and cheesecake.

As an adult, I had mostly forgotten the plot of every American Girl book, but I always remembered how important friendship was to the story. The same is true in my life. Thanks to dear friends who offered so much love and support through this process (and in life generally). Thanks to Abby Southwell, Nazmus Nasir, Jordan McMillan, Terri Laue, Tanya Lane, Winnie Maloney, Joshua Murphy, Cara Pavlak, Alison Moore, Krystyna Soljan, Sophie Gocheva, Heather Parker, Kristin Van Ness, Eric and Lindsay Sacco, Aimee Loiselle, and Allyson Yankle. Thank you to members of vital group chats: Agatha Christie Dinner Club, Dolly Parton's Backup Singers, and Bakes and Books.

As a person of Irish-Italian descent, I live in fear of excluding or forgetting the many family members whom I cherish, so I hope thanking all of my cousins (real and chosen) will cover my bases. For you, I would steal fur pelts from a dead man whose body I discovered in a cave, but thank you for not asking that of me (yet). I love and appreciate all of you. I want to especially thank my aunts Rosemary Benoit and Mary-Ellen Rogers for all their love and support through the years.

I want to acknowledge and remember my grandmother, Mary Sposato, aka Fluffy. I will always cherish the time we shared and the gift of your friendship. While I know for a fact you would never read this book, I also know you would embark on an unsolicited and completely phone-based marketing campaign to promote it to everyone you knew (and complete strangers). You were pure love, chaos, and fun, and I miss you every day.

Thanks to my parents, Rick and Ann Mahoney. My dad's love of history surely put me on a path to being a historian. When I was growing up, my mom read me all of the American Girl books (and countless others), which is one of my most treasured memories. Thank you for the gift of reading, never saying no to buying more books, and always saying yes to "Can't we read one more chapter?" You always made me feel like a major character in your story, and I'm so glad you're a part of mine. To my brothers, Rick and Pat, thank you for always being more fun and interesting than any sibling who has ever appeared in any American Girl book. I really appreciate your love and support. I also want to thank my brother-in-law Josh Cruz, sister-in-law Síobhra Aiken, and my in-laws Tom Newman, Gale Brancato, and Ben Newman. Thank you for so warmly accepting me into your family.

My most important thanks goes to my wife, Anna. It is a gift to share my life with you, and I am so honored to be your wife. This book would not have happened without you. How can I possibly thank someone who threw me a pandemic *Glitter* watch party on Zoom for my birthday because you knew I needed it? Or a person who made me a zine with your reactions to every Beatles song because they matter to me and you had never heard many of their songs before (!?!?) Or, in a move echoing an American Girl cookbook, made me Pop-Tarts from scratch even though you don't support my "every meal can be breakfast food if you believe in yourself and try hard enough" lifestyle? Thank you for reading drafts, talking me down, and generally being the most sane person in this marriage. To quote Dolly Parton, I just love you, "pure and simple."*

To young readers reading this, I want you to know that this part of my life is very fun and very possible, even if you've never read about it in an American Girl book.

*In case Dolly Parton is reading this, thank you for everything. I will always love you, and not in the "I'm about to break up with you, but with poetry" way you originally intended.

Allison's Acknowledgments

How do you thank the people who provided you with the gift of reading and the gift of life? My parents took me to endless bookstores, libraries, and hobby shops to nurture my love of American Girl and much more. They also encouraged my interest in history and showed me so many underexplored parts of the United States. While following many of their own dreams, my parents told me it was a good thing to have my head in a book as long as I also had a bigger vision for myself. Mom and Dad: You gave me roots, wings, and lots of bookmarks. I love you, and I appreciate you more than you will ever know.

My brother, Daryl Horrocks, and my sister, Kate Treloar, have been tremendously supportive during the past few years of my life. I am so grateful for the postcards, texts, check-ins, and, going back a bit further, books you gave me through the years. Together with your spouses, both of you are raising beautiful, kind humans who make me proud to call us a family.

To the people I am honored to call friends: Thank you for choosing to make me a part of your life. Your kindness and humor mean the world to me. Friendship is a major through line of this book, and that is no accident. The friendship I was lucky to develop with Mary has changed my life for the better and changed my life for good. Thanks also to Mark, who told me early on that I could and should write. These are debts that can never be repaid.

Several teachers have made an especially profound impact on my life. Now more than ever, I am in awe of people who give their lives to the teaching of others. My

NPS colleagues have also been extraordinarily encouraging of me and of this project. I strive to be half as good as my mentors, who made me believe in the magic of interpretation.

Andrew, Colin, and Lyla are three of the most special people I know, and not just because we share some DNA. Watching you grow up is a joy and privilege in my life. May you all find stories that speak to you.

Thank you for reading this Feiwel & Friends book.
The friends who made *Dolls of Our Lives* possible are:

Jean Feiwel, Publisher
Liz Szabla, VP, Associate Publisher
Rich Deas, Senior Creative Director
Holly West, Senior Editor
Anna Roberto, Senior Editor
Kat Brzozowski, Senior Editor
Dawn Ryan, Executive Managing Editor
Kim Waymer, Senior Production Manager
Emily Settle, Editor
Rachel Diebel, Associate Editor
Foyinsi Adegbonmire, Associate Editor
Brittany Groves, Assistant Editor
Ellen Duda, Designer
Mallory Grigg, Senior Art Director

Follow us on Facebook or visit us online at mackids.com.
Our books are friends for life.